Composition as a Human Science

1295.

COMPOSITION AS A HUMAN SCIENCE

Contributions to the Self-Understanding of a Discipline

Louise Wetherbee Phelps

New York   Oxford
OXFORD UNIVERSITY PRESS

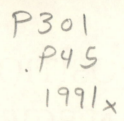

Oxford University Press

Oxford New York Toronto
Delhi Bombay Calcutta Madras Karachi
Petaling Jaya Singapore Hong Kong Tokyo
Nairobi Dar es Salaam Cape Town
Melbourne Auckland

and associated companies in
Berlin Ibadan

Copyright © 1988 by Oxford University Press, Inc.

First published in 1988 by Oxford University Press, Inc.,
200 Madison Avenue, New York, New York 10016

First issued as an Oxford University Press paperback, 1991

Oxford is a registered trademark of Oxford University Press

Portions of the present volume previously appeared in the
following journals and are used by permission:
"Dialectics of Coherence: Toward an Integrative Theory," *College English*, vol. 47, no. 1, January,
1985; "The Dance of Discourse: A Dynamic, Relativistic View of Structure," *Pre/Text*, vol. 3, no. 1,
Spring 1982; "Possibilities for a Post-Critical Rhetoric: A Parasitical Preface 6," *Pre/Text*, vol. 4,
nos. 3–4, Fall/Winter 1983; and "Foundations for a Modern Psychology of Composition," *Rhetoric
Review*, vol. 3, no. 1, September 1984.

Library of Congress Cataloging-in-Publication Data
Phelps, Louise Wetherbee, 1940–
Composition as a human science: contributions to the self-
understanding of a discipline / Louise Wetherbee Phelps.
p. cm.
Bibliography: p.
ISBN 0-19-504269-7
ISBN 0-19-506782-7 (pbk)
1. Rhetoric. 2. Discourse analysis. 3. Literacy. I. Title.
P301.P45 1988
808′.00141—dc 19   87-34467

9 8 7 6 5 4 3 2 1
Printed in the United States of America

For my children
Alexander, Christopher, Lon

If we live profoundly, we are taught by everyone, especially by children, by students and those without public intellectual portfolio. Who is to sort out my ideas from yours? Is it not more genuine and fruitful to work on behalf of a community of inquiry, such that these essays take as their task the relating of otherwise disciplinarily isolated wisdom to our common needs?

JOHN J. MCDERMOTT

Preface

Theory Is Autobiography

When I was writing my master's thesis on a discourse model for teaching, my thesis adviser didn't help much. (He was in Renaissance literature, not composition, and I'm not an easy writer to help anyway.) But he was a poet, so he knew about form, and he said one true, perceptive thing that made up for everything he didn't know or say: "This isn't exposition, it's really autobiography."

Autobiography? *Of course!* No wonder I was struggling with the structure. I reversed field. Instead of aiming for exposition punctuated with narrative bits, I rewrote the thesis from scratch as narrative with expository bits: as the autobiography of an idea transformed by the experience of trying to make it work in practice. It came out awkward, neither fish nor fowl, but no matter. I had taken one of those leaps after which nothing is the same.

Theory is autobiography. Exposition is narrative. (Just the opposite of the classic developmental schemes for writing—or maybe one stage beyond them.) These paradoxes have structured my writing ever since, as conflicts and tensions, not achievements. I'm not alone. We're working, all of us in theoretical discourse from anthropology and psychology to composition and literary theory, toward new genres with the expressive power to represent in their very form what we now believe and feel about the personal nature of knowledge. Meantime we are seeing hybrid, tortured, mixed, and often unsuccessful discourse forms.

This volume of essays will be taken as "theoretical," part of the scholarly effort to define, locate, and legitimize composition studies as a discipline. But theory is autobiography. So from one perspective this collection is a repressed, dislocated narrative of not one but two autobiographies, intricately tangled. One story is the development of composition from an adolescent stage in the 1970s toward self-reflective maturity; the other is my personal growth as a writer trying to help bring about that maturation. Both are searches for identity, for a place and a voice in an ongoing conversation.

I want to bring out these suppressed narratives and their relationships in order to make the point that theory doesn't exist for its own sake, or shouldn't. However formidably abstract, it is a form of intelligibility that the theorist tries to give to personal dilemmas, deeply felt. Like all writing, theory is a way to make sense of life. For oneself, for others. In composition, theory is irrevocably committed to practice: begins there and returns, in recursive loops.

I started to theorize because as a high school teacher I couldn't understand what I was doing, or why. I only knew, thanks to a father and mother who showed me two very different writers writing, that the course of study and textbooks about composition were bunk. By the time I ended up at Case Western Reserve University in the mid-1970s, constructing my own doctoral program in composition and rhetoric, I was looking for an interdisciplinary "framework" as a tool for thinking out answers to the practical problems I had encountered in teaching writing. I imagined such a framework as a synthesis of knowledge from various disciplines about language, thought, social action, and the relations among them.

The story of my development as a writer of theory, and its intersection with the transformation of composition into a self-conscious discipline, hangs on the *idea* of framework rather than its specific content.

My dissertation was to be a group of essays dealing with a set of practical problems by reconceptualizing the terms of the problem. The three problems I selected were discourse structure (how could you deal with it in early forms like notes and drafts?); coherence and transition (what did these terms mean and how did they work?); and reading student writing (how did teachers understand the meaning of drafts in order to give advice?). The rub was, I couldn't make sense of any of these problems in isolation; I needed a comprehensive framework for relating writing, reading, thinking, texts, and context that simply wasn't available in composition at that time. Necessity drove me to invent one in order (as it turned out) to analyze in the dissertation just one of the original problems—discourse structure.

By the time I got this far, though, my purposes in "framing" had broadened. Originally I wanted the framework for myself, as an instrument for thinking clearly about the pedagogical problems I was experiencing. But in trying to construct it I encountered an emergent field in an exciting state of ferment and came to identify myself as a member of a community. My personal need for theory had linked up to the intellectual and political pressures for composition to establish itself in the academy as a coherent disciplinary enterprise. Whereas before I had thought of other fields as providing information and ideas for understanding writing, now I thought that the power of ideas and the ability to interest other language-related disciplines was the only way for composition to overcome its marginality in English departments and the academy at large.

Following this first try at constructing a framework, I began to work—or rather to continue working—on the set of philosophical sketches that are put together here as part 2, "The Process of Reconstruction." I started with the practical problems identified earlier, but these essays (now chapter 6 on discourse structure and chapter 7 on coherence) were composed over long periods of time and reflect further transformations of my concept of framework. My thinking was taking a reflexive turn demanding a new logic and a new form of writing that embeds theory—"frames" it—in metatheory. In my original notion framework operated straightforwardly as an instrument for thinking or theorizing: one attended *from* the interdisciplinary framework *to* acts of writing, reading, and learning in order to understand them. But as a writer trying to speak persuasively to a community of thinkers *about* a framework, my task was to explain and justify my own act of theorizing. I thus needed a framework of frameworks, as an instrument for understanding acts of framing and the selves that enact them. Because of the reciprocity of autobiographies—myself and field—my attention turned to the way communal acts of writing theory construct a disciplinary self.

In deciding to collect and re-present (in a new "frame") the work of this period, I began while still in the old frame to reperceive my purposes and thus select a different set of problems for analysis. When I formed the plan for this book, I listed a set of features that could define composition as a discipline:

an inexhaustible topic (a subject of adequate scope and permanent interest)
a connection with, or relevance to, the intellectual life of the culture
principles for differentiating itself from other fields with similar or overlapping interests
a mission: a moral imperative, social responsibility
methods that are mutually compatible and complementary with respect to assimilation, testing, critique, and use

social/territorial motives and professional/institutional settings where
     it has an accepted role (journals, conventions, departments, pro-
     grams)
an educational system for reproducing the discipline, providing schol-
     ars with a sense of professional identity and common points of
     departure
irony, self-reflexivity about its own projects and discourse

The work in progress became an effort to articulate the study of
specific theoretical and metatheoretical problems as part of a *reflective
project* in the self-understanding of a discipline, and to present this
view of its enterprise to composition itself. The essays in part 2 reflect
these preoccupations and more and more explicitly present them in
the framework of organizing and characterizing disciplinary study.

This philosophical sketchwork culminates in an effort to enfold
the essays of part 2 in a structure of hermeneutical interpretation
(part 1) and application (part 3)—yet another reframing. But in the
two-chapter essay of part 1, "Constructing an Ecology of Composition," the metaphor of frame becomes fully conscious and, in becoming its own content, undergoes metamorphosis. In this essay I make
explicit the project of theory as autobiography in terms of two principles: context and change. The central metaphor of these chapters is the
concept of *field* as self-organizing system, a kind of system that is
dynamically capable, through its openness to the environment, of
innovation and unpredictable evolution. Composition is imagined as
in *resonance* with other cultural fields; its project of self-construction
is redefined as a problem of understanding itself through themes of
identity and difference with larger or parallel cultural fields. Composition is further understood, by its own developmental orientation
turned inward, to be in transition from an ethic of care to an ethic of
truth—a formulation from developmental psychology that reveals
composition to be engaged in a renegotiation of the balance between
feminine and masculine principles in its makeup.

These transformations of the idea of framework, as reflected in
the different processes of framing in these essays and their treatment of
framework as content, bear a complex relationship to the increasing
self-consciousness with which composition wrote of its self-under-
standings during the period of their composition. Over this time span
(approximately 1976 to 1986) the reflective project of forming a discipline became the object of *my* reflection, the process that I sought to
interpret. I wrote to explain, and thus to catalyze, the "interpretive

turn" in composition wherein its own reasoning, its own discourse, its own knowledge became reflexive, critical, and thus newly problematic. When theory becomes its own object it can no longer be presented as product, but must be *written* with irony, to express its own rhetorical self-understanding and development over time.

Every writer knows that to "write" such a narrative is to give personal shape and form to a flux of events; it is to "reframe" the unfinished story in the minds of participants and by doing so to change its meaning and direction. But at the very intersection of autobiographies where writer, constructed *as* theorist by perceiving discipline as story, narrates and thus rewrites it through her own theoretical discourse, the connection is least transparent. Narrative as persuasion resists the writer's effort to represent herself and her theorizing processes autobiographically, perhaps most of all when she writes of the autobiographical nature of theory.

Writing is always hard for most composers; writing theory is damnably hard. It is doubly hermeneutical: interpretation and self-interpretation, but where the *self* is simultaneously myself as writer, ideas as text, ourselves as disciplinary community. Worse than that, it is self not as static, autonomous entity, but (in each case) self as stream of thought interpenetrating others.

How as writer do I locate myself in my text, within our collective reflections? There are severe difficulties—I should like to write more about them sometime—of language, voice, audience, and especially ethos. As a writer I at first felt lonely, adversarial, inarticulate and voiceless in a climate unfavorable to philosophical thinking. I wondered often how I dared think large thoughts or different thoughts, and if I succeeded, how I might ever be heard. Composition has not nurtured its theorist-writers; as a practice it resists theory, refuses to grant the theoretical voice authenticity. It pictures the theorist as the professional con man trying to impress people with pompous, impenetrable jargon. It does not believe theory is *felt* or *written*. There are good reasons why composition distrusts theory. I've talked about them in part 3, where, in the last irony of this book, an essay originally intended to argue the personal and professional need to theorize experience became a defense of praxis against the oppression of theory. But as long as composition does not understand its theorists as writers, it will not understand itself.

In the end I discovered that, because theory is autobiographical, if writers and field are in resonance they develop symbiotically, each dependent on the other for understanding and self-understanding. I have come to understand my work here as on the one hand articulating themes half-tacit, half-explicit in our disciplinary discourse, and on the other hand expressing personal identity themes. Theory as autobiography: the creation of self as writer, thinker.

I have argued my positions, made my commitments, intellectual and ethical. They have changed, will change, being continually constructed and reconstructed by experience, by others. Something endures, in these and beyond these. I read what I read, notice what I notice, listen and respond, because of resonances with recurring life themes. Development as theme is a profound expression of my commitment to my children and my new understanding of myself, at forty-seven, as entering the life stage of disinterested mentorship to another generation. There is a sense in which this is what one's writing is really about: such consolidated commitments and emergent understandings and, even more deeply, the characteristic way a writer perceives problems and resolves them. For me, at that level, this book (and probably everything I write) plays out a fundamental tension that I experience in both self and world: the dialectical relation between yin and yang, feminine and masculine principles. Many of the oppositions treated in this work—nature and art, interpretation and criticism, experience and reflection, praxis and theory—refigure this relationship as a productive conflict that simultaneously enriches us and invokes limits. The attraction that Paul Ricoeur's work had for me during this period was my recognition of the same identity theme (tension and response) in his philosophic method. Carol Gilligan[1] clarified the gender sources for this theme and linked it to development, to my experiences as daughter, parent, teacher, mentor.

This habit of mind requires me to acknowledge formally, in preface, the limits of my work as contribution to a disciplinary conversation. As the work of a conceptualizer it is inherently schematic and programmatic, and invites others to take it up more fully and more concretely. This quality is not just a product of the historical situation; it is both the strength and the limits of my chosen method. Beyond this intrinsic limit of approach, much is missing. Not, perhaps, what some will suggest: reference to Lacan, Foucault, Marxism, deconstruction, or other movements, ideas, and thinkers. Or if they are missing, it is not accidental, but again an aspect of theory as autobiography. In a postmodern culture the writer reads what she needs in order to think, to make sense, not in order to know what is fashionable. There can be no canon of theory, any more than of literature. Composition is a field for generalists because it accepts anything with relevance to its praxis; in this light theory—writing—must be judged for what it does with what it learns. What *is* missing, however, is the problem of power that is raised by many of these thinkers. If rhetoric is a set of relations among language, power, and knowledge, I have neglected power and the political dimension of composition and its praxis. Retrospectively, I think I did so because I found most current frames for discourse about power uncomfortably masculine. I hope in the future to explore the possibility of a more feminine concept of power and the way these differing ideas enter into the practices of classrooms and institutions.

Manlius, N. Y.   L.W.P.
September 1987

Note

1. Carol Gilligan, *In a Different Voice: Psychological Theory and Women's Development* (Cambridge, MA: Harvard Univ. Press, 1982).

Acknowledgments

Though there are many compositionists whose work I respect and have learned from, my intellectual debt in this work is primarily to thinkers in other disciplines. They include, particularly, Paul Ricoeur, Michael Polanyi, Kenneth Burke, Hans-Georg Gadamer, Susanne Langer, Paulo Freire, Lev Vygotsky, Jerome Bruner, Chögyam Trungpa, and most recently Mikhail Bakhtin and his translators, along with the ecological and life-span developmental psychologists.

Friends with mutual interests in writing and rhetoric have shaped my thinking more directly by their constructive involvement with my work-in-process. They provided me not only with the incredible gifts of attentive reading, creative interpretation, and serious criticism, but even more important, with the chance to engage in what one friend, Margaret Himley, calls "deep talk." For these essential dialogues I thank my colleagues Ross Winterowd, Sam Watson, and especially Janice Lauer; and my former graduate students at the University of Southern California, especially Mary Kay Tirrell, Sandra Mano, Barbara Gleason, Lee Leeson, and participants in my seminars on the psychology of composition, literacy development, and ideologies of composition. My mother, Virginia Wetherbee, introduced me to deep talk and remains my most constant and stimulating partner. Other friends have contributed at different points to the evolution of this work, not least by their encouragement: Jan Swearingen, Dallas Willard, Bob Sweeney, Jim Kinneavy, Sharon Bassett, and Janet Emig.

Finally, I am lucky in the stoic grace and practical generosity of my husband Fred, who, while I was writing, listened endlessly, cheered me up, cooked, critiqued, helped the boys with their homework, applauded, fixed my computer, complained, and forgave.

Contents

Part One

Constructing an Ecology of Composition

1

The Cultural Ground

I will begin by developing the observation that composition awakens in the initial moment of its disciplinary project to find itself already situated, prereflectively, within a specific cultural field of meaning— that of postmodern thought, with its characteristic preoccupations and world vision. To put this point another way, the problem of inventing a discipline has an ecological dimension implicit in the term "field" for a scholarly community and its activities. An ecological perspective treats entities like disciplines as systems within larger systems. An ecology is constituted through interdependence and transactions among all levels of a system, both horizontally (the relations of parts within the whole at a given level of organization) and vertically (the relations among elements at different levels). The problem for composition of constructing its studies as a self-coherent and well-differentiated domain of inquiry is, therefore, not capable of autonomous resolution; it requires an ecological strategy bringing out both the internal structure of the "field" and its embedding in larger fields of meaning. This insight provides the organizing scheme and governing metaphor for part 1 of my work, comprising an essay in two chapters.

The first step in constructing an ecology of composition is to make the cultural scene manifest and to disclose latent relationships between its themes and those of composition studies. Accordingly, chapter 1 will be concerned rhetorically with identities, exploring those forms of a postcritical philosophical framework with which composition has the closest affinities.

Locating composition within this sociocultural matrix, however, immediately poses a new question: how can composition individuate itself from this background and, specifically, distinguish itself as an autonomous study of language and writing? The answer hinges on our reply to the question of identities. It is the developmental paradox: in order to grasp his own identity, the child must sharply appreciate the quality of the "other"—the world of objects and persons. The self cannot recognize itself except correlatively and contrastively. The same point is expressed in the basic phenomenological figure of indirect or reflexive understanding: only by interrogating the world can we constitute and understand ourselves. It is precisely by examining the identities and relations between composition and postmodern culture that the second moment of reflection becomes possible, whereby composition itself comes into relief as a distinctive structure for organizing work and thought.

With this shift, "field" takes on additional meanings. In one interpretation it suggests clearing a space of open ground to provide a site where different theories and practices can play against one another. From this perspective, a conceptual framework for composition serves not to eliminate competing approaches or views but to hold them in tension through their mutual relevance and difference. The interplay among them defines a "field" in the sense of a self-organizing system.[1] Such a system is a dynamic process rather than an equilibrium structure; it maintains its integrity through continual self-transformation and possesses the capacity for novelty. At the same time it is logically organized—differentiated, elaborated, hierarchical. The second task, therefore, of an ecology of composition is to articulate its coherence as a field structured by its shared relevancies and oppositions yet capable of continual evolution. This part of my analysis, developed in chapter 2, stresses the rhetorical principle of "division" or difference in order to bring out the particularity of composition studies in their dialectical internal structure and as figure against ground.

The story I want to tell in this introduction is one of loss and recuperation. Figured in broad terms, this pattern is the parallel I will develop between postmodern consciousness in general and composition in particular. I have spoken of composition as "awakening" from a prephilosophical state to find itself already embedded in a matrix of concerns with which it has complex and unexamined relationships. This point was obscure at first to a field preoccupied with its adolescent growth while trapped by historical accident into an exclusive and dependent relationship with literary studies. As recent work begins to break down this isolation, composition faces an exciting but frightening expansion of its horizons. Composition comes to maturity at just the moment when discourse (especially writing) and its interpretation stand at the epicenter of a great change, a fundamental crisis in human consciousness some regard as one of the revolutionary transitions that transform history. Physicist Fritjof Capra calls it the "turning point."[2]

Capra draws the picture of a planetwide cultural crisis, becoming acute in the 1960s when the erosion of the Cartesian-Newtonian view of reality opened the way for a new vision. Like many others, Capra adopts and extends Thomas Kuhn's concepts of paradigm and paradigm change in science to characterize this broad cultural transformation.[3] The postmodern world is marked by themes of loss, illusion, instability, marginality, decentering, and finitude. Just as the physical universe has, in modern physics, become unstable, transitory, fluctuating, indeterminate, and inaccessible to common sense, so has our intellectual universe. Across the disciplines all the old realities are in doubt, placed under radical critiques—critiques that challenge reason, consciousness, knowledge, meaning, communication, freedom, and other values asserted by the Enlightenment and developed in modern sciences, humanities, and public life. These assaults destroy absolutes and leave us in fear of an ultimate meaninglessness that will paralyze action and thought.

The deconstructive, negative purging of beliefs generates the need for a new, positive framework for human life. Many observers are now arguing that the shadowy form of such a schema is emerging from an extraordinary convergence of themes in the sciences, philosophy, and the humanities to take the place of a discredited mechanistic-formalist paradigm. It would be risky to accept uncritically these sweeping global syntheses, or to imagine that Cartesian thought has lost its grip. Scientism and technical reason still rule our search for knowledge. But it does seem that developments on all fronts point to the growing counterinfluence of a new world hypothesis that may transform our understanding even of empirical science itself. The intellectual work of articulating, elaborating, arguing, and applying this view is well advanced.

If so, we are talking about a vast cultural change whose sources, causes, and manifestations I cannot hope to adequately trace. Rather, it provides a hypothetical point of departure for me to explore this changed consciousness through a focus that will bring out its relevance to our project. A key issue that seems promising for this purpose is the questioning that surrounds the theme of rationality as it relates to the possibility of knowledge, the forms of inquiry, the nature of human consciousness, and its relation to a world. This debate parallels the revival of hermeneutics as an interpretive theory of inquiry (though it is more than that), which derives most directly from nineteenth-century efforts to distinguish the human or cultural sciences from the natural sciences. As we will see, hermeneutics is important in both the critical and restorative phases of the debate about reason.

My purpose in examining the cultural ground through this particular lens is to bring out the close correspondences between different levels at which the drama of loss and recuperation is played out, and especially to show that composition itself echoes this pattern and has something to contribute to it. I wish, first, to identify the pattern as it manifests itself in the problem of the human sciences, where it is resolved through a complex relationship between criticism and a positive notion of interpretation; next, to assimilate this result to a world hypothesis called contextualism; and finally, to show how it is relevant to the project of composition. I shall argue that the framework on which the positive directions of postmodern culture converge is an essentially rhetorical one, and as such both fits the needs of composition for a global philosophy of knowledge in relation to praxis, and also opens the way for composition to help articulate and realize this paradigm. The new relationships between interpretation and criticism, reason and rhetoric, science and hermeneutics provide a model for organizing composition productively around oppositions conceived as "key" and "challenge" or "critical moments" to one another.

Finally, I should say a word about the relationship between my project in this introduction and the chapters that follow in part 2. These philosophical sketches, essays written over a ten-year period, record my attempt to discover what problematics of postmodern culture lie behind the dilemmas of composition, and to confront the problem of finding a positive rhetorical framework within which to construe and address the conceptual and practical problems of the discipline. I was trying to formulate, at the level of specific difficulties and antinomies, a conception of the discipline generous enough to accommodate all the strands of its scholarship while preserving the centrality of its practical mission. Such a conception was slowly unfolding during this period in the ongoing dialogue of composition studies, but it needed systematic and reflective exposition. In this introduction I attempt to pull together the themes, choices, and discoveries of those essays in light of that conversation, and to make global sense of them.

Chapter 1 will examine the cultural ground for composition in two steps. First, we will follow the attack on positivism, which ultimately deconstructs the subject-object opposition and the related operations of critical reason on which the claims of modern science rest. The success of this critique, conjoined with parallel or complementary developments in other fields, plunged philosophy, science, and the semiotic disciplines into the "abyss" in what some construe as the triumph of irrationality. From this condition arise the specifically postmodern dilemmas. Second, we will look at how a postmodern consciousness reinterprets this impasse so as to rescue reason and formulate a set of novel problems for which rhetoric, discourse, and praxis are key terms.

The Rise of Postmodern Consciousness: The Critique of Scientism

The attack on positivism is not directed at science itself, nor at scientific thinking as actually practiced. Rather, it targets the position I will call "scientism" or positivism, which refers to the demand of science that the explanatory method used by natural science should be the model for intelligibility in all cases where humans attempt to develop valid knowledge. Jurgen Habermas calls this attitude "science's belief in itself: that is, the conviction that we can no longer understand science as *one* form of possible knowledge, but rather must identify knowledge with science."[4] Scientism may be contrasted to the hermeneutical view of science as one of a number of enterprises by which humans have attempted to understand, and change, themselves and their world. Modern science is distinguished by its refusal to recognize this historicality in its own project.

Through its universalizing and imperialistic tendency, scientism denies the power of communication to develop values and apply them dialogically. Josef Bleicher, drawing on work in critical theory and the philosophy of science, remarks that this ideology represents a social danger insofar as it attempts to reorganize society in its image, through the application of technical reason to social processes. In doing so, it renders practical reasoning ineffectual and undermines democratic control of social life, since "communicative interaction which is based on socially shared norms is supplanted by instrumental action which proceeds in relation to pre-given ends and follows technical, formalizable rules."[5]

The distinction between scientism and the hermeneutical dimension of human life has its roots in nineteenth-century German thought about the distinctive nature of the human sciences. Building on the work of Schleiermacher and inspired by the great German historians of the period, Wilhelm Dilthey tried to establish that the human sciences could rival the natural sciences in constructing true knowledge.[6] He argued that the sciences of the "spirit" (*Geisteswissenschaften*) have an interpretive method appropriate to a different object of study, namely, human experience as fixed in texts, cultural objects and institutions, and history. Accepting the self-rationalization that was then becoming explicit in the natural sciences—the claim to produce apodictic knowledge in the form of causal explanation—he proposed that in contrast the human sciences characteristically develop "understanding," a form of knowledge equally capable of universality and objective truth.

This defense of interpretation and the project of the human sciences did not succeed, in part because of internal flaws but more importantly because it was overwhelmed by the irresistible advances of explanatory science. Now, however, the failure of the positivist rationale for successful scientific practice has coincided with the reformulation and extension of hermeneutical themes by phenomenological philosophers and others to infuse an interpretive dimension into empirical-analytical science itself. Richard Bernstein makes this point in discussing the "recovery of the hermeneutical dimension" in both the social disciplines and the postempiricist philosophy and history of science:

> In the critique of naive and even of sophisticated forms of logical positivism and empiricism; in the questioning of the claims of the primacy of the hypothetical-deductive model of explanation; in the questioning of the sharp dichotomy that has been made between observation and theory (or observational and theoretical language); in the insistence on the underdetermination of theory by fact; and in the exploration of the ways in which all description and observation are theory-impregnated, we find claims and arguments that are consonant with those that have been at the very heart of hermeneutics, especially as the discipline has been discussed from the nineteenth century to the present.[7]

In its nineteenth-century form hermeneutics, shaped by the need to respond to the universalizing claim of positivism (the doctrine of the "unity of science"), tried to gain equality for the human sciences by showing that they developed general, objectively valid knowledge about social and artistic expressions of life. In other words, the debate remained on the level of method and was conducted in the terms set by positivism. But with the phenomenologists' reconstruction of hermeneutics, beginning with Heidegger and continuing with Gadamer, Ricoeur, and others in this tradition, it became possible to challenge scientism's basic premises through an ontological emphasis on the experience of being in the world. We will see how that challenge introduces a pretheoretical understanding into the practice of science. What I want to emphasize here is that it takes just such a powerful critique to weaken the hegemonic claims of what has been called the "orthodox consensus." Experimental science and its self-understanding as positivism remain the great exemplar for new disciplines, given the astonishing success of the Western scientific-technological enterprise as against the weak cognitive claims of the social and humanistic fields.

But scientism itself, as a historical research program, has followed the classic course of development described by Thomas Kuhn and others. What we see now is a paradigm in crisis. Advocates of positivism made a series of efforts to respond to anomalies that they themselves encountered, or to problems that critics raised, by making modifications and additions to their account of hypothetico-deductive science. As these repairs failed, the core assumptions and goals that motivated all these variations on positivism came into question. As a project, scientism rests ultimately on arrogating to itself the responsibility for deciding what constitutes knowledge through (as Walter Weimer says) an equation of knowledge, truth, and proof.[8] In the positivist interpretation, scientific inquiry develops theories (networks of logically connected propositions) that constitute permanently valid knowledge through their reference to some absolute authority. There is a close connection between this claim for science and philosophy's claim to stand above the particular disciplines and, in the form of epistemology, lay out the criteria for truth and knowledge.[9] In both cases, the ultimate commitment is to avoid falling into irrationality, which is thought of as the necessary consequence of giving up a conception of knowledge "justified" by some absolute foundation. It is because of this fear that a negative critique alone is not enough, and scientism will yield only when a new, positive alternative comes into view.

The positivist position evolved to combine logic and empiricism ("logical empiricism"), reflecting the two philosophical bases for knowledge as proof: (1) sense data and (2) universal reason.[10] Positivism originated in the "verification theory of meaning," the doctrine that a proposition is meaningful only if subject to empirical verification. Knowledge then would involve the concatenation of true (i.e., empirically verified) statements. Although this strong thesis had to be liberalized (from a theory of verification to one of confirmation and finally falsification), the emphasis on empirically testable propositions—"hard data"—remained.

A number of ideas cluster around the notion of propositionalized "facts" as ultimate authority. First, facts are required to be open to public and replicable test. Such an ideal of verification rules out of science anything having to do with a unique, nonrepeatable event (such as the hypothesized Big Bang origin of the universe) and makes descriptive sciences like geology and astronomy marginal. In addition, this notion of fact leads to behaviorism, because mental events are neither directly observable nor repeatable. Thus physicalism is a tenet of positivism: the position that all phenomena can be reduced to material terms and causes.

A second important aspect of a strong empiricism is the independence of phenomena from one another and from the framework of observation. Science concerns itself with a world in which facts are discrete atomic bits linked by cause-effect relations. Such facts are context-free: they do not depend on their relations to other facts, or on a situation where they function in a particular way, or on the interpretation of an observer. The independently real world that science studies is seen as fully accessible, transparent to human senses and their extensions. Both our senses and our scientific instruments are open channels for the flow of undistorted, unlimited empirical information. Scientific theories, like propositions themselves, are supposed to mirror reality veridically without changing it, in what is called the "correspondence theory of truth." These beliefs led among other things to idealization of the "objective" attitude of the neutral scientist, who comes to his observations without preconceptions, historicity, or values. In an important corollary, positivists thought that scientists had available to them, or should construct, a neutral observation language that would carry with it none of the connotations, prejudices, emotion, and other contaminations of ordinary or literary language. Instead, it was to be exact, formal, literal, and univocal.

The goal of positivist science was to construct explanations that would link these facts of nature according to universal laws of reason. Harold Brown summarizes the resulting hypothetical-deductive model as stated classically in the work of Hempel and Oppenheim:

> It is generally agreed among logical empiricists that the basic pattern of scientific explanation is the deductive pattern and that this applies equally to the three major areas of scientific explanation: explanation of events by means of laws, of laws by means of theories, and of theories by

means of wider theories. . . . [Hempel and Oppenheim] propose four conditions of adequacy for a scientific explanation. Three of these are labelled "logical conditions": (1) The explanadum [*sic*] must be logically entailed by the explanans; (2) the explanans must contain general laws which are necessary for the deduction of the explanandum (in the case of explanation of an event, the explanans must also contain statements of antecedent conditions, i.e., statements which refer to specific empirical objects or events;) (3) the explanans must have empirical content. The fourth condition, referred to as an "empirical condition," is that the explanans must be true, not just well confirmed.[11]

In ideal practice, then, the scientist proposes hypotheses representing tentative generalizations inductively derived from observation, predicts facts that are deductively related to these generalizations, and tests (supports or refutes) his theory by confirming or disconfirming the facts. In the classic form of positivism, explanation was conflated with prediction, although this equation came under wide attack.

Founded on the twin foundations of logic and fact, this paradigm of scientific method was supposed to guarantee progress. It was believed that as each theory established itself in a given science through these principles, knowledge would accumulate. In this view science is concerned with universals that are timeless and ahistorical. That is why science itself is not conceived as a historical practice whose results are contextually limited and subject to change. Advances in science do not invalidate earlier theories but incorporate and add to them.

While I have abstracted and oversimplified an evolving position, I think my description is faithful to the spirit and ideals of scientism. The most telling expression of those ideals is found in the summaries of "scientific method" offered by practitioners in other disciplines writing about problems of method and the possibility of knowledge. Most often these are the social disciplines. Whether supportive or critical of positivism, such accounts tend to identify this theory of science with science itself. To these writers, for whom the complex history of positivism as a research program is irrelevant, the "scientific method" is transparently well defined and provides an accurate description of practice, at least for the hard sciences. Many, even in opposing it as a model for their own disciplines, see alternatives as falling away from an ideal or at best as preliminary to empirical-analytic studies (e.g., they limit ethnography to generating hypotheses to be tested). In tone their language seems to mourn the inability of their own disciplines to produce true knowledge, to become genuine and rigorous sciences, to achieve certainty or make progress, to agree on an organizing paradigm.

Composition itself can serve as a case in point. Robert Connors has accurately discerned the yearning toward scientific status that permeates much writing in the field (although I would not agree that efforts to articulate a paradigm are necessarily scientistic). However, in the midst of rejecting this ideal, understanding as he does the challenge to positivism posed within philosophy of science and elsewhere, Connors can nevertheless list as characteristics of "science" those very tenets that I have attributed to scientism.[12] Similarly James Kinney, in debating N. Scott Arnold about the values and differences between naturalistic research (ethnography or case studies) and empirical-analytical methods, fails to shake off the influence of the positivistic ideal of scientific practice, leaving himself on the defensive.[13] Each has missed the crucial point that the critique of positivism deconstructs scientism rather than simply circumscribing it. It requires us to redescribe the scientific project itself in terms that reverse its primary assumptions.

Composition, like many other disciplines, does not realize that the ideal it alternately longs for and rejects is an illusion, a nostalgic dream. The professional defenders of positivism have long since abandoned it as untenable. As Anthony Giddens puts it, "What was an orthodoxy is an orthodoxy no longer, and consensus has given way to dissidence and disarray."[14] This is not to say that the scientistic spirit is defeated: efforts persist, as we will see, to rescue the project at its most fundamental level, where it tries to overcome the finitude of reason.

An important document in the demise of the classical view is Thomas Kuhn's *The Structure of Scientific Revolutions*. This work has drawn fierce fire since its publication (and subsequent revision in a second edition, with replies to critics), but whatever its defects, it remains one of the most widely read and influential books of our time. What his book argued (persuading the social scientists, in particular) is that science and the empirical method have no claim to immunity from the subjectivity of practitioners and the historical conditions and contexts of their practice. Instead, science is itself a social, historico-cultural process that proceeds by basically rhetorical strategies.

While many philosophers of science reject this thesis in its strongest form, it has set a new agenda and shifted the ground on which reason could be defended. The new program of the inheritors of positivism is to show that in scientific practice, now viewed universally as a historical project, choices between theories are made on rational grounds that can be made fully explicit. Such objective, universal criteria of assessment, appealing to evidence and logic, would permit philosophers to "demarcate" science from nonscience or pseudo-science. I will argue that this project too fails: the criticisms that undermined the orthodox view preclude its repair and demand instead a new, rhetorical conception of reason, anchored in praxis rather than formalism and neutral data.

Many of the arguments against positivism can be reduced to a single principle: the idea that scientific practice is rife with unformaliz-able elements, many of them inaccessible to consciousness and some of them crucial to the claim of rationality. These elements are both structural, in the form of "tacit knowledge" that is brought to bear upon tasks, and procedural, in the form of the human skills and operations that underlie purposeful activity. According to Michael Polanyi, who established the distinction between tacit and focal di-mensions of activity, the tacit dimension consists of all the cognitive structures, bodily parts, and extensions of either that bear on human action at a given moment and are instrumental to it.[15] Culturally available information and values, represented in the individual mind as a map of concepts and beliefs, act as tacit schemas to guide human intention and response. In addition, Polanyi includes in the tacit the individual's know-how, skills, and even the physical and symbolic tools that extend the body into the environment. For example, in a given experiment a telescope is tacitly part of the entire system of observation whereby the individual participates in and interacts with the environment.

Polanyi's distinction is functional, not substantive (a point often misunderstood). Elements of action are not intrinsically tacit, so that it is possible for what is tacit in one instance to become focal at some other time, though never simultaneous with its instrumental or subsid-iary function. However, there are kinds of tacit knowledge or tacit processes that remain always inaccessible to direct consciousness—the work of the operational rather than the theoretical mind. Since they are not experienced consciously, such elements cannot be formulated and subjected to criticism or direct control by the person using them, as she or he uses them. Instead, the user controls something else— carries out an action such as a linguistic utterance or bicycle riding or scientific measurement—*through* the tacit elements of grammar, mus-cles and nerves, microscopes, and so on.

Polanyi's insight that human experience depends on presupposi-tions and anticipatory schemas that actively "construct" reality is

almost a cliché of contemporary thought. It is supported by philosophical analyses from Kant onward, by psychological research on
perception, learning and development, and by studies in linguistics,
biology, and neurology. At the most fundamental level, the sensory
channels (the source of our "empirical data") cannot deliver "information" except in terms of individual and cultural structures of expectation that not only select and give meaning to facts, but determine what
we are able to notice and grasp and in what terms. Heidegger and
other phenomenologists developed the concept of forestructures of
understanding to explain the same condition of human life at an
ontological level.

This characterization of ordinary perception, supported by both
science and philosophy, has been extended to scientific observation by
philosophers of science such as Polanyi and Kuhn. Beyond the perceptual and cognitive pretheoretical understandings that scientists share
with all human beings, they bring to the simplest act of observation the
elaborated cultural schemas that we call theories and paradigms.
These actively determine not only what the scientist looks for, what
counts as a relevant fact, and what it signifies, but even to some degree
what is perceptible at all. This point is dramatically illustrated by the
work of Barbara McClintock, Nobel Prize–winning geneticist. Her
biographer, Evelyn Fox Keller, says of her:

> Through years of intense and systematic observation and interpretation
> (she called it "integrating what you saw"), McClintock had built a
> theoretical vision, a highly articulated image of the world within the cell.
> As she watched the corn plants grow, examined the patterns on the
> leaves and kernels, looked down the microscope at their chromosomal
> structure, she saw directly into that ordered world. The "Book of
> Nature" was to be read simultaneously by the eyes of the body and those
> of the mind. The spots McClintock saw on the kernels of corn were
> ciphers in a text that, because of her understanding of their genetic
> meaning, she could read directly. For her, the eyes of the body *were* the
> eyes of the mind.[16]

For years McClintock's work was ignored because scientists simply
could not see what she saw under the microscope, hence could not
even grasp what her papers espoused. Only when some of them began
to visit her laboratory and to look over her shoulder as she pointed out
the patterns on the corn, could they finally, literally, see them and
appreciate her theories.

McClintock's case illustrates not only the influence of theory on perception, but the way in which a combination of instrumentalities—vision, theoretical understandings, the microscope and slides, the technologies of drawing, photography, writing and print, among others—work together to comprise know-how, for which Polanyi uses the old-fashioned word "skill." He has examined how skills operate within processes of inquiry in his book *Personal Knowledge*. He remarks there that skills, like other kinds of "personal knowledge" in science or everyday life, are forever unspecifiable because they are originally discovered or learned as tacit instruments of a focal effort: "It [the effort] relied on an act of groping which originally passed the understanding of its agent and of which he has ever since remained subsidiarily aware, as part of a complex achievement."[17]

The constructivist notion of human perception and the role of theory in constructing scientific data pose a strong threat to empiricism by destabilizing and subjectivizing the "facts" on which theories are supposed to be based. This threat is the more poignant because the premise is itself supported by scientific inquiry. However, as we might expect, different values and preconceptions about human rationality lead thinkers to interpret and respond to this threat differently. Beyond accepting the dependence of fact on theory, there is no agreement.

With sense data now discredited as an absolute, neopositivists retreat to the second authoritative foundation for knowledge, formal reason. Here are two examples of their attempt to rescue rationality by finding rulelike criteria, the first on the level of unconscious cognition and the second on the level of theory choice. In both cases I will look at them through the eyes of their critics.

In his 1972 book *What Computers Can't Do*, Hubert Dreyfus examined the effort to model human cognition on digital computers (the converse of the effort, by computer scientists and psychologists, to construct an artificial intelligence).[18] The core of this view is the image of human cognition as information processing. The notion of knowledge it expresses, which Dreyfus traces back through philosophy to Plato, is the idea that all knowledge worthy of the name must be capable of explicit formulation in rules that anyone can apply. With the invention of the computer, this ideal came within reach, because computers need not appeal to a transcendental subject in the mind (a little man, or homunculus) to interpret and apply such rules. Thus artificial intelligence specialists are the heirs to an idealist or rationalist tradition that appears in positivism as the hypothetical-deductive method.

Dreyfus succinctly lays out this view of man as a general-purpose symbol-manipulating device in terms of the following four assumptions:

1. A biological assumption that on some level of operation—usually supposed to be that of the neurons—the brain processes information in discrete operations by way of some biological equivalent of on/off switches.
2. A psychological assumption that the mind can be viewed as a device operating on bits of information according to formal rules. . . .
3. An epistemological assumption that all knowledge can be formalized, that is, that whatever can be understood can be expressed in terms of logical relations, more exactly in terms of Boolean functions, the logical calculus which governs the way the bits are related according to rules.
4. Finally, since all information fed into digital computers must be in bits, the computer model of the mind presupposes that all relevant information about the world, everything essential to the production of intelligent behavior, must in principle be analyzable as a set of situation-free determinate elements. This is the ontological assumption that what there is, is a set of facts each logically independent of all the others. (p. 68)

Dreyfus mounts a sustained attack on each of these premises in turn. He demonstrates for a number of human activities that computer scientists have tried to model—including pattern recognition, chess playing, and certain types of problem solving—that they depend in large part on unformalizable and largely tacit structures and processes. For example, he suggests, pattern recognition in humans does not involve explicitly searching memory for templates and then comparing the perceptual item to the template. Instead, people quickly and economically recognize a pattern by at least four unformalizable means: (1) distinguishing the essential from the inessential features; (2) using tacit cues on the fringe of consciousness; (3) taking account of context; and (4) relating the individual to a paradigm (p. 40).[19]

Dreyfus's argument does not depend on the empirical fact that we are unconscious of these processes. He faces the issue at a more fundamental level, where the question is whether (regardless of human awareness) our successful performance of such activities can be explained by formalizations and be simulated on computers. If that were the case—that is, if one could create an artificial intelligence indistinguishable from humans in its functioning—one might conclude that there exists in the human mind a level of behavior that works like a computer, through explicit rules carried out rapidly and automatically.

Dreyfus argues on both philosophical and empirical grounds that this is not how the human mind works: that in principle a formal system of rule application cannot match the economy, speed, and flexibility of human performance, which depends on making explicit only as much as the situation demands and relying otherwise on tacit, global knowledge. Drawing on the work of Wittgenstein, Heidegger, Merleau-Ponty, and others, Dreyfus proposes a phenomenological explanation of intelligent behavior as rooted in the experience of living bodily in a pragmatically structured human world. It is here that he departs from the ground of agreement that I outlined earlier between neopositivists and their opponents regarding the interdependence of theory and data. For far from locating this problem in the observer, Dreyfus makes the totality of human-and-situation, and their interdependence, the unit of analysis. Facts are not imposed on a separate reality by an observer's theories; rather, the observer understands them as a total function of his own relation to the context—historical, cultural, situational. Just as the "bits of data" can no longer be abstracted from the situation, there can be no such things as rules for thought and behavior that would function the same in every context. Instead, there is context-guided orderliness, which, following Wittgenstein and Heidegger, Dreyfus compares to the regular but unformalizable flow of traffic.

The view taken by Dreyfus in the context of the problem of artificial intelligence corresponds closely to that of Kuhn in dealing with the problem of how scientists resolve anomalies and decide between theories. However, many philosophers of science, while admitting the role of theory in observation and the historical development of science, are unwilling to accept Kuhn's emphasis on unformalizable elements and nonempirical, nonlogical factors, which leads to his thesis that rival theories are partially "incommensurable" because they involve different ways of seeing the world.[20] Like the advocates of the computer model of the mind, Kuhnian critics who follow the lead of Karl Popper identify reason with following context-independent rules. Hence they attempt to show that there are universal criteria for theory choice that can be made explicit, even if only in a reconstruction after the fact. This position, called critical rationalism, emphasizes the possibility of criticism rather than positive justification of theories. This view claims that a theory is scientific if it can in principle be falsified by data, and that science progresses by a process of demonstrating error.

In his detailed analysis of this position in *Notes on the Methodology of Scientific Research*, the psychologist Walter Weimer values Popper's principle of critical rationalism because it separates criticism from the notion of proof, or justification by appeal to ultimate authority. Under this principle, science becomes a *"comprehensively critical endeavor; all* its conjectures, including the most fundamental standards and basic positions, are always and continually open to criticism" (p. 40). But Weimer shows that this position implies that even "refutation" itself becomes subject to future refutation; there is no end to testing. It becomes clear that what constitutes adequate criticism, what it should be applied to, how far it should be carried, and so on, are interpretive, context-dependent matters. In other words, even criticism itself is rhetorical: discursive and social rather than formal and rule-governed; a search for "good reasons" for scientific statements that remain always subject to new criticism.[21]

In the Kuhn-Popper controversy within the philosophy of science, the critical rationalists, having given up a positivist theory of instant rationality, would still like to describe scientific progress solely in terms of an "explicit conception of rationality . . . one which is consciously available to the individual in a form that can guide his or her behavior in given cases" (Weimer, *Notes,* p. 89). In contrast to this demand for a philosophical reconstruction of scientific growth, Weimer emphasizes implicit elements in rational decisions and acknowledges psychosocial factors in science as a practice. He replaces the notion that theory influences observation and scientific judgment with the broader idea that tacit knowledge provides a language for the scientist to think with, a lens to see through, a world view to dwell in.

Weimer agrees, then, with Kuhn's project to reconstruct scientific practice historically and psychosociologically rather than only philosophically, focusing on the "psychology of concept formation, inference, and expectation" (p. 92). A psychologist, Weimer abjures a subjectivist or exclusively cognitivist approach to science. Drawing on the work of the physicist David Bohm, he regards science as a system of perception-communication. Says Bohm:

> Science is *primarily* an activity of extending perception into new contexts and into new forms, and only secondarily a means of obtaining what may be called reliable knowledge [as codified in theory]. . . . The very act of perception is shaped and formed by the intention to commu-

nicate. . . . It is generally only in communication that we deeply understand, that is, perceive the whole meaning of what has been observed. So there is no point to considering any kind of separation of perception and communication.[22]

Thus, concludes Weimer strikingly, the logic of science is rhetorical; social, psychological, and philosophical analyses of scientific practice fall within the larger domain of understanding the rationality of science as communication and instruction. "Rhetoric has as its domain all aspects of the argumentative mode of discourse including logic, dialectic, and the methodology of science" (p. 84). Knowledge becomes a matter of "warranted assertion" within the context of a community of language users who form its rhetorical audience.

The critique of scientism reintroduces into postmodern thought the themes of rhetoric with which composition will come to identify itself. I should like to clarify this trend further by examining more closely the hermeneutical perspective on inquiry as it pertains to the relationship between the human and the natural sciences.

Toward a New Order: The Hermeneutical Alternative

While the critique of positivism in philosophy of science did not originate in the hermeneutical tradition, Kuhn himself has acknowledged that it represents an infusion of hermeneutical themes into the self-description of natural science.[23] These affinities have become clear in part because the social disciplines draw on both sources to elucidate new conceptions of their nature and methods as interpretive sciences. In doing so they fill a curious gap in hermeneutics itself, which was revived by Heidegger and his followers in an antiepistemological mode that treats the issue of method in the human sciences as derivative from a more fundamental hermeneutic in which understanding is not a special mode of knowledge but a primordial condition for human existence, reflecting the fact that man is situated in history. This move takes away the privileged status of the natural sciences (by making them derivative from a prephilosophical hermeneutical situation), but does not clarify the status or nature of interpretive methods in the social sciences and humanities. Nor, for that matter, does it explain how the natural sciences can reconstruct their own method to encompass reason and the claim of truth in a postempiricist world.

In this situation the social sciences have taken up the challenge with some sense of urgency. Although neopositivist positions and goals continue to have a tenacious hold on social thought, Paul Rabinow and William Sullivan argue in a cogent and elegant essay that the human disciplines have taken a decisive "interpretive turn."[24] The critique that they develop focuses on the underlying commonalities of previous projects to unify the social sciences within a framework in which "human actions can be fixed in their meaning by being subsumed under the law like operations of the epistemic subject" (p. 3). Structuralism, although it does replace linear models with concepts of systems and wholes, fails ultimately to overcome the fundamental reductionism of those projects. What is needed is an approach that accounts for the way the subject "knows himself through reflection upon his own actions in the world as a subject not simply of experience but of intentional action as well"—the demands of a practical anthropology as envisaged by Kant (p. 3). Rabinow and Sullivan find such a positive alternative in a focus on cultural meaning, founded philosophically in an ontological hermeneutics.

To understand how such constructive potentials inhere in the hermeneutical enterprise, we must first refute the accusation that hermeneutics simply reverses rather than deconstructs the subject-object polarity. Part of the poverty of scientism is that it can conceive as its alternative only an irrational relativism, often equated with subjectivism (although as we will see there is no necessary connection). In order to create new choices, contemporary hermeneutics must overcome this sedimented Either/Or in the face of suspicion that the hermeneutical project revives all the dangers of psychologism.

The development of postmodern hermeneutics follows a rather classic course for anti-Cartesian movements, in that critics interpreted its initial attempts to formulate positions outside the subject-object framework as simple inversions of that relation. Hermeneuticists struggled here both with the weight of their own Romantic tradition, which had never succeeded in overcoming a psychologistic bias, and with criticism that accused them of unbridled relativism.[25] (These same criticisms greeted parallel critical projects in literary and social theory.)

One can sympathize with these responses and the fears they express of what some critics called "cognitive atheism." The positions at issue often do appear radically subjectivist, and sometimes declare their self-understanding in such terms—for example, in David Bleich's argument for a new subjective paradigm.[26] Some theorists are gleefully iconoclastic about relativism, irrationality, indeterminacy, and other such ideas, which evoke the "Cartesian Anxiety." Writers like Feyerabend and Derrida adopt a playful style to further subvert the institutions and metaphysical agreements that lie behind the history of philosophy and Western science and, indeed, the very language in which these are implicitly constituted. It is no wonder that opponents draw back from what one respected Kuhnian critic, Imre Lakatos, pictured as a nightmare of "sceptical fallibillism, with its 'anything goes' attitude, the despairing abandonment of all intellectual standards, and hence of the idea of scientific progress. Nothing can be established, nothing can be rejected, nothing even communicated: the growth of science is a growth of chaos, a veritable Babel."[27]

Nonetheless, this view that Cartesian critiques necessarily embody a radically subjectivist relativism cannot be sustained. The primary reason is that the subjectivist alternative has been demolished every bit as effectively as its objectivist counterpart, undermined by a multipronged attack on the autonomous subject both as an effective agent (of communication or action) and as a self-present consciousness. One powerful influence on conceptions of the human subject was structurallism, which displaced concerns with individual experience onto the semiotic codes by which selves were thought to be constituted. Says Josué Harari of structuralism, "if reason obeys universal laws of operation, man becomes the product of structure. The notion of self or subject—individual *cogito*—prevalent in the fifties in phenomenology and existentialism, is automatically devalued insofar as human thought functions everywhere according to the same logic. . . . [W]hereas phenomenology and existentialism privileged speech (hence the individual) and claimed that the subject was at the center of the significations it generated, Lévi-Strauss, on the other hand, privileges language (hence the system) in which a subject with no possibility of totalizing the course of his history would inscribe himself."[28]

In the realm of literary interpretation, it might appear that decentering the speaking subject—the author—merely shifts responsibility for meaning to another subject, the reader. Phillip Lewis argues that structuralism does contain a residual subjectivism in this respect,[29] and the same could be argued of reader-response criticism (Fish, Holland, Bleich, and others). However, as Walter Benn Michaels has pointed out, the notion of an autonomous reader is as problematic as that of an autonomous text or author.[30] Ultimately the reader as subject dissolves in codes, becomes a fictional role, or otherwise loses primacy.

A second source for the dethroning of the subject is what Paul Ricoeur calls the "suspicious hermeneutics" of Marx, Neitzsche, and

Freud. Ricoeur has shown that together these masters present a critique of culture centered on a conception of "false consciousness" and revealing that illusion is not an error or lie but "a cultural structure, a dimension of our social discourse."[31] These negative hermeneuticists attack the Cartesian conception of the cogito at its very heart: "The philosopher trained in the school of Descartes knows that things are doubtful, that they are not such as they appear; but he does not doubt that consciousness is such as it appears to itself; in consciousness, meaning and consciousness of meaning coincide. Since Marx, Nietzsche, and Freud, this too has become doubtful. After the doubt about things, we have started to doubt consciousness."[32] Ricoeur sees this demystification of consciousness as opening the way to a new hermeneutics in which reflection can be accomplished only indirectly, through a deciphering or interpretation of cultural meaning.

No contemporary hermeneuticist, then, can have recourse to the subject as foundation, any more than the contemporary philosopher of science can return to a naive empiricism.[33] The specter of irrationality, while real, does not derive from an irresponsible subjectivism but from the loss of foundation itself, which generates the malaise and moral paralysis of the "Cartesian Anxiety." Richard Bernstein demonstrates that the battle between objectivist and subjectivist positions hides their secret unity, in the longing for an Archimedian point on which to anchor philosophy (or communication or science) against radical skepticism. A more profound "objectivism" is how he describes this unity, "the basic conviction that there is or must be some permanent, ahistorical matrix or framework to which we can ultimately appeal in determining the nature of rationality, knowledge, truth, reality, goodness, or rightness."[34]

The reconstructed hermeneutics that forms a base for an interpretive science begins, then, not with a subjective but an intersubjective turn. It takes as point of origin (rather than foundation) the situation in which human beings find themselves before philosophy or science, before the recognition of self as consciousness or world as object. This state of immersion in a pregiven world precedes any questions of method or critical thought, though this is not to say (as Calvin Schrag points out) that it is totally unreflective: comprehension is already at work in a world that presents itself as a field or horizon of human concerns. Schrag undertakes a radical reflection on this prephilosophical experience in order to conceive a philosophical anthropology and the role of the human sciences within it.[35]

In his book *Radical Reflection and the Origin of the Human Sciences*, Schrag distinguishes sharply between two levels of hermeneutics, one ontological (and primary), the other methodological. In the prior, ontological sense, hermeneutics addresses human sociohistorical existence, encompassing the reading of nature as well as cultural texts and history itself. Schrag extends the notion of "text" in traditional hermeneutics metaphorically to designate—in the terms "texture" and "*con*-text"—the interweaving of experience and interests in everyday life (p. 98). In this domain, configurative "world-facts" of perception and human action present themselves to human consciousness "not as discrete data but as experienced totalities in which figure and background are interwoven" (p. 88). The self is not marked off from and against this world but is inseparably embedded in it. Similarly, facts and meanings are not distinct; the facts of perception, practical activity, and sociopolitical action are already ways of comprehending the world. This primordial world of pure experience manifests itself, then, as a totality of experiencer-figure-ground.

Schrag makes an important point—one in which his analysis differs from some other phenomenologists' characterizations of the life-world. This experiential matrix is not mute: it is attuned to "the articulative and expressive function of ordinary language" (p. 90). Schrag argues that the life-world is not a disorganized "blooming, buzzing confusion," not purely perceptual and emotive, but generates all philosophical and scientific meanings. The life-world is cognitive and reflective, a domain of knowledge that preempts the claims of science and philosophy to initiate the operation of reason. Our understanding and comprehension of the experiential field, expressed in ordinary language, underlie the ability of more methodical reflection to create human self-understanding.

This stream of experience is not only the origin of science and philosophy, but the condition and scene of their effective practice. It is through this insight that Gadamer made a crucial new connection between hermeneutics, praxis, and reason.[36] Richard Bernstein has summarized this contribution of Gadamer's in making his case for practical reason as a common theme of apparently conflicting positions in postmodern thought. Gadamer, he says, presents a notion of reason as "historical or situated reason which gains its distinctive power always within a living tradition. For Gadamer this is not a limitation or deficiency of reason, but rather the essence of reason rooted in human finitude."[37] Gadamer supports this view through an analysis of Aristotle's conception of practical reason and practical wisdom as developed in the *Nichomachean Ethics*. This analysis allows Gadamer to develop a practical-moral view of reason in contradistinction to the modern idea of praxis as technical reason, a means by which science dominates values. In its place he revives the notion that decision making is a question not of expertise in logic and evidence, but of dialogic and context-bound negotiation based on values as they are applied to concrete situations. In essence, Gadamer's theory of reason is a theory of rhetoric. He places this rhetorical conception within the heart of hermeneutics, as a moment of "application" inseparable from moments of interpretation (in the special sense of explanation) and understanding that had traditionally been seen as separate stages.[38]

While this conception of reason as rooted in context and praxis is not beyond criticism, it does possess the potential to repair the damage done by the critique of positivism to the possibilities of knowledge based on reason. In his discussion of the work of Feyerabend, Kuhn, Gadamer, Habermas, Rorty, Hannah Arendt, and others Bernstein finds common ground in the attempt to rehabilitate reason as dialogue. Summarizing the new image of science (which incorporates a hermeneutical dimension), he says, "In order to gain a fruitful perspective on the rationality of science itself, it is necessary to see that reasons and arguments employed by the community of scientists are grounded in social practices and that there is an essential openness in the very criteria and norms that guide scientific activity. . . . [C]entral to this new understanding is a dialogical model of rationality that stresses the practical, *communal* character of this rationality in which there is choice, deliberation, interpretation, judicious weighing and application of 'universal criteria,' and even rational disagreement about which criteria are relevant and most important" (p. 172). This view is dominated by the metaphor of philosophy and science as the conversation of mankind.[39]

Let us reconsider now the question of method in the distinct sciences. We begin with the hermeneutical/phenomenological premise that *all* sciences share their origin in the precategorical life-world, where facticity and meaning are seamlessly blended. Further, although sciences differ in the use of measurement, logic, techniques of observation, experiment, narration, and other aspects of method, knowledge in all sciences is ultimately constituted in the same way, through discourse. Science is a rhetorical practice of reason, the ideal of which Bernstein has characterized in terms of these central themes: "dialogue, conversation, undistorted communication, communal judgment, and the type of rational wooing that can take place when individuals confront each other as equals and participants" (p. 223). Thus science arises from praxis, develops through practical reason, and returns to praxis, with different purposes and effects according to the varying interests of the interpretive, natural, and critical sciences.

In Schrag's account, the various scientific and philosophical studies of human nature involve selective constitutions of worlds, and subworlds, from the originary life-world. Each special domain of knowledge (art or science) involves the work of a community of investigators engaged in a dialogue by which they delineate and explore a "world" understood as a particular horizon or field of human concerns. What distinguishes the human sciences is the fact that within their thematic worlds the investigators have a communicative relationship not only with one another but with the object of study as well. "The natural sciences constitute a thematic horizon in which the data under investigation (natural objects and events) do not endow their behavior with meaning. . . . [In the human sciences] the investigatable data are human agents who endow their own gestures, speech, and actions with signification. What is at issue . . . is human actions, motives, purposes, and concerns, which directly inform the self-understanding of the agents and actors under consideration" (*Radical Reflection*, p. 69). This structure of interpretation in the human sciences is the "double hermeneutic." All sciences share a hermeneutical nature, first, through their grounding in a prescientific understanding, and second, in constituting their meanings and truths through dialogue and interpretation. However, only the human sciences operate at the second-order level of hermeneutics; they produce interpretations of interpretations.

Anthony Giddens, in defining this double hermeneutic, remarks that it implies a complex relationship in the human sciences between ordinary language and technical languages.[40] The exigencies of the double hermeneutic also require that the human sciences must recover both the empirical subject and the objectivity of the experienced world. In the first case, in order to conceive culture as a web of signification, we need a theory of the subject not as foundation but as concrete individual capable of reason, intentionality, action, and the dialogic creation of meaning through signs. At the same time, to escape subjectivism or imprisonment within a closed, virtual language or textual system, we must restore the possibility of reference through discourse to a public and intersubjectively experienced "real" world that exerts a claim of truth on the scientist. In both cases it is the primacy of context that allows the human sciences to reconstitute subject and world without lapsing into solipsism or relativism.

Since the effort to reappropriate reason, meaning, and context takes place in a postcritical world, it cannot remain naive. The entire project takes place in terms of a conversation based on the principle of critical rationalism. As a consequence, every positive and affirmative impulse is so checked by critique as to obscure the commonalities among the philosophers and scientists who share goals and concerns. Hermeneutics itself must therefore submit to a critique before we can construct a notion of the spectrum of sciences within a philosophical anthropology. Paul Ricoeur points the way in a philosophy that attempts to reconcile the possibility of recuperating meaning (for example, the meanings of myth) with the requirement for criticism that cannot be escaped in the postmodern world. He calls these the conflicting claims of "depth" and "clarity." His special virtue is his ability to show in what ways they are interdependent.

In his writings Ricoeur has tried to develop a notion of *critical moments* as an intrinsic part of hermeneutics itself.[41] Critical moments are ideas or positions that, through their opposition to a favored stance, define its limits, while in turn their own limits appear through the dialectic. In the most important cases this counterfocus is hidden within the focus itself and provides the possibility for a type of deconstruction, though Ricoeur's approach is very different from those of Derridean poststructuralism. Ricoeur finds such a critical moment in hermeneutics by showing that hermeneutics as a textual theory recognizes an inherent distanciation imposed on the interpreter by the nature of writing, which fixes the event of discourse as a public "saying." Through inscription, writing detaches this "said" from its original context and from intention in the psychologistic sense and makes it accessible to examination in objectifying ways. Analytical methods thus constitute an "explanatory" phase of hermeneutical readings. This phase intervenes and mediates between the first, naive moment of understanding (an initial or anticipatory grasp of the text) and a later moment in which the interpreter appropriates meaning in the form of the world disclosed by the text.

The reason this hermeneutical circle is necessary is that hermeneutics begins (by definition) in an initial situation of misunderstanding. The interpreter finds a text, historical event, or different culture alien and opaque because of her or his own "prejudices" and must overcome this distance through an excursion into analysis. When the interpreter does so, the experience of appropriation is not one of possession but of disclosure and self-transformation. What is disclosed is a projected world, "the proposal of a mode of being-in-the-world." The ability to appropriate that world—to fuse horizons with it—depends on "the sort of universality and atemporality implied by the explanatory procedures. Only the interpretation which satisfies the injunction of the text, which follows the 'arrow' of meaning and endeavors to 'think in accordance with' it, engenders a new *self-understanding*."[42]

Ricoeur takes this pattern to a higher altitude in discussing the relationship between a Gadamerian hermeneutics of tradition and the utopian critique of ideology offered by Habermas.[43] He shows in detail how each presumes and requires the other as complement and critique. From one perspective the critique of ideology, which claims that communication has been systematically distorted by structures of power and domination, profoundly questions the hermeneutical project to restore possibilities of meaning and understanding through discourse. At the same time hermeneutics constitutes a critique of critique. But Ricoeur makes the point that hermeneutics must incorporate within its own method experiences of distance, alienation, and distortion in the form of critical moments. According to Ricoeur, "the major characteristics of the concept of ideology are: the impact of violence in discourse, a dissimulation whose key eludes consciousness, and the necessity of a detour through the explanation of causes. These three characteristics constitute the ideological phenomenon as a *limit-experience* for hermeneutics."[44] The critique of ideology corrects a tendency in Gadamer to privilege tradition and prejudice uncritically; for this bias Ricoeur wishes to substitute a dialectic between belonging and alienating distanciation, based on the model of text interpretation. In this light he sees distanciation as the very condition for interpretation. The emancipation of the text through its self-decontextualization in inscription and subsequent recontextualization through interpretation is projected onto the general phenomenon of understanding itself.

By building criticism into the conception of postmodern inquiry, we can overcome some of the problems that Richard Bernstein has identified in the effort to move beyond objectivism and relativism. In his discussion of Gadamer, Bernstein points out that critical theory, among other positions, suggests that we can no longer count on members of a culture to share a common set of values and similarly construed world-facts. These taken-for-granted aspects of tradition have been eroded by the conditions of modern life, including the

negative intellectual critiques themselves. Bernstein speaks of the paradox "that the desired coming into being of community already presupposes an experienced sense of community" (*Beyond Objectivism*,
p. 226); the possibility of dialogic construction of values through
practical and political reason depends on a vanished polis.

Criticism helps us to identify these limits to reason, meaning, and
community insofar as they constantly impose themselves on the positive effort toward reappropriation. But it also becomes part of the very
process and project itself. The critical spirit embeds moments of distance, irony, analysis, and judgment within the interpretive effort. At
the same time it invokes the claims of truth and the regulative ideals of
communication and community, which function as utopian possibilities against which human inquiry measures its progress.

This notion of the dialectical spirit of inquiry allows us now to
reconceptualize the spectrum of sciences within a philosophical anthropology. Gerald Radnitzky has suggested that the relationship
between the cultural and the natural sciences should be approached
through a principle of "detotalizing" the claims of each.[45] Both the
hermeneutical-dialectic (i.e., the interpretive and critical) sciences and
the natural sciences make a claim that their models account totally for
phenomena within a particular sector of reality. If it can be demonstrated that each has internal limits even within its own sector that can
be defined through the other, "*the apparent polarity of the two models
dissolves and they are hence seen as complementary*" (p. 63).

In the natural sciences this demonstration has occurred, essentially, in the critique of positivism and objectivism. The natural sciences have been shown to have no authorized point of departure;
instead, they derive from a situation of primordial experience in which
meanings are already given (as "prejudices"). Their methods of construing data and evaluating theories rest on shifting criteria dependent
on the discourse of history and interpretive communities, criteria that
can never be made fully explicit nor stabilized.

The human sciences arise too from this matrix of experience,
from which they construct their own perspectival worlds. Through
their interpretive method they become doubly hermeneutical. But we
have seen that hermeneutics itself is not unequivocally an experience
of belonging or of immediate understanding (any more than the natural sciences can rest on instant rationality). Rather, hermeneutics at
the level of method is characteristically mediated by critical moments
of explanation that permit reappropriation of the lost or alien cultural
meanings in historical or aesthetic events and objects. Radnitzky

(drawing on the example of psychoanalysis offered by Karl-Otto Apel) calls these "quasi-naturalistic" moments in which objectifying methods must interrupt dialogue because understanding fails (pp. 44–45). He postulates a constant alternation and feedback between these two stances and practices in any human science.

Following Ricoeur, I will broaden the notion of critical moments beyond naturalistic methods to include a spectrum of objectifying modes that can serve as limit ideas for a hermeneutical philosophy. They become necessary just to the degree that we encounter the finitude of human will and consciousness. Even our own bodies represent an opaque zone whose workings we cannot completely know or control. Our consciousness is not only limited in its field of awareness but sometimes illusory or deceptive. Our actions, as Anthony Giddens points out, have unanticipated conditions and unintended consequences. His proposal for a hermeneutically informed social theory assumes that such a theory must deal with the ways in which human action and intentionality derive from recurrent practices through a process of *structuration* whereby human agents encounter, learn from, affect, and are affected by institutions.[46] I suggest, therefore, that appropriate critical moments for hermeneutical disciplines are those methods dealing with aspects of human experience that are, for whatever reason, outside our direct, intuitive knowledge or control. Within ourselves bodily and mental activity may be unconscious or inaccessible to direct observation and will. "Outside" us, much that we experience is felt as resistant to control or even as imposing itself upon us in the form of the will of others, brute fact, or logical necessity.[47] Phenomena at many ecological levels, including political and social institutions, are too large and complex to be affected by an individual in simple and immediate ways. Examples of counter-methods that might help us to account for this objectivity in the world within a human science include, for example, any of the suspicious hermeneutics such as psychoanalysis or Marxist theories; structuralism in any form; the biological, chemical, and physical sciences; cognitive science; critical theories concerned with violence and repression through cultural institutions (including language and communication); and structural or analytic treatments of language as symbol system.

Once we have conceived the possibility that interpretive and objectifying methods enter into a mutually limiting dialectical relation within a given field, the sharp division between human and natural sciences blurs. For this reason Radnitzky envisions a dimensional system with naturalistic and hermeneutical principles as the two poles within which specific sciences are located, depending on the practice by which they mix the two approaches. Discriminations and choices would depend on a variety of factors: the object of investigation, the instruments or media of observation, accessibility of meaning, or, as Stephen Toulmin suggests, the sensitivity of objects to disturbance and interaction. Toulmin remarks: "Dilthey had, pardonably, taken it for granted that the difference between the objectivity of material objects and the subjectivity of states of mind was absolute. . . . Yet it now appears that these two cases lie, rather, at the opposite ends of a spectrum. At one extreme, there are objects that respond to us only minimally when we observe them; at the other, there are people who interact with us in a highly responsive manner. In between, there are all kinds of more or less complex and subtle processes and organisms."[48]

In this long yet unavoidably sketchy development of the postmodern situation, with its special conditions, assumptions, and problems, context has become perhaps the predominant theme. The central insight shared by these divergent approaches is the irreducibility of the human world as a web of significations constituted through social practices, most especially through discourse enacting practical reason. This affirmative notion of context as providing meaning and the possibility of knowledge represents the precise counterpart (as God-term) to the discredited ideals of an autonomous, context-free authority—presence, logos, reason, an empirical world, and the like. But there is a certain incompleteness in the notion as I have so far explicated it. It seems to oppose rather than to include the naturalistic, extratextual, and essentially nonhuman (or unself-conscious) world that needs to be accounted for through critical moments of objectification and explanation. In the last section of this chapter I would like to climb to yet another altitude, above the level of a philosophical anthropology (the study of human nature) to that of world hypothesis. I want to show that at this level an enlarged concept of context is operating in postmodern thought, not explicitly articulated in the disciplines and movements considered thus far, but capable of unifying and explaining them in its terms. This contextualism encompasses more than the human world because it projects on the universe at large the metaphor of dramatistic event. Furthermore, it adds to the picture presented so far a dimension of process that clarifies certain radical possibilities in postmodern themes.

The Contextualist Hypothesis

To show the true scope of a contextualist paradigm, I am going to present it through the lens of a borderline discipline in which naturalistic and hermeneutical methods are equally important. This is psychology, especially developmental psychology, which has explicitly placed itself within a contextualist framework that is usually derived from the work of Stephen Pepper.[49] Members of other subdisciplines of psychology, including ecological, social, personality, and cognitive branches, have taken a similar position, drawing on a variety of sources ranging from Pepper and philosophy of science to Eastern philosophies and systems theory. Life-span developmental psychology is unusual in the clarity with which it explores the premises of this framework and its implications for method. These implications, we will see, do not remain at the dramatistic level of motive, consciousness, and intention, but extend to physical causality itself, drawing together biological, cultural, social, and environmental aspects of human development into one open, interactive system.

Robert Hoffman has made the most perspicuous presentation of Stephen Pepper's theories within a psychological framework.[50] Pepper proposed that there are four relatively adequate world hypotheses, each based on a metaphor. Pepper's 1942 book develops a conception of root metaphors as the basis for general "world hypotheses" within which philosophical and scientific questions are framed. His notion anticipates Kuhn's conception of paradigm at the most global level. Hoffman and Nead describe root metaphors as part myth and part logic. As myth they holistically fuse properties in terms of unifying principles or images. As logic they provide categories of analysis.

Although Pepper argued against eclecticism, Hoffman makes a plausible case that world metaphors can be successfully mixed. The familiar Cartesian-Newtonian framework (particularly in logical empiricism) can be seen as combining two metaphors: formism, which describes the world in terms of patterns or logical rules, and mechanism, which sees the world as a machine. As Hoffman points out, these conceptions blend effectively in computer-based models of the mind as a processor of information. The organicist hypothesis imagines the world as a growing organism. It is, in the form of Romantic or early hermeneutical views, a reply to the formist-mechanist synthesis, although it has other interpretations. Organicism has much in common with contextualism and they tend to overlap, but I will restrict my discussion to a strong contextualism.

Contextualism, which Pepper thought was the most nearly adequate hypothesis, frames the world as event. Pepper and his interpreters develop the concept of event in two basic categories: (1) process or change, and (2) context. Context (also system, field, whole, ecology, relation) refers to the total set of relationships from which particular entities and qualities derive. This whole is, by virtue of the principle of change, in a constant state of flux, a dance of information/energy patterns that underlies all the apparent stabilities, structures, and laws we experience in nature or society. Local events, or experiences, reflect these qualities in the system as a whole in being temporal and configured as fields within fields, their elements context-dependent, their meaning inexhaustible and subject to endless interpretation from different perspectives.

Most contextualist theories tend to be realist, in that they assume the underlying event flow (i.e., the context), as well as its manifestation within the explicate order as relatively stable entities or laws of nature, to be real apart from specific instances of human consciousness or participation. For instance, Don Ihde speaks of the realist emphasis in phenomenology: "Writ large and reinterpreted as a totality, it is the World and always the World with which phenomenology begins and from which the descriptive analysis springs."[51] (He contrasts this sense of realism to the residual or explicit idealism in Cartesian and empiricist metaphysics.) On the science side, ecological psychologies stress the richness of the environmental array, which presents itself to humans living (literally) within its perceptual horizons as a set of affordances for actions, as meanings already at hand.[52]

However, we know the world only in terms of human observations, descriptions, and engagements that selectively confer structure upon it, screening out some possibilities and thereby constituting others from its potential energies.[53] Therefore, say Hoffman and Nead, "contextualist theories are relativist theories, that is, relative to specific domains, niches, or purposes, and are expressed in terms of changes and invariants" ("General Contextualism," p. 518). (Relativism here is not construed as pernicious; "pluralism" conveys more accurately the idea that reality is too complex to be encompassed by any single truth or perspective on it.)

A contextualist theory is one in which all parts are not only interdependent but mutually defining and transactive, so that through their shifting relationships they continually constitute new parts or elements as well as new structures. This premise holds for the system in general, and specifically for the relationships between subject and object, observer and observed. Neither is fixed; the line between the two is neither sharp nor stable, because each is derived from and defined by the constantly new relationships in which it participates. Further, transactions in a contextualist system are both horizontal and vertical. All levels are embedded, that is, reciprocally related to all others, so that change spreads through the whole system from any given level. At the same time, change in entities or units on any given level enters into transactional patterns with other units (and changes) on the same level. This is the full measure of an ecology: a total interrelatedness and reciprocity of change for all parts and all levels. Within such a system emergent novelty, unpredictable new orderliness, becomes possible.[54]

Contextualism shares, or perhaps comprehensively articulates, the peculiar reflexivity of postmodern thought. We can see this most clearly in developmental psychology, a case study that demonstrates the possibility for a contextualist natural or quasinatural science. The developmental psychologist deals specifically with the interface between the individual—as subject of consciousness and willed action—and the environment, both physical and social, as an impersonal force that requires causal and structural analysis. Development must therefore confront all the issues and conflicts that lie between the human and the natural sciences, and it is not surprising that in its contemporary evolution this discipline has become centrally concerned with metatheory. According to Richard Lerner and others who have articulated these new perspectives, a major theme in developmental psychology today is the influence and role of philosophical foundations and world metaphors in research programs.[55] This irony about scientific discourse, which Hayden White has described as a tropical or self-constituting element, internalizes (in characteristically postmodern fashion) a critical principle in the foundational self-understanding of a discipline.[56] Lerner presents a relatively new discipline that is building into its research such a Socratic irony, which constantly deconstructs theory by a methodological pluralism.

The pluralism of developmental research recognizes on the one hand the complexity of human experience and on the other the infinite multiplication of perspectives necessary to understand it. These themes are strikingly expressed in a new view of causality as multidimensional. As Dixon and Nesselroade describe it, effects have multiple causes and causes have multiple consequents. They do not expect that any analysis will yield an understanding of human behavior based on a simple cause-effect chain involving one variable. Knowledge of a contingent universe that is "excess and indeterminate" as well as "unified, incomplete, continuously changing" will always remain itself partial.[57]

Within this contextualist framework human individuals appear remarkably various, from one to the other, and remarkably complex, viewed as multidimensional systems not clearly distinguishable from their social and physical environment. Gregory Bateson describes the inseparability of humans and their context with respect to concepts of message, learning, and mind. All three inhere in the whole system, not just the human being. He comments:

> The separation is only maintained by saying that the contexts have location outside the physical individual, while the orders of learning are located inside. But in the communicational world, this dichotomy is irrelevant and meaningless. The contexts have communicational reality only insofar as they are effective as messages, *i.e.*, insofar as they are represented or reflected. . . in *multiple* parts of the communicational system we are studying; and this system is not the physical individual but a wide network of pathways of messages. Some of these pathways *happen* to be located outside the physical individual, others inside; but the characteristics of the *system* are in no way dependent upon any boundary lines which we may superimpose upon the communicational map.[58]

Psychologists of social development now propose that the relationships between individuals and their environments are probabilistic and bidirectional, meaning that they reciprocally influence and define one another.[59] Indeed the individual as such is an open system constantly evolving through the exchange of energies with the world, through interactions (the interdependence of relatively distinct entities and processes) and transactions (their interpenetration and inseparability).[60] These kinds of interplays are called "dialectical" by those who emphasize that they are conflictual as well as cooperative, synergistic, convergent, causal, and so on.[61]

An examination of the cultural ground through the figure of identity or merger suggests that composition is prereflectively in tune with the contextualist and ecological themes of the turning point. Like the mainstream of Western thought, composition is enacting an Edenic drama of loss and reappropriation. Beginning with a negative critique of a played-out tradition, composition has attempted to forge a new positive framework for research and practice, in part by repossessing and reinterpreting its classical heritage. But the field has been hampered by the failure to recognize and reflect on its attunement with the larger cultural pattern. In the next chapter I will pursue this inquiry by trying to place composition reflectively *against* the cultural ground as a distinctive disciplinary enterprise organized by a contextualist premise.

Notes

1. The concept of a self-organizing system was developed by Ilya Prigogine and his coworkers. See Ilya Prigogine and Isabelle Stengers, *Order Out of Chaos: Man's New Dialogue with Nature* (Boulder: Shambhala, 1984). For explanations of its meaning and implications, see Erich Jantsch, *The Self-Organizing Universe: Scientific and Human Implications of the Emerging Paradigm of Evolution* (Oxford: Pergamon, 1980); and, less technically, Jeremy Hayward, *Perceiving Ordinary Magic: Science and Intuitive Wisdom* (Boulder: Shambhala, 1984), pp. 121–35.

2. Fritjof Capra, *The Turning Point: Science, Society and the Rising Culture* (New York: Simon and Schuster, 1982).

3. See Thomas S. Kuhn, *The Structure of Scientific Revolutions*, 2nd ed. (Chicago: Univ. of Chicago Press, 1970). I think pedantic criticisms of these applications of Kuhn's ideas are not only futile—"paradigm" has passed into public domain —but beside the point. While there are certainly abuses and misunderstandings of Kuhn's work, these writings in other fields capture an essential Kuhnian insight: a new recognition of the role of metaphor, presupposition, abstract conceptual structures, and context in determining problems and facts in a discipline. In the shock of self-understanding, the authors reexamine their own disciplines as social practices. This therapeutic role of Kuhn's work outweighs the copycat scientism that some criticize.

4. Jurgen Habermas, *Knowledge and Human Interests*, tr. Jeremy L. Shapiro (Boston: Beacon Press, 1971), p. 4. See Roy J. Howard, *Three Faces of Hermeneutics: An Introduction to Current Theories of Understanding* (Berkeley: Univ. of California Press, 1982), p. 31, on the doctrine of methodological monism, which he traces to a classic article by Carl Hempel.

5. Josef Bleicher, *The Hermeneutic Imagination: Outline of a Positive Critique of Scientism and Sociology* (London: Routledge, 1982), p. 5.

6. For summaries of the work of Schleiermacher and Dilthey within an overview of hermeneutics, see Richard E. Palmer, *Hermeneutics* (Evanston, IL: Northwestern Univ. Press, 1969), and Josef Bleicher, *Contemporary Hermeneutics: Hermeneutics as Method, Philosophy and Critique* (London: Routledge, 1980), as well as Howard, *Three Faces*, pp. 1–23.

7. Richard J. Bernstein, *Beyond Objectivism and Relativism: Science, Hermeneutics, and Praxis* (Philadelphia: Univ. of Pennsylvania Press, 1983), p. 31.

8. Walter B. Weimer, *Notes on the Methodology of Scientific Research* (Hillsdale, NJ: Erlbaum, 1979).

9. Richard Rorty, *Philosophy and the Mirror of Nature* (Princeton: Princeton Univ. Press, 1979), pp. 131–64.

10. For this summary I am drawing primarily on Harold I. Brown, *Perception, Theory, and Commitment: The New Philosophy of Science* (Chicago: Univ. of Chicago Press, 1977), and Weimer, *Notes*. For strong critiques see also Habermas, *Knowledge*, and Rorty, *Philosophy*; Paul Feyerabend, *Against Method: Outline of an Anarchistic Theory of Knowledge* (London: Verso, 1975); and Wayne C. Booth, *Modern Dogma and the Rhetoric of Assent* (Chicago: Univ. of Chicago Press, 1974).

11. Brown, *Perception*, p. 51.

12. Robert J. Connors, "Composition Studies and Science," *College English* 45 (1983), 1–20.

13. James Kinney, "Composition Research and the Rhetorical Tradition," *Rhetoric Society Quarterly* 10 (1980), 143–48; N. Scott Arnold, "Research Methods and the Evaluation of Hypotheses: A Reply to Kinney," *Rhetoric Society Quarterly* 10 (1980), 149–55; and Kinney, "A Rhetoric of Dismissing Differences: A Reply to Arnold," *Rhetoric Society Quarterly* 10 (1980), 156–59.

14. Anthony Giddens, *Profiles and Critiques in Social Theory* (Berkeley: Univ. of California Press, 1982), p. 3. He is actually speaking here of the decline of positivism in social science.

15. Michael Polanyi, *The Tacit Dimension* (1966; rpt. Garden City, NY: Doubleday, 1967).

16. Evelyn Fox Keller, *A Feeling for the Organism: The Life and Work of Barbara McClintock* (New York: Freeman, 1983), p. 148.

17. Michael Polanyi, *Personal Knowledge: Towards a Post-Critical Philosophy* (Chicago: Univ. of Chicago Press, 1962), p. 63.

18. Hubert L. Dreyfus, *What Computers Can't Do: A Critique of Artificial Reason* (New York: Harper, 1972).

19. Insup Taylor and M. Martin Taylor, *The Psychology of Reading* (New York: Academic Press, 1983), pp. 233–67, suggest that these are right-track operations that complement and perhaps have priority over left-track ones that function more like digital computers. However, both work together in perception and comprehension.

20. The issue of commensurability is pivotal in criticism of Kuhn, as illustrated in *Criticism and the Growth of Knowledge*, ed. Imre Lakatos and Alan Musgrave (Cambridge: Cambridge Univ. Press, 1970). See Kuhn's defense in the same volume, "Reflections on My Critics," pp. 231–78, and in the 1969 "Postscript" to the second edition of *Scientific Revolutions*, pp. 198–210.

21. Cf. the "philosophy of good reason" as developed in rhetoric by Booth, *Modern Dogma*; Chaim Perelman and L. Olbrechts-Tyteca, *The New Rhetoric: A Treatise on Argumentation*, tr. John Wilkinson and Purcell Weaver (Notre Dame: Univ. of Notre Dame Press, 1969); and others.

22. David Bohm, "Science as Perception-Communication," in *The Structure of Scientific Theories*, ed. F. Suppe (Urbana IL: Univ. of Illinois Press, 1974), p. 374; quoted in Weimer, *Notes*, p. 74.

23. Thomas S. Kuhn, *The Essential Tension: Selected Studies in Scientific Tradition and Change* (Chicago: Univ. of Chicago Press, 1977), p. xv.

24. Paul Rabinow and William M. Sullivan, "The Interpretive Turn: Emergence of an Approach," introduction to *Interpretive Social Science: A Reader*, ed. Paul Rabinow and William M. Sullivan (Berkeley: Univ. of California Press, 1979).

25. Divisions within contemporary hermeneutics express this struggle (e.g., in the famous Habermas-Gadamer debate and the objectivism found in the work of Emilio Betti and E. D. Hirsch). For discussions see David Couzens Hoy, *The Critical Circle: Literature and History in Contemporary Hermeneutics* (Berkeley: Univ. of California Press, 1978), pp. 43-72, and Bleicher, *Contemporary Hermeneutics*.

26. David Bleich, *Subjective Criticism* (Baltimore: Johns Hopkins Univ. Press, 1978).

27. Imre Lakatos, "Falsification and the Methodology of Scientific Research Programmes," in Lakatos and Musgrave, *Criticism*, p. 113.

28. Josué V. Harari, "Critical Factions/Critical Fictions," introduction to *Textual Strategies: Perspectives in Post-Structuralist Criticism*, ed. Josué V. Harari (Ithaca: Cornell Univ. Press, 1979), p. 20. See also, in the same volume, Michel Foucault, "What Is an Author?" pp. 141-60.

29. Philip Lewis, "The Post-Structuralist Condition," *Dialectics* 12 (1982), 2-24.

30. Walter Benn Michaels, "The Interpreter's Self: Peirce on the Cartesian 'Subject,'" in *Reader-Response Criticism: From Formalism to Post-Structuralism*, ed. Jane P. Tompkins (Baltimore: Johns Hopkins Univ. Press, 1980), pp. 185-200.

31. Paul Ricoeur, *Paul Ricoeur: An Anthology of His Work*, ed. Charles E. Reagan and David Stewart (Boston: Beacon Press, 1978), p. 214.

32. Paul Ricoeur, *Freud and Philosophy: An Essay on Interpretation*, tr. Denis Savage (New Haven: Yale Univ. Press, 1970), p. 33.

33. See Paul Ricoeur, "The Question of the Subject: The Challenge of Semiology," tr. Kathleen McLaughlin, in Ricoeur, *The Conflict of Interpretations: Essays in Hermeneutics*, ed. Don Ihde (Evanston, IL: Northwestern Univ. Press, 1974), pp. 236-66.

34. Bernstein, *Beyond Objectivism*, p. 8.

35. Calvin O. Schrag, *Radical Reflection and the Origin of the Human Sciences* (West Lafayette, IN: Purdue Univ. Press, 1980).

36. Hans-Georg Gadamer, *Truth and Method* (New York: Seabury, 1975), pp. 274-341.

37. Bernstein, *Beyond Objectivism*, p. 37.

38. See E. D. Hirsch, *Validity in Interpretation* (New Haven: Yale Univ. Press, 1967), for a traditional interpretation.

39. Cf. Rorty, *Philosophy*, pp. 389-94, and Kenneth Burke, *The Philosophy of Literary Form: Studies in Symbolic Action*, 3rd ed. (Berkeley: Univ. of California Press, 1973), pp. 110-11.

40. Giddens, *Profiles*, p. 7.

41. See parts 1 and 2 in *Hermeneutics and the Human Sciences: Essays on Language, Action, and Interpretation*, ed. and tr. John B. Thompson (Cambridge: Cambridge Univ. Press, 1981), especially "Hermeneutics and the Critique of Ideology," "Phenomenonology and Hermeneutics," and "The Hermeneutical Function of Distanciation." See also "Structure, Word, Event" and "Explanation and Understanding" in Reagan and Stewart, *Paul Ricoeur*. Those who see Ricoeur and Derrida as poles apart have not noticed that the notion of distanciation based on the textual metaphor corresponds closely to Derrida's view of the nature and priority of writing. See Jacques Derrida, *Of Grammatology*, tr. Gayatri Chakravorty Spivak (Baltimore: Johns Hopkins Univ. Press, 1974); Lawrence Lawlor, "Event and Repeatability: Ricoeur and Derrida in Debate," *Pre/Text* 4 (1983), special issue on *Ricoeur and Rhetoric*, ed. Louise Wetherbee Phelps, 317-34; and Paul Ricoeur, "Toward a 'Post-Critical Rhetoric'? A Reply," *Pre/Text* 5 (1984), 9-16.

42. Ricoeur, in Thompson, *Hermeneutics*, pp. 192–93.

43. In addition to "Hermeneutics and the Critique of Ideology," see Paul Ricoeur, "Ideology and Utopia as Cultural Imagination," *Philosophic Exchange* 2 (1976), 16–28.

44. Ricoeur, in Thompson, *Hermeneutics*, pp. 85–86.

45. Gerald Radnitzky, *Continental Schools of Metascience*, vol. 2 in *Contemporary Schools of Metascience* (Göteborg, Sweden: Akademiförlaget, 1968), p. 62.

46. Giddens, *Profiles*, pp. 35–39. Cf. Henry A. Giroux, "The Politics of Educational Theory," *Social Text* 5 (1982), 86–107.

47. On this duality of experience, see Peter L. Berger and Thomas Luckmann, *The Social Construction of Reality: A Treatise in the Sociology of Knowledge* (Garden City, NY: Doubleday, 1967).

48. Stephen Toulmin, "The Construal of Reality: Criticism in Modern and Postmodern Science," in *Politics of Interpretation*, ed. W. J. T. Mitchell (Chicago: Univ. of Chicago Press, 1983), p. 103.

49. Stephen C. Pepper, *World Hypotheses: A Study of Evidence* (Berkeley: Univ. of California Press, 1942).

50. E.g., Robert R. Hoffman, "Context and Contextualism in the Psychology of Learning," *Cahiers de psychologie cognitive* 6 (1986), 215–32; and Robert R. Hoffman and James M. Nead, "General Contextualism, Ecological Science and Cognitive Research," *Journal of Mind and Behavior* 4 (1983), 507–60.

51. Don Ihde, *Existential Technics* (Albany: State Univ. of New York Press, 1983), p. 161.

52. For some examples of ecological psychology, see *Perceiving, Acting, and Knowing: Toward an Ecological Psychology* (Hillsdale, NJ: Erlbaum, 1977); and *Cognition and the Symbolic Processes*, ed. Walter B. Weimer and David S. Palermo, 2 vols. (Hillsdale, NJ: Erlbaum, 1974, 1982).

53. See Constance Weaver, "Parallels between New Paradigms in Science and in Reading and Literary Theories: An Essay Review," *Research in Teaching English* 19 (1985), 298–316, on the "quantum leap." Note that she conflates the organic and the contextualism metaphors in this article.

54. Cf. Prigogine's open system, discussed earlier.

55. Richard M. Lerner, "The History of Philosophy and the Philosophy of History in Developmental Psychology: A View of the Issues," in *Developmental Psychology: Historical and Philosophical Perspectives*, ed. Richard M. Lerner (Hillsdale, NJ: Erlbaum, 1983); and Lerner and Nancy A. Busch-Rossnagel, "Individuals as Producers of Their Development: Conceptual and Empirical Bases," in *Individuals as Producers of Their Development: A Life-Span Perspective*, ed. Richard M. Lerner and Nancy A. Busch-Rossnagel (New York: Academic Press, 1981), pp. 1–36.

56. Hayden White, *Tropics of Discourse: Essays in Cultural Criticism* (Baltimore: Johns Hopkins Univ. Press, 1978), p. 1.

57. Roger A. Dixon and John R. Nesselroade, "Pluralism and Correlational Analysis in Developmental Psychology: Historical and Philosophical Perspectives," in Lerner and Busch-Rossnagel, *Individuals*, p. 140.

58. Gregory Bateson, *Steps toward an Ecology of Mind* (New York: Ballantine, 1972).

59. Robert B. Cairns, *Social Development: The Origins and Plasticity of Exchanges* (San Francisco: Freeman, 1979), p. 21.

60. For an explanation of the difference, derived from John Dewey, see Louise Rosenblatt, "Viewpoints: Transaction versus Interaction: A Terminological Rescue Op-

eration," *Research in Teaching English* 19 (1985), 96–107. I find both terms useful within a contextualist framework.

61. E.g., John A. Meacham, "Political Values, Conceptual Models and Research," in Lerner and Busch-Rossnagel, *Individuals*, pp. 447–74; and Klaus F. Riegel and John A. Meacham, "Dialectics, Transaction, and Piaget's Theory," in *Perspectives in Interactional Psychology*, ed. Lawrence A. Pervin and Michael Lewis (New York: Plenum, 1978), pp. 23–47.

2

The Idea of Composition
as a Discipline

In the first chapter I tried to show how a great transformation in our view of reality forms a background for the effort of composition to constitute itself reflectively as a unified discipline. The two decades in which we have striven toward that goal coincide with movements in many spheres of inquiry toward a contextualist understanding of knowledge, thought, and communication. The patterns of change vary locally and unfold at different rates in different fields, but they have a synergistic effect as interdisciplinary thinkers begin to perceive, formulate, and argue their coherence in philosophical terms.

In brief, this epistemic revolution counters the still powerful Cartesian-Newtonian model of Western science and metaphysics with a dialectic emphasizing pluralistic perspectives on a world characterized by change, holism, multiplicity, relationship, and openness. The old paradigm does not consist simply of a dominant scientism, as is sometimes thought. It is instead the relationship that developed historically between a formist-mechanist synthesis and the Romantic (organicist) reply to it, which tries to restore the lost values of feeling, spontaneity, freedom, and closeness to nature. The two together perpetuate an intractable set of dichotomies in which the opposed terms confirm and reinforce each other: reason and intuition, alienation and belonging, explanation and understanding, and other familiar dualities of the Western tradition.[1]

Contextualism avoids this dilemma by envisioning dialectic, duality, in fact a multiplicity of voices and perspectives, as the human condition: a way of knowing that corresponds to the infinite complexity and inherent possibilities for chaos or order in nature itself. This new vision, which twenty years ago existed only in fragments and obscurity, has become a powerful force not simply in intellectual circles where it is explicitly argued, but in the popular consciousness. To the academic disciplines it opens the possibility of overcoming specialization without the specter of totalization. Contextualist concepts blur genres, in Clifford Geertz's phrase, and provide a principle for multivocal dialogue among previously insular discourse communities. And finally this vision reincorporates a notion of practical wisdom within the very project of reflective thought itself, proposing the even more radical hope of reuniting doing and saying, work and word.[2]

This is an auspicious moment for composition to burst on the scene and assert a newfound intellectual identity in which praxis plays a decisive role. The problem before us in constructing an ecology of the discipline is to locate composition within the mainstream of these cultural changes and to establish its own special importance to them. The potential contributions of composition to contemporary intellectual life arise, first, from the "discourse connection," through which composition touches base with the root metaphor of contextualism; and second, from the commitment to open this new relation between human and world to every developing person.

On what basis can we articulate an idea of composition as a discipline? The movement established by the ecological strategy is from identification to difference. Having broadly sketched in the cultural ground, we must now make the affinities between composition and postmodern thought explicit and self-conscious. We will proceed in two stages. The first involves examining the "process shift" at the moment of awakening to grasp both its resonance with trends in the broader cultural system and its inadequacy to articulate a comprehensively ecological framework for composition. The topic of the second stage is contextualism itself, reexamined to discover its connection with discourse. We saw in chapter 1 that discourse is the thread linking postmodern debates of diverse origin and focus. But the centrality of discourse is not immediately evident in contextualism, the worldview that appears to encompass all these movements. I will argue that the metaphor of "event" that Pepper proposed for contextualism is frequently specified as "discourse event" or, more broadly, semiosis. Hence from one angle discourse is a trope for construing the qualities and values associated with a contextualist worldview. In reverse perspective, contextualism is an order of thought that requires certain qualities in our conception of discourse, requirements that are not met in most of the theories of discourse familiar to composition.

All this is preliminary to the work of individuating composition from the cultural ground. In the last part of the discussion, three concepts will emerge as distinctive organizing principles around which we might build a conceptual framework for composition: *reflection*, *experience*, and a *developmental orientation*. These are proposed as abstractive projections for constructing an array of working concepts and hypotheses to account for activities that fall within the proper subject matter of the field. This subject matter consists of discursive practices at three levels of responsibility: writing, or literate behavior; teaching; and inquiry. The logical exploration of these principles suggests how the discipline may negotiate its position within a network of parallel and intersecting fields.

Resonances

When process was introduced as a key term for the reformation of composition, it seemed to express a fruitful, necessary, even obvious conception of subject matter in the field. If composition as praxis was an educational art, primarily the teaching of freshman writing, then to ask "What is the nature of the composing process?" defined a new fundamental level of inquiry that was to found that practice. Such a question broke sharply with what came before in claiming, first, that teaching should rest on systematic knowledge about writing as an activity, and second, that writing is a fundamental act of the human mind worthy of the serious, sustained study that marks a discipline. These propositions, put forth in the face of the prevailing belief that writing (other than literary production) was trivial and mechanistic, transformed a marginalized profession into a potential discipline at one stroke. It was a simple but brilliantly successful move.

It was also a philosophically naive one. In hindsight (and to some observers at the time) the notion of process that was argued and celebrated by the new breed of compositionists appears underconceptualized and significantly restricted, principally because they did not understand that process was a concept rather than simply an object to study.[3] The *idea* of process promulgated throughout the late 1960s and 1970s is almost entirely unanalyzed. The term functions indexically to call for empirical description of the named event rather than for theoretical construction of its meaning. During this whole period composition has lacked any sense of irony about its own terminology, premises, and recuperative project.

Since composition, like psychology before it, originated its research without systematic definition or philosophical formulation of its terms, it took as subject matter "writing" in the most literal sense and "composing process" as the underlying psychology of that activity. In doing so, composition unwittingly perpetuated or reinstituted a number of pernicious antinomies that are now being wrung out of the research framework with great difficulty, among them speech/writing, writing/reading, drafting/revision, doing/saying, expression/communication, and of course process/product. At the same time the tacit logic of this formulation set the stage for a paradoxical and conflicted development of composition toward an explicate contextualism. For as a key term "process" was, to borrow an image from Ricoeur, "a battle field transversed by two opposing trends" that it proceeded to realize differentially. These consisted of an explicitly Newtonian interpretation of process undermined by tacit pressures toward a contextualist one.

In an essay of the early 1970s David Smith describes how speech communication encountered the same ironies and paradoxes in embracing the term *process*.[4] Communication scholars throughout the 1960s made programmatic theoretical statements compatible with a quantum relativistic (i.e., contextualist) concept of process, developing out of physics and the work of philosophers like Alfred North Whitehead. But their actual research enacted a linear, deterministic (i.e., Newtonian) concept of process as causal sequence, expressed in notions of dependent and independent variables taken over from behaviorism. Smith chastises communication scientists for this contradiction and urges them to practice what they preach.

In composition the situation is complicated by the fact that not one but both interpretations were largely tacit, owing to the philosophical naiveté of the new discipline. However, the Newtonian model dominated conceptions of process because it was assumed as a corollary of the positivist ideal that governed the legitimation of research and the expression of disciplinary goals and standards. These assumptions were not effectively questioned in relation to the research tradition until the 1980s.[5] Until then the challenge to them was posed on different planes of discourse: in vitalist or expressive views of language and learning applied primarily to practice, and in the revival of rhetoric as a parallel, semi-independent strand of the new composition. These challenges could not succeed, first, until they confronted the Newtonian conception directly on a theoretical level (and in the case of Romantic teaching, surpassed its own participation in the objectivist paradigm); and additionally, until they were reinforced by contact with other movements (e.g., Marxist theories, poststructuralism, ethnography of communication) that thematized context.

From our present perspective, however, we can see that contextualist themes are latent in the very origins of process. The rhetorical tradition never lost its grip on the imagination of the new discipline, and rhetorical scholarship always lay outside the boundaries defined by the process-product axis. Insofar as process was assimilated to this tradition, it tended to expand from a psychological to a social (i.e., contextualized) framework and attempted to account for more of the complexity and wholeness of the discourse event. At the same time, process research brings new facts into view and, when applied in the classroom, begins to reveal its oversimplifications in a self-correcting fashion. Throughout this period these tendencies are a subversive force that gradually deconstructs the concept of process, fostering an increasing self-consciousness that culminates in the kind of philosophical project undertaken here.

It should be remembered that the new compositionists imagined the process shift as a drama of loss and reclamation of a heritage, even though they did not understand the correspondence between their story and the broader pattern of postcritical thought. In this light we can understand the implicit logic of the process shift and its position within the ecology of ideas more profoundly than it understood itself. Here are some of the recuperative changes that make this point:

1. By making the act of writing a primary subject matter, the process shift implicitly downplayed notions of language as system, code, and structure in favor of language as event.
2. The focus on event introduced a temporal/historical dimension into composition, even though dynamic axes have not been fully exploited at all levels of subject matter.
3. Process restored the concrete subject to written language and thus the possibilities of agency, intention, purpose, felt experience, and effective action in a world.
4. Process reconnected thought to language and prepared the way for overcoming other oppositions that, at first, it seemed to reinforce.
5. Process initiated empirical investigations that pointedly challenged assumptions and maxims of the tradition on the grounds of their irrelevance to the actual experience of concrete individuals.
6. The process shift was a catalyst for breaking down the intellectual/political bondage of composition to literature and transforming it into a vital, intellectually open system.

Connections to the trends we have been examining should be obvious, with the exception of the last point. On this matter, many have pointed out that the subordination of composition to literature in the political structure of English departments is part of a larger apparatus of binary oppositions. This hierarchy valorizes poetic language, texts, consumption, and theory over ordinary language, discourse events, production, and practical activity respectively.[6] I will touch on this structure at various points in this chapter and later ones that deal with the significance of praxis to composition. Here I am concerned only with the intellectual ecology of composition.

The accident whereby composition became an apparent adjunct to or even a branch of literature completely misrepresents and distorts its proper relation to other disciplines. There is no historical or logical reason why composition should define itself exclusively by its opposition to the discipline of literary studies as currently defined (criticism and theory), rather than through its positive relationships to linguistics, speech communication, rhetoric, cognitive psychology, philosophy, and a host of other disciplines. Historically composition as literacy aligns with rather than opposes literature, while as rhetoric its dialectic with philosophy is arguably more important than that between rhetoric and poetic. In taking the polarity with literature as its point of departure for self-understanding, composition got caught in the same kind of aporia that hermeneutics did with positivist science, and with less justification. (It should be remembered that such an aporia works both ways, as the literary establishment may be discovering.)

The process shift did not immediately dissolve this structure. Composition still struggles against the hegemony of literature both institutionally and intellectually, vacillating between attempts to "bridge the gap" or reverse the polarity. But process indirectly undermined the exclusive nature of this frozen relationship, because it multiplied contacts between composition and other disciplines where the whole array of postcritical thought came into view. In this respect it did on a contemporaneous level what the revival of rhetoric did historically, repositioning composition within the global ecology of knowledge.

Why is it that, despite the resonances I have pointed to, process is ultimately too frail a concept to support what Susanne Langer calls "the heavy strains of bold speculative hypothesis"? The original conception of process that emerged from the shift is deeply flawed, being burdened by scientism, psychologism, dichotomization, severely restricted scope, and ecological blindness. Many but not all of these problems can be traced to the fact that those using the term were simply unreflective about its meaning and provenance. As long as process remained a spontaneous rather than a precise scientific concept, thinkers could not treat it as a productive abstraction and systematically exploit its denotations and connotations. Instead, it brought about shifts in attention, focus, emphasis, and value that initiated a period of transition. That period was marked by great diversity, conflict, fragmentation, inconsistency, and compartmentalization. But during this time the inner logic of the process conception worked itself out in action and became slowly more visible and subject to critique.

Perhaps this is enough to rule out process as a generative term for composition: it just carries too much baggage that needs to be cleared away before we can perceive the contextualist possibilities it evokes only partially and distortedly. But I think there is more to it than that. In developing concepts we treat ordinary language as trope, then exploit the associations evoked by the term we choose. But in the case of process there are a number of words better suited to this purpose. Among them are many used here for contextualist ideas: event, act, activity, interaction, transaction, open system, relation, ecology. It is questionable whether we should choose any one of these terms to carry the whole weight of developing a framework, as I myself and others have previously attempted.[7] They are at once too powerful—being essentially root metaphors for reality itself—and too unspecific to be generative terms for composition.

Instead, we can assimilate our themes to a worldview while working to develop our own key concepts at various levels of abstraction appropriate to the needs and topics of composition. In choosing a root metaphor (whether as event or discourse), we would do well to proliferate what Peirce calls "interpretants"—signs that refigure and resymbolize the key term in a process of "unlimited semiosis."[8] As Derrida says, "What we do know, what we could know if it were simply a question of knowing, is that there never has been and never will be a unique word, a master name . . . not even the name of Being."[9] Even with interpretation, such God-terms will never generate our own working concepts by metaphoric transference, branching, or some other derivative process. They must spring directly from our own subject matter. This was the intent of the term "composing process" (which evokes but was not derived from either the Newtonian or the contextualist usage). It simply turned out in practice to be inadequate to the purpose—for example in its inability to deal with reading and textual artifacts (see chapter 7).

It is that failure, as much as the problems created by the resonances of process to conflicting epistemological frameworks, that
demands of us now the courage to look harder for productive abstractions that do not simply designate phenomena but describe them. Such
projections have the function of reconceiving facts in fresh and surprising ways, so that we can assign negotiable meanings to vague but
important terms like audience, coherence, discourse structure, felt
meaning, semantic intention, and so on.[10]

The contradictions and transitional nature of the process decades seem
abstract and lifeless in summary. Let me make them more vivid with a
representative anecdote. My example is the tagmemic grid, introduced
to composition by Richard Young, Alton Becker, and Kenneth Pike in
their 1970 textbook *Rhetoric: Discovery and Change*.[11] The context
for the grid is the authors' attempt to reformulate the writing process
as a problem-solving act on the model of science. Now ubiquitous in
composition textbooks and classes, the tagmemic matrix is associated
with the reincorporation of invention into classroom rhetoric and is
widely taught (in modified forms) as a means of systematically generating content for writing.

The grid is built around a matrix in which two sets of concepts are
played against each other. The first, drawn from physics, is the triad
"particle, wave, field"; the second, drawn from structural linguistics, is
the triad "contrast, variation, distribution." In practice most teachers
do not actually use the grid because they find it too difficult. Instead of
following the principle of playing classification *systems* against one
another, they select one of the axes and use its three *perspectives* to
provide systematic variation of angles on reality. Theorists who try to
rationalize the confusingly overlapping categories of the whole grid
often end up reducing it to an intersection of dualities (dynamic/static,
unit/system, and so on), reflecting the fact that the original choices are
not natural triads (a pair mediated by a third element).[12]

The tagmemic heuristic has come in for a certain amount of
criticism and reevaluation over the years. Most of this—as I have
suggested—is instrumental, having to do with the difficulty of applying or teaching it and, more deeply, the illogicality of its categories.
Originally the grid was also the focal point for an argument over
whether rhetoric is properly an art or an unanalyzable act of the
imagination—the famous exchange between Janice Lauer and Ann
Berthoff.[13] The debate concerns the legitimacy of heuristics as part of
composing acts, their alleged scientism, rival conceptions of writing/

thinking as problem solving or an expression of the "forming" power of the imagination, and related issues. These arguments evoke the conflict between formist and organicist conceptions of process, in that Young, Becker, and Pike drew their grid from science and modeled composing on scientific creativity, while Berthoff presented an explicitly antiscience protest shaped by New Critical thought about literature. At the same time, insofar as Lauer and Young drew on the rhetorical tradition, they expressed latent contextualist meanings in the grid, which show up openly in later reinterpretations such as Charles Kneupper's.[14]

What is missing in all these discussions, though, is a critical, philosophically oriented consideration of the original choices that constructed the grid. To my knowledge, no one has asked this question: why (not in a logical but a cultural sense) these particular axes? What is the significance for composition that one of these dimensions is drawn from modern physics and the other from structural linguistics? Why, when the grid is reduced, do people always use the physics terms rather than the linguistic ones? Are these choices compatible? Why not some other triad—from Peircean semiotics, for example? Why triads at all, instead of pairs or the Burkean Pentad?

These questions operate on a different level in aiming to elucidate the meaning of the theoretical (and practical) choices themselves, where the meaning lies in the cultural influences and themes that these choices reflect. To reply that the grid is borrowed from tagmemic linguistics is not a philosophical answer. It would be interesting and perhaps relevant to discover why tagmemicists made these choices, but that does not mean that composition can accept them uncritically. Once the grid is proposed, it implies the possibility of an infinite number of alternative matrices, not necessarily nine-celled, in which different classification systems are played against one another. We must justify the choice of these particular ones for our own purposes. And that justification must be context-sensitive at the intellectual as well as practical level.

However, this point reveals that the specific categories do not really matter, after all. The grid is less important for what it says than for what it does: it multiplies perspectives on phenomena and systematically varies them. In other words, the grid enactively conveys that reality is multiple and our understandings of it pluralistic and relativistic. Further, the matrix structure embodies interaction in requiring that we never look at reality from a single perspective but simultaneously, from the intersection or ratio of two. At the same time the two systems from which these perspectives are chosen represent new insights into structure and relation along with the dynamic nature of the world and the relativity of knowledge. The particle/wave duality was specifically put forward in physics as a principle of complementarity— the covalidity of incompatible truths.

The grid has a further meaning that derives specifically from its use for composing. The grid establishes a distance between ourselves and our own thinking such that we question our own reasoning and attempt to control its course. This is the reflexivity of consciousness, which—we will see—is intimately connected with writing. We name that property of reflection with terms like metacognition, self-consciousness, irony, criticism, and art (as in the "art" of rhetoric). This principle is the serpent in the Garden of Eden. The real reason for the acrimonious debate over heuristics is that they trigger the postcritical dilemma in a field that was formerly in a state of nature with respect to its own activity. To many, heuristics and their advocates represent from this point of view the threatening forces of structure and system, of science (despite their allegiance to "art"), of abstraction. Projecting this dilemma on the activity of writing itself, the strong Romantic strain of composition attempts to preserve the values of a "natural" relation between an individual, her discourse, and her community—values that are vulnerable to the skeptical, rational spirit. At another level, this may be understood as the effort of praxis to resist the alienating potential of self-conscious inquiry.

One measure of such resistance is the simple fact that no one thought to turn the grid on the discipline itself. That is the real meaning of the failure to grasp the grid more abstractly: we do not comprehend, or do not wish to understand, that it demands systematic reflection about our own projects. In one sense, this meditation on constructing an ecology of composition is simply an application of the tagmemic heuristic. It reveals that, in terms of the grid, composition has taken an almost exclusively particle/contrast view of its own activity. Only now are we beginning to view composition systematically from all these perspectives—as historical, evolving, systematic, embedded in greater systems, varying across contexts, distinct from other fields, and so on—and to examine their relationships. It is thus that we will position ourselves to understand how the two imperatives of contextualism, change and relation, apply to and define our subject matter.

Contextualism: The Discourse Connection

Discourse as Root Metaphor

Pepper's formulation of contextualism in terms of the metaphor of event was not really tested until contextualist theories began to proliferate. These theories did not arise deductively from his hypothesis but as the very specific results of powerful forces operating in a given universe of discourse. The language in which they express themselves is usually invented in response to those forces and not consciously borrowed from an existing metatheory like Pepper's (although his work has influenced many psychologists). For that reason it is remarkable how many of these theories turn to the sphere of discourse for a vocabulary of process and relation with which to describe reality. (Not exclusively, of course; some other sources of imagery are music, dance, mystic experience, and drama.) Very frequently verbal communication in its dynamic aspects serves as a prototype or analogue for the flux of reality, from the subatomic to the cosmic, the material to the psychic levels.

The discourse metaphor is closely related to dramatism, which projects human activity onto the universe on the model of the theater along with other narrative forms including history itself. Among the best-known dramatistic theories are those of Kenneth Burke, George Herbert Mead, and Erving Goffman. Theodore Sarbin, a personality psychologist, has given a useful synthetic account of dramatistic views as one important variety of contextualism.[15] However, in most cases these theories are explicitly chosen to describe human action in contrast to processes that are not intentional and conscious (in Burke's terminology, organized as movement). For this reason they cannot easily account for contextualist natural sciences or naturalistic elements in cultural sciences, while they have special relevance for human studies.

The discursive version of contextualism models reality on the communicative relation. The term "discourse," from a Latin root meaning "to run to and fro," expresses the intuition that this relation is *primarily* diachronic or in motion, projecting the temporality of utterance even on system. On this model, objects, events, entities, and structures are described as:

1. *Semiotic*: organized as sign/meaning relationships; mediated, triadic in Peirce's sense.

2. *Transactive*: deriving any autonomous or stable units from a holo-movement, the parts constantly influencing, defining, and modifying one another.
3. *Holistic*: functioning as a system in which all elements are interconnected and interdependent.
4. *Dialogic*: developing conversational relations such as question/answer, statement/qualification, hypothesis/implication, and so on.
5. *Dialectic*: characterized by conflict, opposition, competition. A further specification of dialogue: the two are often equated. Both dialogue and dialectic are frequently broadened from the face-to-face dyad, which produces the vocabulary and images of duality, to metaphors of conversation, as in Burke's cocktail party or Bakhtin's multivocal dialogue.

These qualities are often summarized in the terms "rhetorical" or "semiotic," depending on whether the emphasis is interpersonal or systemic.

Discourse metaphors are found everywhere, in the most unexpected contexts. Thus Prigogine, a chemist, describes the relationship between the scientist and nature as a dialogue:

> The experimental dialogue thus corresponds to a highly specific procedure. Nature is cross-examined through experimentation, as if in a court of law, in the name of a priori principles. Nature's answers are recorded with the utmost accuracy, but relevance of those answers is assessed in terms of the very idealizations that guided the experiment. All the rest does not count as information, but is idle chatter. . . . The experimental method is the art of choosing an interesting question and of scanning all the consequences of the theoretical framework thereby implied, all the ways nature could answer in the theoretical language chosen.[16]

Or there is Klaus Riegel, the developmental psychologist who builds his theories on the concept of dialectic. In one article written with John Meacham, Riegel takes dialogues such as those between mother and child as a model for dialectical development and change generally. He and other developmental psychologists such as Ethel Tobach extend the transactional (conversation) model to encompass multiple exchanges throughout the entire ecological system as it affects and is affected by organisms.[17]

In two important articles the anthropologist Myrdene Anderson and her colleagues attempt to show how semiotics pertains to the synthesis of a new scientific paradigm focused on open systems that "include the real and ideal, the material and abstract, the natural and artificial, time-independent and time-dependent, active and inactive, directional or transactional."[18] She defines semiosis as shaping transactions in systems of matter/energy, information, and mixed modes. "Signs can best be understood as carriers of both information and energy, across space and through time" (Synthetic Potential," p. 368). Her work recognizes that the convergence of scientific thought and language studies requires changes in semiotics (to incorporate pragmatics, set sign systems in motion, account for matter/energy systems), even as semiotics is becoming a universal principle for explaining order (and disorder) at all levels, from the genetic code and the cell to the cosmos.

These few examples suggest the great generative power implicit in coupling the vocabulary and imagery of event with that of discourse. The metaphor gets its flexibility and range from the possibility of interpreting it at different levels of abstraction (conversational exchange, semiotic system); applying it to different aspects of reality (psychic, material, ideal); and emphasizing different qualities of discourse (wholeness, transaction, temporality, conflict). In one sense we may characterize contextualism as a habit of construing reality in similar tropes. But this habit does not necessarily lead to comparable or even compatible descriptions, since it can be applied to different elements of reality and, more important, can express a variety of attitudes toward what is revealed. Different temperaments, situations, prejudices, and conditions of inquiry, among other things, can lead one person to moods of despair or skepticism, another to playfulness, and another to political activism—all in response to similar images of life or world.

I feel it necessary, in setting forth a conceptual structure for composition, to select certain values and attitudes from this range and argue for them, while recognizing the personal nature of such choices and acknowledging the right of others to assert different ones within the same framework. (One of the advantages of contextualism is its tolerance for internal conflict and differences, fostering the novel and unpredictable.) The choices of other compositionists become, in the framework I propose, a set of copresent values that, for me as an individual working within it, serve to criticize and limit my own, just as mine do those of others. These same relationships apply to values and emphases asserted by interest groups or schools of thought within the field. Contextualism is intended to make these different approaches and perspectives coherent, but not through a totalizing mechanism.

It seems to me, from a practical-moral standpoint, that a discipline needs at a minimum to take its subject matter to be real, to allow its topics to set the terms of inquiry, and to take an affirmative view of its own projects. By affirmative I do not mean uncritical or utopian, merely that our working program, like any science or praxis, must envision success, not failure, salted with the saving grace of irony. The objects of our study—which need not be material—must nevertheless compel our interest and curiosity by presenting themselves to us as vivid, concrete realities of experience. Finally, our approaches must fit themselves to these realities rather than the other way around—as in the technological imposition of Method. The last problem is addressed in later chapters, particularly chapter 9. The other considerations lead me to affirm two commitments; first, to realism, and specifically to the concrete variety of ordinary life in which written discourse is a significant activity; and second, to a positive appreciation of those features of reality unfolded by the contextualist insight: alterity, multiplicity, change, the ubiquity and multivocity of dialogue, the historicality of thought, and all the rest.

As a beginning, let us recall that contextualism assumes a flow of information/energy in an open system. In other words, it presumes that communication is the norm of life and of semiotic systems like human society. This premise does not have to be proved empirically: it is, within the root metaphor, the experiential reality responded to by the inquiring scientist. Contextualism also asserts the irreversibility of time (while admitting reversibility in some domains). That means we may take development as a given for any living, psychological, or semiotic system, in the sense that changes must occur within any human event, human life, mental act, or text, reflecting and responding to the in- and outflow of energy and information in the system. This exchange subjects the system to the constant threat of disorder and breakdown, but also creates opportunities to create novel order from complexity.

Far from adopting a skeptical attitude toward the possibility of communication, then, we take the position that the flow of messages (information, meaning, feelings, images, percepts, concepts—however we wish to categorize the semiotic flux) continues ceaselessly throughout the entire organism-environment system, which is a symbiotic unity. We assume the natural entry of human individuals into this flow at birth and their ability to develop powers within it as part of their normal growth. Composition separates out a strand of that growth and semiosis for study, so as to characterize its nature and describe its complexities. Because of our teaching mission, we have a special interest in asking what interferes with or distorts the flow of communication and the movement of development (i.e., what are the opposing forces associated with chaos on the one hand and with order on the other).

Contextualism supplies, then, in its first premises, the basis for treating discourse and the life-world as intertwined realities. I remarked in chapter 1 that contextualist theories tend to be realist, in that they acknowledge the facticity of phenomena in a world presenting itself to human consciousness as given, not only materially but as a web of signification. I use the term "real" here in the sense defined by Berger and Luckmann: "a quality pertaining to phenomena that we recognize as having a being independent of our own volition (we cannot 'wish them away')."[19] They tie this notion to the life-world:

> Among the multiple realities [we experience] there is one that presents itself as the reality par excellence. This is the reality of everyday life. Its privileged position entitles it to the designation of paramount reality. The tension of consciousness is highest in everyday life, that is, the latter imposes itself upon consciousness in the most massive, urgent and intense manner. It is impossible to ignore, difficult even to weaken in its imperative presence. Consequently, it forces me to be attentive to it in its fullest way. I experience everyday life in the state of being wide-awake. (p. 21)

They present language as the primary instrument by which we experience everyday life as both objective and open to our own shaping influence.

This kind of common-sense realism may appear at odds with contextualist emphases on transience, illusion, indeterminacy, difference —ideas conspicuous in poststructuralist theories where texts, authors, and readers tend to disappear. However, there is no necessary conflict. In general, contextualist theories tend to multiply realities rather than deny them. David Bohm has distinguished the explicate order—the world of phenomenal experience—from the implicate order that it unfolds, called the holomovement.[20] Human understanding always remains partial, relative to the totality of implicate orders, while developing multiplistic, multiperspectival insights (simultaneously and successively) that unfold aspects of that whole within the explicate order.

> Our basic proposal was then that *what is* is the holomovement, and that everything is to be explained in terms of forms derived from this holomovement. Though the full set of laws governing its totality is

unknown (and, indeed, probably unknowable) nevertheless these laws are assumed to be such that from them may be abstracted relatively autonomous or undependent sub-totalities of movement (e.g., fields, particles, etc.) having a certain recurrence and stability of their basic patterns of order and measure. Such sub-totalities may then be investigated, each in its own right. . . . [B]ut . . . we have always to be ready to discover the limits of independence of any relatively autonomous structure of law. (p. 178)

In addition, contextualist psychologies do not perpetuate the subject-object distinction that poses the problem of realism to begin with. Like Heideggerian phenomenology, they simply begin with the fact of the person-in-the-environment or, more broadly, with the coevolution and mutual adaptation of life to the universe.[21] They assume very practically that this adaptation means humans perceive reality directly (at some level and order), since they are successful and thriving organisms.

Because not all contextualist theories profess a frank, everyday realism, such realism represents for composition a choice—not merely intellectual but moral in nature. As experience, discourse is real; so are thought and the world to which discourse refers and addresses itself. Because composition is a praxis and studies a praxis, it is concerned with human life as concretely lived by individuals in perceptual, social, economic, and political worlds where literacy (or illiteracy) and texts have both vivid consequences and explanatory contexts. Written discourse suffuses cultural experience in a literate society and requires that we understand it in relation not only to abstract thought, personal development, learning, and literary art, but also to work and power.

I am emphasizing this commitment because it is uncommon in the humanities, which, especially with respect to texts, betray an underlying uncertainty about the existence of their objects of study that shakes the foundations of their disciplines.[22] Perhaps this is one reason for the extraordinary passion with which text-based disciplines scorn composition as "practical," while composition embraces the concrete to the extent that it still struggles with a profound anti-intellectual bias. As W. Ross Winterowd wittily puts it, in the history of English departments "literary studies were purified *to* theory, and rhetoric was purified *of* theory."[23] Recently composition has found the courage and eloquence to condemn what Hairston calls the Mandarin attitude, "an elitist mindset that prefers that which is accessible only to the few and that despises the useful or the popular."[24] These protests are the other side of a commitment affirming ordinary life and the potential of ordinary people for reflection and participation in the conversation of mankind. This commitment has a historical basis in rhetoric as an organizing principle for education, and composition is becoming conscious now of its cognitive as well as ethical content.

The second choice I wish to explore has to do with the attitude we take toward the realities revealed by contextualist interpretations. I suggest that praxis is again decisive, in that it inclines composition toward postcritical, restorative forms of contextualism that offer a model for engaged and committed activity even in the face of human finitude. I do not want to put this point invidiously, since many find such a spirit in positions like poststructuralism, critical theory, Marxism, and "edifying" philosophy that others find gloomy, skeptical, and paralyzing.[25] I am only asserting that, in order to construct a philosophy of composition, one needs more than critique. Among the thinkers whose attitudes and tone I find most congenial for these constructive purposes are Burke, Bakhtin, Ricoeur, and Polanyi. To suggest how such attitudes affect cognitive content, I will take the concept of "friendly alterity" as an example: a principle derived from the discourse metaphor and projected on human life and the universe in general.

The term "alterity" is taken from the work of Mikhail Bakhtin, where it represents a contrast, opposition, and connection between "I" and "other." In a magnificent biography of Bakhtin, Katerina Clark and Michael Holquist explain the values attached to this concept:

> If man is the language animal, he is fated to dualism, insofar as the order of signs never coincides with the order of things they name. The word is always other to consciousness, so alterity is in human nature. . . . In dealing with these dualities, Bakhtin emphasizes not so much the gaping dichotomies at the center of human existence as the strategies by which they might be bridged. This emphasis finds expression in Bakhtin's term for the condition of the word as it presents itself to consciousness, "addressivity," which implies that our relation to the world is essentially communicative. Thus, the nature of human beings is dialogic. The structuring force that organizes communicative relations—whether between self and self, self and other, different selves, or self and the world—is what Bakhtin calls "architectonics," the activity of forming connections between disparate materials.[26]

Bakhtin's attitude toward the friendly alterity of existence contrasts sharply with the sense of alienation that accompanies some contemporary accounts of "difference," or what Clark and Holquist identify as the centrifugal forces that drive entities and objects apart in a contextualist reality. Bakhtin's dialogism is a "merry science" that does not regret the loss of Edenic wholeness, even while he acknowledges the centripetal forces striving toward unity. For him these forces and their interplay constitute the interdependence of mind and world. Dialogism is a productive principle that through difference, struggle, and conflict generates possibilities for freedom, novelty, order, and meaning.

The same joy in alterity marks the work of Kenneth Burke, who develops a view of rhetoric as communicative, or addressed, by exploring the relationships between identification and division as principles of transformation: "*The Rhetoric* deals with the possibilities of classification in its *partisan* aspects; it considers the ways in which individuals are at odds with one another. . . . Identification is affirmed with earnestness [as a principle of rhetoric] precisely because there is division. Identification is compensatory to division. If men were not apart from one another, there would be no need for the rhetorician to proclaim their unity."[27] Like Bakhtin, Burke relishes the Human Barnyard in all its wild variety and scramble and prefers humanity in its state of Babel after the Fall (p. 23).

Later we will see that reason is another discourse-related principle that need not be given an exclusively negative interpretation, even though the negative, that is, critical, side of its meaning is crucial.

Contextualist Theories of Discourse.

Having shown the pervasiveness of the discourse metaphor for contextualist theories, I am now faced with the awkward prospect that available discourse theories are not comprehensively contextualist, either as specific images and systematic analyses or as the loose agreements I have called process theory. I cannot undertake to propose here a unified discourse theory, nor do I think that such a goal is desirable, if it means a characterization of discourse intended to supersede all others. Instead, I want to suggest how contextualism provides criteria for (relative) completeness and adequacy in a discourse theory.

Unlike theories in the physical sciences, theories of discourse tend to be simultaneously valid and, in the case of productive ones, not to be superseded, although they may be neglected and later rediscovered (just like great literature, art, and philosophy). In their general form they serve three major functions for composition.

First, they provide distinctions and concepts for understanding discourse in general. Most familiar discourse theories are comprehensive taxonomies that analyze, characterize, or classify discourse according to type, genre, function, form, and so on. Such descriptions serve many practical purposes, for example defining varied genres for use in testing or in organizing textbooks. They tend to codify common-sense experiential knowledge rather than provide new abstractive principles, although, again like art, they may resymbolize these understandings insightfully. Some examples influential in composition are the taxonomies of Jakobson, Britton, and Kinneavy.[28]

Theories that surpass classification or formulation of common understandings of discourse are far rarer. We can often recognize them by the new vocabulary that struggles to capture their original abstractions, provoking complaints about the author's difficult, obscure, technical style. (Bakhtin is one example, Burke another, and in the sphere of language system, Chomsky, as well.) Such theories are so rich that they spill over, either directly or metaphorically, into other domains. Thus Bakhtin's theory of authorship becomes an architectonics of human existence, his rhetoric a model for biology.

In their second function, discourse theories provide conscious schemas for analyzing or in some cases producing discourse, especially texts, in concrete situations. An important distinction is that between intrinsic and extrinsic features of the events and situations analyzed. These terms discriminate features of an event itself (intrinsic) from those of its context (extrinsic), a distinction made by anyone experiencing or describing an event as such. Intrinsic features are those that participants or observers construct from the stream of events (or the specific discourse event) as a perceived element or aspect of the concrete instance. This is a typical contextualist analytical principle because it produces boundaries that can shift over time or by perspective. Perspective is a variable rather than a criterion, that is, participants' views are not privileged over observers', or vice versa. This is so because, since one cannot observe discourse in most important dimensions without understanding it, observers are only a different type of participant. The differences lie in skill, degree of involvement, purpose, scope of observation, and so on.

Constitutive features *created* in the concrete activity of discourse contrast with extrinsic ones *associated* with it: preexisting or coexisting factors, underlying or contextual. Extrinsic features include, for example, the discourser as historical person rather than persona (e.g., his or her language habits and talents); facts in the world as distinct from their representation in discourse as propositions; language as a virtual structure available for use; and the more remote layers of contextualization wherein discoursers and events participate in institutions, large-scale intellectual movements, and other broad patterns in the ecology.[29]

Finally, in their third function, discourse theories provide normative descriptions that guide activity. The relationship between cases and discourse theories in composition is subtle, variable, and crucial. Discourse theories provide generalizations about relations between observed events or elements in events. Such generalizations are not usually predictive of behavior in detail.[30] Instead, they illuminate possibilities intrinsic in situations, conventions, genres, structures; feature some factors as more salient than others; help explain (reconstructively) complex interactions of cause or motive; and otherwise structure interpretations. But they exhibit their meaning only in application to the concrete instance. There, discourse descriptions and norms guide the subject's perception in analyzing the case of a situated, ongoing discourse event or the flow of discourse over time within a larger system.

Examples of cases in composition classrooms might be a composing event involving several drafts and responses; the body of texts written by one student over time; the exchanges, written and oral, among class members and teachers over a given topic or assignment; or a dialogue journal between student and teacher over a year. Only through such direct observation of specific cases can subjects—here, students and teachers—bring norms or ideals of discourse to bear on actual decisions and actions. (It is clear that discourse theories are deficient for such purposes unless they have a developmental dimension or are supplemented by theories of literacy development.)

We might compare the significance of cases in composition to the situation in medicine, where empirical observations may be conducted on the one hand to develop or support theories of health and disease, and on the other hand to understand the situation of an individual patient and act accordingly. In the latter instance the doctor is interested in how the case fits into expectations and norms for disease, and how it can be explained in terms of laws and well-understood causal relationships. However, every case is also novel, blending known and unknown factors unpredictably in ways that call for context-specific response guided, but not determined, by generalizations about normal and abnormal physiology, biochemistry, immunology, properties of drugs, and so on.

Within a contextualist framework, any discourse descriptions (abstract or applied), analytical schemes, and images or metaphors will be adequate only insofar as they display or account for the contextualist qualities in reality. (It will be remembered, though, that contextualism provides for an internal moment of opposition in the form of stabilities, identities, laws, "universals," and so forth.) This is not a criterion for truth, since contextualism is only a relatively adequate perspective from which to construe reality. What we ask here is that discourse theories match in some way what we perceive as the wholeness and complexity of the phenomena. Our existing theories are not so much wrong as they are thin and bloodless. They seem partial and incomplete even on their own terms, when compared to the vitality and copia of discourse itself. It helps if we regard such theories as variations and supplements to one another.

Composition has available to it many schemes for characterizing discourse. Most of these represent discourse as a set of discrete components (units and correlated functions) based on variations and elaborations of the traditional communication triangle. Such schemes are useful because they speak to the realities of our common sense experience. One way to make discourse theories of this kind more adequate in contextualist terms is to apply operators to their terms. This approach seeks to understand each element contextually. In part that means first explaining how an element (e.g., the writer as "ethos") is discriminated from a flux and perceived as invariant, stable, and autonomous. (This is a major goal of Bakhtin's theories of authorship.) Natural and traditional categories acquire greater depth and scope as concepts when we apply operators to them: temporalize them, interpret them as metaphors, expand their range of variation, multiply their interpretants, pursue their logic to the limit, or treat them in historical-institutional terms. The point of such operations is to open and critique the meanings of concepts in the hope of giving them descriptive power beyond mere designation. One example of this approach is the recent effort to reconsider audience as a concept in light of contemporary reading theories.[31] Another is my own work on process theory, which tries to select and transform terms within a comprehensive, synthetic framework.

Another route to a more adequate and fruitful discourse theory begins with inherently transactional concepts as a way of overcoming the entrenched gaps, clichéd meanings, and frozen oppositions of established taxonomies. This approach, contextualist at the origin, acknowledges a relationship as starting point and proceeds to differentiate strands from it horizontally, along the grain of the relationship, so as to capture a quality in the whole system. In addition to coherence (my topic for this kind of integrative analysis in chapter 7), many other ideas lend themselves to this approach, for example sign, purpose, message, and voice.[32] Once such a concept is formulated, it tends to have comprehensive applicability throughout a conceptual system as an interpretant or operator for other elements. This is the case with the principles developed in the next section.

The Structure of the Discipline

In this section I want to sketch a set of interconnected principles that determine a unique structure for composition. To do so we must return to the discourse metaphor. Our previous discussion failed to reveal that this metaphor incorporates its own internal dialectic in the form of an antithesis between speech and writing, or orality and literacy. Exploring this dialectical figure will help us to grasp what the focus on writing means for the identity of composition.

The Speech/Writing Pair

On the face of it, speech is primary both historically in human culture and developmentally for the individual. Whereas all human beings learn to speak, they learn to write only in literate societies and usually by virtue of formal instruction. Speech saturates culture in daily life, while writing is often restricted in particular societies to certain groups and activities. It appears from this perspective to be a derived, secondary form of language. On the other hand, for the same reasons one might consider writing an advanced form of language that introduces new possibilities for thought and communication. In Western civilization it is closely connected with the rise of rational thought in Greece and the later developments of science, along with a high culture of literary texts.

From the beginnings of Greek literacy this contrast has carried a metaphorical weight. Speech and writing were associated with different modes of thought and experience, starting with Plato. These associations permitted thinkers to elaborate the contrast as a double metaphor standing for two important sides of human life potentially in conflict as different ways of being, knowing, doing, and making. Different conceptual systems regard one of these sides of life as more basic or important than the other, expressed in the figure as the superiority of speech or writing. The consistent associations that historically attach to and distinguish speech and writing, orality and literacy, are a structure of opposition that I will call the orthodox interpretation of these pairs. Both sides of the opposition share an understanding of the meanings of speech and writing in a hierarchy that can be read in either direction.

The orthodox interpretation identifies speech with the real, the concrete, with the flow and change of life itself, with process, event, and a sense of belonging and participation in culture. Culture here is naturalized so that, through speech, we are at home in the meaningful world of objects and events. Taking these values to be paramount, Plato and others following him criticized writing as abstract, static, unresponsive to questioning, and empty of life and passion. For these thinkers, writing is the absence of the vital, dialogic qualities found in face-to-face speech.

Equally old, however, is the idealization of literacy for these very qualities. This side of the tradition understands literacy as freeing humans from their bondage to the immediate and the irrational. It equates writing with the possibility of reason, science, reflection, criticism—with the decontextualization of thought and thus the opening of hypothetical worlds. This view carries the immensely powerful weight of the success of Western science and its metaphysics, supported in the popular mind by the associations between literacy, economic power, and social status. In technological societies speech itself has assimilated the qualities and values of print writing.[33]

Without going into the complex history of these opposing trends, we can say that the symbolic turn of inquiry early in the twentieth century began a new series of debates over the relations between speech and writing. Subsequent to Saussure's structuralism, which privileged speech, literacy and textuality have come to stand at the center of postmodern discussions, but with a difference. We now have revisionist theoretical accounts, notably by Derrida, that challenge the orthodox interpretation itself. These radical reformulations of the conceptual opposition coincide with a separate set of investigations questioning the empirical basis for linking literacy to cognitive advances and thus the validity of the traditional contrasts between oral and written language.

Jacques Derrida's influential reanalysis of writing in *Of Grammatology* inverts the orthodox identifications of speech with event, and of writing with reason, abstraction, and death.[34] Speech is conventionally thought of as eventful or "present" in the sense of immediate, transient, changeable, living. But Derrida takes presence (and therefore speech) as a metaphor for foundation, that is, for the desire on the part of Western metaphysics to locate an ideal, unchanging order of meaning behind phenomena. He names this yearning "logocentricism." Philosophy takes the unmediated natural relationship between speech and meaning as metaphor for reason, logos, truth, the Word—not as processes of discourse but as final cause, the goal toward which philosophy reaches. Speech/writing is the central figure in a cluster of oppositions. Culler explains:

> In oppositions such as meaning/form, soul/body, intuition/expression, literal/metaphorical, nature/culture, intelligible/sensible, positive/negative, transcendental/empirical, serious/nonserious, the superior term belongs to the logos and is a higher presence; the inferior term marks a fall. Logocentricism thus assumes the priority of the first term and conceives the second in relation to it, as a complication, a negation, a manifestation, or a disruption of the first.[35]

Through Derrida's elaboration of the notion of "différence"—emphasizing absence, alterity, difference, deferral—it is now writing that becomes shifting, indeterminate, endlessly mediated: the antithesis of a totalizing principle.

In making these iconoclastic and outrageous claims for writing (as "archewriting," that is, as metaphor), Derrida refigures writing *as* rhetoric rather than Logos, or conversely, he reconceives Logos *as* rhetoric. In other words, his deconstruction of the opposition between speech and writing expresses at the level of metaphor the same movement I have already examined in hermeneutics and science in order to understand reason itself as rhetorical and to make discourse practices within ordinary life the model for developing knowledge.

Newton Garver makes this connection in his preface to Derrida's *Speech and Phenomena*. He takes rhetoric to be "not a matter of pure form but . . . [of] the relation of language to the world (to life) through the relation of linguistic expressions to the specific circumstances in which their use makes sense.[36] Garver aligns Derrida firmly on the side of rhetoric against the hegemony of logic in Western understandings of reason, truth, and language. In Garver's analysis Derrida emerges as a quintessential postmodern contextualist who rejects the analysis of the world into "simples," the foundationalism of empiricism and rationalism, the derivation of the finite or temporal from the timeless, and the possibility of a private language independent of social context; and who emphasizes the contextual basis of meaning, the priority of event (utterance), and the continuing dialogue of humanity ("It remains, then, for us to *speak*, to make our voices *resonate* throughout the corridors in order to make up for the breakup of presence"[37]).

In this way Derrida attaches contextualist qualities to *both* sides of the speech/writing pair and therefore to the dimensions of human life that each connotes. There remains an important distinction between the two terms and their meanings that a deconstructive analysis does not eliminate and in fact depends on. But now they are seen as interpenetrating, similar as well as different, mutually qualifying, and interdependent. Here we see the convergence of Derrida's abstract analysis with efforts to reexamine the empirical basis for the distinction. That work addresses the relationship of orality and literacy at many levels, including historical and contemporary studies of the shift from oral to literate societies, cross-cultural ethnographic and experimental research on literacy practices, and developmental studies of the cognitive and social aspects of speech and writing.[38] Such approaches develop fine-grained descriptions of causality, interaction, and variation in the relations between speech and writing in concrete situations, displaying an indeterminately rich range of ways whereby language modalities can enter into the experiences of individuals and cultures.

When we use speech and writing as metaphors, we are abstracting away from those experiences selectively, to emphasize certain qualities we perceive as normative or significant. Just as we apply those metaphors to understanding reality, new scientific descriptions of the root experiences modify our metaphors and their applications. Thus studies of orality and literacy are showing us, among other things, that ordinary speech contains prereflective possibilities; that writing can be naturalized, in other words, that literacy can develop in the unselfconscious way that speech does; that the nature and functions of literacy depend on social practices; and that writing is not decontextualized but open to recontextualization. Many of the differences between the two can be reanalyzed as concepts that cut across mode.

The Composing of Meanings

The next part of this discussion considers how writing operates metaphorically at the heart of composition to determine its first principle, which I call *reflection*. To begin, I will take up this idea within the orthodox interpretation, as associated with reason and especially critical reason. I will qualify this interpretation, however, in light of the deconstructive analyses and revisionist investigations of writing and literacy just discussed. By this means I will place reflection in relation to its complement, *experience*, and view both in light of the *developmental orientation* proper to composition.

As a working hypothesis, let us say that composition studies written language in general as a symbolic activity. At the same time, it is engaged as a profession in teaching this activity. This joint hypothesis immediately commits us to three levels of subject matter on the following grounds. Composition must examine its own teaching and research practices because in a postmodern world all disciplines are born reflexive. Also, these two levels are themselves discursive practices and specifically literate ones. Thus, we arrive at the following levels of responsibility:

3. INQUIRY INTO PRACTICES OF WRITTEN DISCOURSE
2. TEACHING WRITTEN DISCOURSE AS A PRACTICE
1. WRITTEN LANGUAGE AS A DISCURSIVE PRACTICE (COMPOSITION)

This hierarchy is a little misleading, but I will correct it later.

The first premise suggested by this definition of level 1 is that the responsibility of composition is not simply for writing as the production of a text by a writer, even in the psychological sense. It is for written language as a human activity that can be understood from many perspectives, which include but are not exhausted by the experiential states of authors and readers. I propose to define writing in the wider sense as

> a type of discursive practice whereby individuals *compose meanings* in relation to (1) the correlative composing of meanings by significant others and (2) concrete situations in semiotically constructed worlds.

The intersubjectivity of meaning-composition not only applies to brief discourse transactions (i.e., the reciprocity of writing and reading acts), but also implies an ongoing flux of meanings and their ordering in various systems of communication having temporal dimensions including event-time, life spans, and historical evolution of languages and cultures. Individuals both participate in and internalize, not a fixed system, but an ideological holomovement of discourse that is, in Bakhtin's term "heteroglot"—stratified, random, diverse, multiplanar, dialogic.[39] This definition allows us a great deal of freedom to consider the activity from different perspectives, for instance as joint (between dyads), as collective (in social groups or within institutions), as individually experienced (by authors, readers, observers, and so on), or as abstractly structured.

I am attempting here to take a concept native to the discipline and implicit in its ordinary vocabulary, and make it more precise. The notion of composing meanings has come into use in the context of efforts to account for the similarity in the work of writers and readers, both now understood as actively constructing meanings mediated by texts.[40] I want to build this into an abstractive principle based on qualities normatively associated with writing (i.e., with writing/literacy as metaphor). By expressing these properties abstractly we acknowledge that they are neither necessarily nor uniquely characteristic of written inscriptions. Instead, writing is the prototype for the possibility of composing meanings, and conversely the composing of meanings essentially characterizes writing as a discursive practice, though that does not exhaust the meaning of literacy.

Writing stands, in this abstraction, for the possibilities introduced to discourse events by inscription, specifically inscription via a visual symbol system in a semipermanent form. What distinguishes writing as a type of inscription is the way it combines permanence—the fixing of the symbol—with freedom for discoursers to change both the symbol (the writer) and its meanings (both writer and reader). That is to say, the discoursers can *compose* meaning as distinct from generating them spontaneously, "naturally," without self-consciousness. Ricoeur speaks of writing as a work, that is, something worked and formed, "the object of a praxis and a technique" on the part of both author and interpreter.[41] Writing suspends the temporality of the text act and expands indefinitely the time of the discourser to do this work. Such spatialization opens symbol-meaning-world and self-other relations and their elements to many new attitudes and processes: systematic anticipation (planning), feedback and correction, criticism, second thoughts, replay, revision, social influence, control, deliberate forming and shaping. Readers and authors have different but comparable opportunities to practice discourse as labor in this sense.

Since the properties of written inscription have been extensively discussed, I will only stress two points sometimes overlooked. It is not simply the fact of recording that matters; audiotape preserves discourse, but does not have the same potential as writing to facilitate the composing, as opposed to the spontaneous creation, of meanings. What does matter is the specific quality of writing as a basically visual system of representation. Visual signals, as distinct from audio signals, are not transient by nature, and they transform time into space, facilitating parallel as well as serial processing. (Touch—Braille—is an inferior though acceptable substitute; replayable sound is less so.) Second, writing is realized in technologies such as ink, typewriter, print, and computer that are both fixable and extraordinarily fluid, easy and cheap for writers to modify or for readers to supplement (as in marginal commentary). Writing as a medium (a symbol system and its technologies) is thus a standard against which other forms of language can be measured for a complex of properties that facilitate composing.

In its highest realization the potential for composing meanings becomes the principle of reflection, which, as we have seen, connotes the deliberative as opposed to the spontaneous, the operations of consciousness and reason, and especially the critical spirit. This principle allows us to generalize from the notion of composing meanings in acts of writing or reading (narrowly construed) to the complex of activities that Shirley Brice Heath calls "literate behavior": "analogical reasoning, verbalization about abstract topics, quick and ready skills in conversation, and sustained focus in writing exposition and narrative."[42] We can thus reconnect the concrete activities of literacy to the abstract potential in writing for composing meanings without being naive about the nature of literacy as a concrete practice.

In regarding reflection rather than literal authorship of text as the fundamental responsibility of composition, we gain ourselves a great deal of flexibility and scope to account for what the discipline actually studies, teaches, and practices. Among these are acts of writing, reading, speaking, listening, and inner speech, along with nonverbal images and other kinds of symbolism that are interdependent in literate behavior. As Jerome Harste and his colleagues show, particular literacy events are orchestrations of different forms of symbolism, not purely writing.[43] In addition, Heath is suggesting that reflection opens out into a complex of attitudes and behaviors—she emphasizes talk *about* language—not tied directly to specific writing and reading acts but associated with being literate. Because of the originary character of writing for reflection and its continuing empirical importance in encouraging and facilitating the composing of meanings, it remains the focus of composition, but now in relation to a matrix of related verbal and nonverbal activities, capabilities, and habits.

We need now to acknowledge the complexities of reflection itself in its relation to experience. The history of this concept goes back at least to Socrates and has been important for many contemporary thinkers.

My formulation is especially indebted to Dewey, Freire, Langer, Polanyi, and Ricoeur. As a point of departure, here is Dewey's definition in a book written for teachers: "*Active, persistent, and careful consideration of any belief or supposed form of knowledge in the light of the grounds that support it and the further conclusions to which it tends* constitutes reflective thought."[44] Earlier he speaks somewhat more generally of reflection as "turning a subject over in the mind and giving it serious and consecutive consideration" (p. 3). "Reflection involves not simply a sequence of ideas, but a *con*-sequence—a consecutive ordering in such a way that each determines the next as its proper outcome, while each outcome in turn leads back on, or refers to, its predecessors" (p. 4).

This definition expresses some, though not all, of the meanings I want to capture in the term "reflection." Among other problems, Dewey speaks of reflective *thought* as mental act, whereas I prefer to emphasize both the social nature of reflection and the formative role of discourse, especially textual symbolization, or writing, in facilitating deliberative consideration of subjects. As we have seen, in much theoretical discourse and in educational contexts writing/textuality stands metonymically for reflective activity. Dewey is trying to characterize that activity concretely as a process and product. More abstractly, reflection is a term developed in many philosophies to describe a process of consciousness contrasting with the naive natural state in which human beings find themselves originarily (and in which animals remain).[45] Reflection, which brings into being the subject-object split, involves the systematic and deliberative operations of reason to understand the world and our situation in it.

In chapter 1 we saw that reflection as the operation of reason objectifies and distanciates phenomena in order to come to an understanding of them that is mediated by processes of analysis, deconstruction and reconstruction, hypothesis and testing, and so on. In other words, reflection establishes an effortful relationship of knowing between human and world. (Note the correspondence to writing as work.) Reflection in this sense is associated with criticism and a concept of the negative—in Ricoeur's phrase, the "dubitative word." He and Burke both make the negative a primary feature of human language; Eco makes a similar point in his emphasis on the capacity of language to lie.[46]

The reflexivity of reflection, however, alienates reason from itself and produces the aporias discussed earlier. In those discussions we saw that an emergent postmodern consensus accepts this reflexive property of reflection without despair, since, in order to curb the totalizing and absolutist tendencies of reflection, it is necessary for consciousness to undergo what Ricoeur calls the "second Copernican revolution," which will establish its limits.[47] This is a process of submitting reason to rhetoric and history.

In coming to grips with this problem, however, many postmodern theorists fail to preserve the positive/generative aspects of reflection itself, before it is qualified by its subjection to praxis. Reflection as derived from Enlightenment ideals contains both critical and creative dimensions. The generative aspect of reason is the principle of intellectual intuition or insight, by which reflection connects us to the realities that contextualism affirms. This principle is strongly asserted by scientists like Bronowski, Polanyi, Bohm, and McClintock.[48] They stress the capacity of intuition, first, to directly apprehend order in reality under new abstractive principles that Bohm calls "insight" and Polanyi "tacit anticipations"; and then, through the complementary principle of judgment (the dubitative word) and the systematic work of observation and reflection, to rigorously develop and establish the validity of that insight.

The commitment to realism resurfaces here as a response to the world that presents itself to our consciousness in a communicative relation, such as Prigogine described in his metaphor of science as questioning nature, or Bakhtin calls the condition of "addressivity," in which we stand with regard to other and world.[49] Instead of making a claim *to* truth (in some absolute sense), we respond to the claim *of* truth made by the world on us. Reflection, broadly understood to include the empirical supports for intuition and judgment, is our response. Objectivity is in its proper sense our respect for nature as a dialogic partner, our rigorous effort to "dwell in the variety and complexity" of nature as did Barbara McClintock, with the unprecedented powers of attention that her biographer calls "a feeling for the organism."[50] For all these thinkers, reflection is deeply felt, suffused with passion. As Ricoeur points out, reflection as response to nature in this spirit of truth is always in tension with the rhetoricality of reason, its dependence on discourse and history, its insertion into a situation of human interest and sedimented belief.[51]

Reflection and Experience

Reflection is complex by virtue of its inner duality of insight and criticism; it becomes more so when we turn to its relationship to experience.

We have seen that, in the postmodern period, inquiry and reason have come to be understood as discursive practices modeled on rhetoric rather than an idealized logic. In making reflection itself rhetorical we bring it closer to ordinary human experience, but the two may still be distinguished. If science and philosophy are the praxis of reflection, daily life is praxis at a different, prereflective level. Both are discursive (i.e., rhetorical), but their discourse is different. In much European thinking about reflection this distinction is sharply maintained. What I would like to do is Americanize the concept of reflection—that is, bring it closer to experience and develop a more contextualist sense of their interrelations—along lines suggested by John J. McDermott in his interpretation of American pragmatism.

As a first step we need to examine more closely the distinctions and relations earlier formulated as three levels of subject matter:

3. INQUIRY INTO PRACTICES OF WRITTEN DISCOURSE
2. TEACHING WRITTEN DISCOURSE AS A PRACTICE
1. WRITTEN LANGUAGE AS A DISCURSIVE PRACTICE (COMPOSITION)

I have developed the concept of reflection directly from the idea of composing meanings, drawing on the metaphorical interpretation of writing to characterize written language as a symbolic activity (level 1). But now it is clear that this characterization is entirely parallel with the concept of inquiry (level 3), since organized inquiry is the praxis of reflection at its most rigorous, active, and responsible and is conducted largely through literate behavior. (We must qualify the last part of this statement by incorporating the idea of measurement, which stretches the idea of literacy further than I want to, and by acknowledging the many other nonverbal elements of empirical research. Even in the case of measurement, however, literacy mediates these elements and is decisive in formulating and arguing theory.)

What interests me at the moment is how teaching (level 2) connects levels 1 and 3. If we give level 1, writing as discursive practice, its broad interpretation, then it *encompasses* the other two levels, both teaching and inquiry being practices of literacy. However, if we conceive level 1 in its narrower aspect as that which teaching teaches, we are looking at the emergent reflective discourse of learners.

But what is it, then, that teaching teaches? Not literally writing as a discursive practice, as our working definition proposed. Teaching teaches writing to developing persons within concrete life situations. Thus it teaches the development of literacy, addressing itself not simply to particular discourse events and texts but to the whole life process by which literacy—and reflection—become habitual, skilled, mature, and subject to self-understanding, within a complex of literate abilities, attitudes, and practices.

If we apply contextualist criteria, there is no principled way to restrict the responsibility for such teaching to a particular age or setting. We will admit a close relationship between reflective uses of writing and schooling. But it has been shown empirically that literacy as a practice is not reflective in origin. In favorable circumstances it develops naturally like speech through cultural instruction that is not itself highly self-conscious or systematic. Furthermore, as a developmental phenomenon it must be assimilated to development over the life span, rather than reaching some predictable end point in late adolescence. Thus we have grounds for enlarging the teaching responsibilities of composition to encompass the origins of literacy in cultural experience and its continuing growth and application to practical contexts, such as work or public life, within the individual's personal history.

This pattern of cultural instruction moves from a prereflective stage, on the part of both teachers and students, to become an increasingly metacognitive and metalinguistic activity. In the home the child learns from the entire print environment (billboards, cereal packages, television), from stories read to him or her, from literacy events that have practical meaning. In school the teacher (representing the mainstream literate culture) constructs an environment that is reflective in many dimensions: through the teacher's thoughtful planning and implementation of instruction; through the teacher's reliance on organized knowledge about literacy; through texts that present literacy as a system; through the student's efforts to learn that system consciously; through the student's use of literacy to think, communicate, and learn about the world.

In this way the domain of responsibility designated by level 1, through the "developmental orientation" to literacy, has expanded to include something more than, and in some sense opposed to, reflection itself. That something is everyday or practical experience, with its connotations of naturalness, community, purpose, value, and context.

Since teaching is a praxis that *applies* organized inquiry (research and theory) and personal reflection in order to help the developing person move through literacy toward reflection, education in literacy may be thought of as a channel through which the two streams—reflection and experience—flow together, mingling and separating. There are more currents in this confluence than we could name. But some of them are: the teacher's decisions within the concrete situation of the class-room, where she reads, writes, and talks about texts; the teacher's reflections on these activities; experiences that the student writes about reflectively; reflections by others in cultural works that students read; reflective talk among students and teachers about their own texts. All these concrete instances are embedded in layers of other experience and reflection on the part of participants outside the classroom.

It seems now that the term *levels* of responsibility fails to capture the parallel between organized inquiry and developing literacy, both of which are reflective practices, nor does it grasp the role of teaching in mediating the two. Instead of a hierarchy, we might picture the activities of composition as forming three *regions*, each of which is both an intellectual responsibility for the discipline and the focus of practical-moral concerns. These regions (inquiry, teaching, and per-sonal literacy) are separately and together the scene of a dialectic between reflection and experience. The developmental orientation expresses a relation between cultural instruction and the development of reflection/literacy that is generalized to apply in all regions (thus, for example, it implies the reflexive study of inquiry itself as a develop-ing practice).

Figure 1 represents this conception as a new dynamic triad in-spired by David Bohm's image of atomic particles as "world tubes" (p. 10).

McDermott's work on the culture of experience in American thought provides a deeper theoretical context in which to understand the complex, multiplistic relationships created by the interplay of these three principles within and between regions of activity and responsibility. McDermott characterizes American culture as one in which experience *disciplines* reflection, "forc[ing] theoretical state-ments to respond more to the language of events than to its own mode of discourse."[52] American culture asserts the priority of experience over reflection in response to the "pressing and omnipresent collective experience of a situation that was novel at every turn" (p. 3). In a new land, values and ways of acting emerged from the context, and tradi-tional wisdom seemed "inept" to aid in managing practical life. But, McDermott argues, this openness to experience has not been properly understood as expressing a new philosophical idea of inquiry itself, in which reflection and experience are brought into a complementary and interpenetrating relation (characteristically contextualist). That is Dewey's "method of experience."

EXPERIENCE

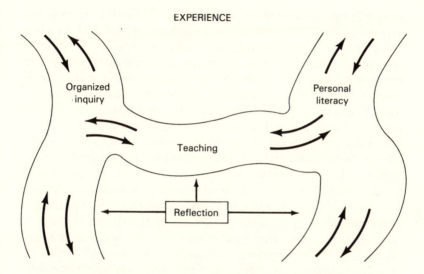

Figure 1. Regions of responsibility in composition: organized inquiry, teaching, and personal literacy.

In the method of experience, theoria and praxis become coprinciples of inquiry:

> Rather than honoring a simple dualism between thought and action, the American bent toward the practical should be viewed from a wider perspective. Both the method of reflection and the method of action are to be seen as cojoined and rotating functionaries of an experimental approach. Neither method is self-contained nor totally reliable but assumes priority relative to the nature of the problem to which it is directed. It is the problem and its resolution, or at least reconstruction on more enhancing terms, that occupies the place of importance in this approach to inquiry. (McDermott, *Culture*, p. 10)

In this view experience is not unreflective but prereflective, prefiguring tacitly in practical consciousness the systematic reflections of discursive consciousness. Anthony Giddens defines practical consciousness as "the vast variety of tacit modes of knowing how to 'go on' in the contexts of social life."[53] According to McDermott, American culture contends that "experience, as such, has informing, directive, and self-regulating qualities which are ordered and managed as subject to intelligence and as responsible to the burdens of the various contexts in which inquiry finds itself" (*Culture*, p. 10). Dewey, he says, saw experience itself as "shot through . . . with implicitness and meaning" and experimental in its vital form (p. 12).

In this view of experience American pragmatism agrees with phenomenologists (e.g., Calvin Schrag, whose views were discussed in chapter 1) and with social theorists like Giddens, and converges with schools of contemporary psychology, developmental pragmatics, and learning theory that emphasize the way organisms actively construct knowledge in experience and conceive human development as moving toward increasingly self-reflective relationships with the world. McDermott points out that the American concept of reflection as being "native and constant" (Dewey's phrase) in experience is an effort to reconstruct the idea of education and relocate the role of learning in American culture (p. 6). Dewey's method of experience is intimately connected with ideas of personal development and with the responsibilities of reflection for aiding growth. Says McDermott: "From the very outset, the notions of growth, experiment, liberty, and amelioration have characterized inquiry in American life. . . . In such a world view, the most profound recesses of reflection are themselves burdened by the obligation to reconstruct experience so as to aid in the resolution of those difficulties seen to hinder growth" (p. 9).

This philosophy seems to me profoundly illuminating for composition as simultaneously a discipline and an educational praxis. Its conception of reflection recovers, through the relationship with experience, the values and insights lost through too exclusive an emphasis in literacy on analysis, criticism, systematic thought, and the rigorous rhetoric of truth in philosophy and science. It allows us to recognize, accommodate, appreciate, and appropriate in our inquiries and teaching many other aspects of discourse as a concretely experienced practice. Among these are the naturalness of literacy; the experiences of community and belonging; the competitive, rhetorical motives and conflicts of everyday discourse; literacy as an expression of the artistic impulse; and the relations between individual experience and social institutions. At the same time we can place the focus of composition on reflection as it comes into tension with these facets and values of experience.

In composition, what we think of as knowledge *about* written discourse—the product of organized reflection—takes on a much more dynamic and open aspect through its constant testing against and within the framework of formal education. Teacher and student alike experiment with such knowledge and reflect on its relevance and validity to the minutely particular and situated literacy events of the classroom—reflections that are not simply psychological processes but a concretely interpersonal dialogue.

At the same time, the flow of organized reflection through experience implies the flow of experience toward reflection. Teachers and students alike become subjects rather than objects of reflection, so that we come to see the teacher as researcher and the student as scientist, each learning *about* written language and *with* it.[54] Their own personal experiments with reflection and symbolic action, in and out of classroom discourse, critique knowledge about literacy and about development proposed by researchers on the basis of systematic inquiry (science). As composition moves concretely into a broader field of cultural education (e.g., into homes, workplaces, prisons), this experimental relation is reproduced within other spheres and levels of society.

Dewey understood that the power of reflection tacit in experience must be subjected to elaboration and critique through the development of discursive consciousness, both in the individual and in society generally. Accepting the American premise regarding the power of experience, Dewey nevertheless "demands also an articulation of this assumption relative to the major problems faced by each generation and subject to the logical structures of the various approaches as embodied in the disciplines of intellectual life" (McDermott, *Culture*, p. 11). This demand corresponds to the two imperatives of composition: as a discipline, to develop or synthesize organized knowledge about human experiences of writing, reflection, literacy, and development; and as a praxis based on this knowledge, to cultivate personal growth in literacy and discursive consciousness. (Some would add a third: to make literacy an effective force for social critique and change.)

The American interpretation of reflection ties it directly to the developmental orientation as both an intellectual and an ethical principle. Composition is ameliorative in nature. As a representative of the intellectual community and the literate tradition, composition envisages the utopian possibility that through education the individual will be drawn into multiple universes of literate discourse rather than being merely the object of their applications. This is the hope put forth by Paolo Freire, making literacy as critical consciousness the basis for constructing communities characterized by undistorted communication.[55]

In this aspect, composition is not only a human science but what Ira Progoff calls a "humanic art," a field that goes beyond the analysis of man in society to encourage the growth of individuals in everyday experience.[56] In a humanic art this commitment has intellectual import in a way that it does not for traditional humanities and social sciences. In conceiving composition as a rigorous discipline, one cannot emphasize too strongly the significance of teaching as a daily, concrete, personal experience of the entities and activities that are the object of inquiry. In these encounters, which are saturated with meaning and feeling, teachers come to appreciate poignantly and vividly the complex, difficult relationships among reflection, development, and experience. They are not detached but participate humanly in these relations, as actors struggling to make decisions in a practical-moral situation, as thinkers reflecting on the relevance of their abstract knowledge. They themselves experience, engage in forms of literate discourse, reflect, and develop in ways that are synchronous with the ways that students do. They cannot help, therefore, but perceive the comprehensive, reflexive applicability of those terms to every region, element, and entity of the discipline.

A Discipline among Disciplines

We have found, then, a structure by which the intellectual project of composition and its teaching praxis come into harmony. The notion of writing as a discursive practice—the composing of meanings—becomes the abstractive principle of reflection. Composition acknowledges the complex, mixed character of reflection: its generative and critical sides, its rhetoricality, its roots in prereflection and speech, its semiautonomy (once developed) from writing in the literal sense. Reflection is not opposed definitely to experience, but is a way that the values of work and word come productively into dialogue. From this perspective both reflection and action are modes of learning that literacy supports and connects. In its own organized inquiry, the commitment to cultural instruction directs composition to emphasize the ways whereby these principles affect and are affected by development.

Composition associates, but does not identify, the development and practice of reflection with the acquisition of literacy. On both metaphorical and concrete levels the elements and forms of each exclude some aspects of the meaning of the other. This fact gives composition certain interests that fall outside the domain of reflection and within literacy, and others that fall outside literacy but within reflection.

This point can help us to formulate the relationship between composition and other disciplines when, having discriminated it as a unique field, we resituate it in the ecology of knowledge. Broadly, my characterization of composition places it as a human science within a philosophical anthropology. The idea is developed in later chapters that composition has no intrinsic methodology, but draws on approaches from across the range of disciplines falling within the natural, critical, and hermeneutical sciences. To these I would add praxis as a source of knowledge, both the praxes of composition itself (discourse, teaching, inquiry) and analogous arts of performance or creation (acting, sports, music, building). I see composition as favoring hermeneutical and dramatistic methods of inquiry because it is primarily interested in the terms that make events and processes of literacy or reflection intelligible to their participants. However, other methods play a critical role in constraining such descriptions and interpretations.

By virtue of its new autonomy, composition is able to reconstruct its relationship with literature, reinterpret its sometimes parasitical relationships with other disciplines, and participate in complex networks of inquiry. These relationships are of two kinds. First, there are the relationships with other specific disciplines which develop knowledge that can contribute to or benefit from the project of composition. Examples are developmental psychology, linguistics, speech studies, education, and literature. The three principles and regions that give composition its structure provide criteria for selecting and using the work of other fields.[57] Composition tends to be a synthesizing force in relation to these disciplines, incorporating their work as information and as alternate perspectives on its own topics and issues. Its principles of integration and critique are precisely those proposed by Dewey; reflection dominated by experience. In other words, composition is interested in the practical significance and validity of insights that have their own context of meaning and justification in another discipline. In addition, composition may contribute insights to such disciplines as it develops theories that explicate general properties of discourse and thought (for example, insights bearing on a philosophy of science) or specific processes and structures of discourse.

In the second instance composition participates in what van Dijk and Petöfi call "cross-disciplines."[58] These are relationally constituted genres or foci of inquiry defined by the intersection of interests among separate disciplines. (Admittedly, the distinction between disciplines and cross-disciplines is breaking down because new disciplines tend to be interdisciplinary in nature, as is composition, while old disciplines become more and more open systems. The institutional reality of such cross-disciplines changes historically, but they constitute enduring perspectives.) The cross-disciplines most crucial for composition are, historically, rhetoric and, contemporaneously, an emergent intersection of studies in literacy. Composition is logically subordinate to these fields if looked at from their own altitude, which is why composition, dealing with written discourse, is so often described as a branch of rhetoric or literacy. However, from the perspective of composition itself, it has a *surplus of meaning* with respect to any cross-discipline within which it falls. Part of that surplus is simply the region in which composition participates in one cross-discipline where it does not coincide with another, for example, the areas of difference between rhetoric and cognitive science. The rest arises through the uniqueness of composition, in the ways that it brings together these overlapping topics and concerns in terms of fresh abstractive principles that create a distinctive domain of inquiry.

The relationship between composition and other specific disciplines, in areas of overlapping and complementary responsibilities, is a matter for negotiation on logical, historical, and political grounds. Boundaries and alliances will shift as disciplines grow and develop new interests and emphases. For example, from one point of view the focus in composition on reflection distinguishes it from a primary focus in literary studies on felt experience, corresponding to a difference between discursive and presentational discourse.[59] However, this distinction has been superimposed on many other dualities, as for instance production versus consumption, specialized versus ordinary literacy, and a developmental as opposed to a cultural-historical orientation to literacy. Some of these oppositions are more productive than others. They need not be pernicious, if they become principled ways to reinscribe the complementarity of the two within shared cross-disciplines like rhetoric, literacy, semiotics, or cross-cultural discourse studies. Through such negotiations new alliances will emerge (I have worked out some here for composition with philosophy, science, and human development), many with political consequences for divisions in academia, including the possible reconstruction of English studies in terms of one or more cross-disciplines of discourse and culture.

Over and above these relationships, composition has a very special role in the ecology of knowledge because of its unique relationship to the contextualist themes of postmodernism. It is not simply that composition echoes these themes in its theoretical studies, or even that it can contribute new descriptions of the nature and elements of writing, reading, rhetoric, discourse, and all the other preoccupations of contemporary debates. The significance of composition is that it is *experimental* in the Deweyan sense. Composition *enacts* as practical-moral commitment the relations that postmodernism *proposes* between theoretical and practical wisdom, self and world. Its teacher-scholars do so in their daily work, which is a fluctuating movement between reflection and experience.

There is a new element in this experiment. In the flow of reflection from research to teacher to student there is no point at which reflection ceases and a person becomes the technological object or instrument of a static knowledge. *Both teacher and student are part of the reflective movement, which flows both ways.* There is ideally no imposition of research on teacher or of teacher's knowledge on learner. In *principle* composition understands teacher and learner themselves as critically conscious; understands experience as their primary mode of experiment; and understands reflection as their potential power to shape experience. In this way composition *generalizes* ideas put forth in the context of professional inquiry and specialized practice (ideas about systematic, collective reflection on idealized experience) to the sphere of personal, everyday experience, and places these two realms of reflection into a dialogic relation. On one level this is an intellectual achievement that establishes a continuum from the reflection and experience of daily life to that of science and philosophy, deconstructing the hegemony of the one over the other and replacing it with a transaction. On another level, this conception corresponds to the emancipatory hope of the field to open the freedom and dialogue of a contextualist world to everyone.

Ricoeur, a philosopher-educator, speaks on behalf of composition in these eloquent words about reflection, discourse, and experience:

[O]ne need not be ashamed of being an intellectual, as is Valery's Socrates in *Eupalinos*, doomed to the regret of having made nothing with his hands. I believe in the efficacity of reflection because I believe that man's greatness lies in the dialectic of work and the spoken word. Saying and doing, signifying and making are intermingled to such an extent that it is impossible to set up a lasting and deep opposition between "theoria" and "praxis." The word is my kingdom and I am not ashamed of it. To be more precise, I am ashamed of it to the extent that my speaking shares in the guilt of an unjust society which exploits work. I am not ashamed of it primordially, that is, with respect to its destination. As a university professor, I believe in the efficacity of instructive speech.[60]

Notes

1. An excellent short account of how these two perspectives developed symbiotically is found in Ilya Prigogine and Isabelle Stengers, *Order Out of Chaos: Man's New Dialogue with Nature* (Boulder: Shambhala, 1984), pp. 27–99.

2. See Paul Ricoeur, *History and Truth*, tr. Charles A. Kelbley (Evanston: Northwestern Univ. Press, 1965), pp. 197–219; and Richard J. Bernstein, *Beyond Objectivism and Relativism: Science, Hermeneutics, and Praxis* (Philadelphia: Univ. of Pennsylvania Press, 1983), pp. 171–231.

3. For my own critiques, see chapters 6 and 7 in this volume and Louise Wetherbee Phelps, "Acts, Texts, and the Teaching Context: Their Relations within a Dramatistic Philosophy of Composition," retitled "Composition in a New Key," diss. Case Western Reserve University, 1980.

4. David H. Smith, "Communication Research and the Idea of Process," *Speech Monographs* 39 (1972), 174–82.

5. E.g., see Janet Emig, "Inquiry Paradigms and Writing," *CCC* 33 (1982), 64–75; Robert Connors, "Composition Studies and Science," *CE* 45 (1983), 1–20; Lester Faigley, "Competing Theories of Process: A Critique and a Proposal," *CE* 48 (1986), 527–42; and changes in the editorial policy of *Research in Teaching English* under the editorship (beginning in 1984) of Judith Langer and Arthur Applebee. In her "Musings" in the May 1984 issue, Langer writes of a "post-process paradigm."

6. E.g., Robert Scholes, *Textual Power* (New Haven: Yale Univ. Press, 1985), pp. 6–11. For recent commentary on the politics of English, see W. Ross Winterowd, *Composition/Rhetoric: A Synthesis* (Carbondale, IL: Southern Illinois Univ. Press, 1986), pp. 323–53, and "The Purification of Literature and Rhetoric," *CE* 49 (1987), 257–73; Maxine Hairston, "Breaking Our Bonds and Reaffirming Our Connections," *CCC* 36 (1985), 272–82; Terry Eagleton, *Literary Theory: An Introduction* (Minneapolis: Univ. of Minneapolis Press, 1983), pp. 194–217; James Kinneavy, "Restoring the Humanities: The Return of Rhetoric from Exile," in *The Rhetorical Tradition and Moden Writing*, ed. James J. Murphy (New York: MLA, 1982), pp. 19–28; and various essays in *Composition and Literature: Bridging the Gap*, ed. Winifred Byran Horner (Chicago: Univ. of Chicago Press, 1983).

7. Phelps, "Composition in a New Key," develops a Burkean framework for composition based on "act." Other researchers have proposed "transaction" as the key term for literacy: see Jerome C. Harste, Virginia A. Woodward, and Carolyn L. Burke, "Examining Our Assumptions: A Transactional View of Literacy and Learning," *RTE* 18 (1984), 84–108; and Constance Weaver, "Parallels between New Paradigms in

Science and in Reading and Literary Theories: An Essay Review," *RTE* 19 (1985), 298–316.

8. I am following Umberto Eco's interpretation of C. S. Peirce's term "interpretant": Umberto Eco, *A Theory of Semiotics* (Bloomington: Indiana Univ. Press, 1976), pp. 15, 68–72. See Charles S. Peirce, *Philosophical Writings of Peirce*, ed. Justus Buchler (New York: Dover, 1955), 98–119, and *Selected Writings*, ed. Philip P. Wiener (New York: Dover, 1985), pp. 389–93.

9. Jacques Derrida, *Speech and Phenomena and Other Essays on Husserl's Theory of Signs*, tr. David B. Allison (Evanston: Northwestern Univ. Press, 1973). p. 159.

10. See Susanne Langer's discussion of conceptual bases of science in *Philosophical Sketches* (Baltimore: Johns Hopkins Univ. Press, 1962), pp. 11–16.

11. Richard E. Young, Alton L. Becker, and Kenneth L. Pike, *Rhetoric: Discovery and Change* (New York: Harcourt, 1970), pp. 126–35.

12. See Peirce's concept of "thirdness," *Selected Writings*, pp. 158, 380–89.

13. This debate of the early 1970s is accessible in W. Ross Winterowd, *Contemporary Rhetoric: A Conceptual Background with Readings* (New York: Harcourt, 1975), pp. 79–103.

14. Charles W. Kneupper, "Revising the Tagmemic Heuristic: Theoretical and Pedagogical Considerations," *CCC* 31 (1980), 160–68.

15. Theodore R. Sarbin, "Contextualism: A World View for Modern Psychology," in *Nebraska Symposium on Motivation, 1976*, ed. Alvin W. Landfield (Lincoln: Univ. of Nebraska Press, 1977), pp. 1–41.

16. Prigogine and Stengers, *Order*, p. 42.

17. Klaus F. Riegel and John A. Meacham, "Dialectics, Transaction, and Piaget's Theory," *Perspectives in Interactional Psychology*, ed. Lawrence A. Pervin and Michael Lewis (New York: Plenum, 1978), pp. 23–47.

18. Myrdene Anderson, "Synthetic Potential within, beyond, and through Semiotics," in *Semiotics 1984*, ed. John Deeley (Lanham, NY: University Press of America, 1985), pp. 363–72; Myrdene Anderson et al., "A Semiotic Perspective on the Sciences: Steps toward a New Paradigm," *Semiotica* 52 (1984), 7–47. This quotation is from "Synthetic Potential," p. 367. Cf. Eco on broadening semiotics to include communication as well as signification, *Theory*, pp. 3–31.

19. Peter L. Berger and Thomas Luckmann, *The Social Construction of Reality: A Treatise in the Sociology of Knowledge* (Garden City: Doubleday, 1967), p. 1.

20. David Bohm, *Wholeness and the Implicate Order* (London: Routledge, 1980).

21. Examples of these approaches are William M. Mace, "Ecologically Stimulating Cognitive Psychology: Gibsonian Perspectives," in *Cognition and the Symbolic Processes*, ed. Walter B. Weimer and David S. Palermo (Hillsdale, NJ: Erlbaum, 1974), pp. 137–64; Robert Shaw and John Bransford, "Introduction: Psychological Approaches to the Problem of Knowledge," *Perceiving, Acting, and Knowing: Toward an Ecological Psychology* (Hillsdale, NJ: Erlbaum, 1977), pp. 1–39; David Magnusson and Vernon L. Allen, eds., *Human Development: An Interactional Perspective* (New York: Academic Press, 1983); Richard M. Lerner and Nancy A. Busch-Rossnagel, "Individuals as Producers of Their Development: Conceptual and Empirical Bases," in *Individuals as Producers of Their Development: A Life-Span Perspective*, ed. Richard M. Lerner and Nancy A. Busch-Rossnagel (New York: Academic Press, 1981), pp. 1–26.

22. Dallas Willard calls this uncertainty over the reality of their subject matter the central problem of the humanities (personal communication). For some humanists

professing a realist epistemology, see Wendell V. Harris, "Toward an Ecological Criticism: Contextual versus Unconditional Literary Discourse," *CE* 48 (1986), 116–31; Michael Fischer, *Does Deconstruction Make Any Difference?: Post-Structuralism and the Defense of Poetry in Modern Criticism* (Bloomington: Indiana Univ. Press, 1985); and Eagleton, *Literary Theory.*

23. Winterowd, "Purification," p. 257.

24. Hairston, "Breaking our Bonds," p. 276.

25. See Harris, "Toward an Ecological Criticism," Fischer, *Does Deconstruction,* and Jonathan Culler, *On Deconstruction: Theory and Criticism after Structuralism* (Ithaca: Cornell Univ. Press, 1982). Also consider Bernstein's positive view of diverse philosophies in *Beyond Objectivism.*

26. Katerina Clark and Michael Holquist, *Mikhail Bakhtin* (Cambridge: Harvard Univ. Press, 1984), pp. 83–84. This work provides an important summary of Bakhtin's untranslated work and an overview of his philosophy of language.

27. Kenneth Burke, *A Rhetoric of Motives* (1950; rpt. Berkeley: Univ. of California Press, 1969), p. 22.

28. Roman Jacobson, "Closing Statement: Linguistics and Poetics," in *Style in Language,* ed. Thomas A. Sebeok (Cambridge: MIT Press, 1960), pp. 350–77; James Britton et al., *the Development of Writing Abilities: 11–18* (London: MacMillan, 1975); James L. Kinneavy, *A Theory of Discourse* (Englewood Cliffs, NJ: Prentice-Hall, 1971). See also Kinneavy's comparison of his own theory and three others, "A Pluralistic Synthesis of Four Contemporary Models for Teaching Composition," in *Reinventing the Rhetorical Tradition,* ed. Aviva Freedman and Ian Pringle (Conway, AR: L and S Books, 1980), pp. 37–52.

29. For a description of these nested contexts, see Urie Bronfenbrenner, *The Ecology of Human Development: Experiments by Nature and Design* (Cambridge: Harvard Univ. Press, 1979).

30. See Kenneth J. Gergen, "Stability, Change, and Chance in Understanding Human Development," in *Life-Span Developmental Psychology: Dialectical Perspectives on Experimental Research,* ed. Nancy Datan and Hayne W. Reese (New York: Academic Press, 1977), pp. 135–158. Gergen argues for an "aleatory orientation" in studies of development and behavior, emphasizing human freedom and unpredictability because of the complexity of interacting factors. See my discussion in chapter 9.

31. Lisa Ede and Andrea Lunsford, "Audience Addressed/Audience Invoked: The Role of Audience in Composition Theory and Pedagogy," *CCC* 35 (1984), 155–71; Barry M. Kroll, "Writing for Readers: Three Perspectives on Audience," *CCC* 35 (1984), 172–85.

32. See my holographic approach in chapter 4, and in "Cross-Sections in an Emerging Psychology of Composition," in *Research in Composition and Rhetoric: A Bibliographical Sourcebook,* ed. Michael G. Moran and Ronald F. Lunsford (Westport, CT: Greenwood Press, 1984), pp. 27–70.

33. Shirley Brice Heath, "Being Literate in America: A Sociohistorical Perspective," in *Issues in Literacy: A Research Perspective,* 34th Yearbook of the National Reading Conference, ed. Jerome A. Niles and Rosary V. Lalik (Rochester, NRC, 1985), pp. 1–18. See also E. D. Hirsch, Jr., *The Philosophy of Composition* (Chicago: Univ. of Chicago Press, 1977), pp. 14–71.

34. Jacques Derrida, *Of Grammatology,* tr. Gayatri Chakravorty Spivak (Baltimore: Johns Hopkins Univ. Press, 1974).

35. Culler, *On Deconstruction,* p. 93.

36. Newton Garver, preface to *Speech and Phenomena and Other Essays on Husserl's Theory of Signs*, by Jacques Derrida, tr. David B. Allison (Evanston: Northwestern Univ. Press, 1973), pp. ix–xxix.

37. Derrida, *Speech and Phenomena*, p. 104.

38. Examples are Jack Goody, *The Domestication of the Savage Mind* (Cambridge: Cambridge Univ. Press, 1977); Eric A. Havelock, *Preface to Plato* (Cambridge: Harvard Univ. Press, 1963); Walter J. Ong, *Orality and Literacy: The Technologizing of the Word* (London: Methuen, 1982); Sylvia Scribner and Michael Cole, *The Psychology of Literacy* (Cambridge: Harvard Univ. Press, 1981); Deborah Tannen, "Oral and Literate Strategies in Spoken and Written Narratives," *Language* 58 (1982), 1–21; and Elinor Ochs, "Planned and Unplanned Discourse," *Syntax and Semantics*, ed. T. Givon, vol. 12 of *Discourse and Syntax* (New York: Academic Press, 1979), pp. 51–80.

39. M. M. Bakhtin, *The Dialogic Imagination: Four Essays*, tr. Caryl Emerson and Michael Holquist, ed. Michael Holquist (Austin: Univ. of Texas Press, 1981), p. 263.

40. Anthony Petrosky, "From Story to Essay: Reading and Writing," *CCC* 33 (1982), 19–36; Patricia Bizzell, "On the Possibility of a Unified Theory of Composition and Literature," *Rhetoric Review* 3 (1986), 174–80.

41. Paul Ricoeur, *Hermeneutics and the Human Sciences: Essays on Language, Action and Interpretation*, tr. and ed. John B. Thompson (Cambridge: Cambridge Univ. Press, 1981), pp. 136–38.

42. Heath, "Being Literate," p. 12. The article develops this concept at length.

43. Jerome C. Harste, Virginia A. Woodward, and Carolyn L. Burke, *Language Stories & Literacy Lessons* (Portsmouth, NH: Heinemmann, 1984), pp. 34–40, 195–96.

44. John Dewey, *How We Think* (1933; rpt. Chicago: Regnery, 1971), p. 9.

45. E.g., Edmund Husserl in *Ideas Pertaining to a Pure Phenomenology and to a Phenomenological Philosophy, First Book: General Introduction to a Pure Phenomenology*, tr. F. Kersten (The Hague: Martinus Nijhoff, 1983); Husserl's ideas influence Ricoeur's thematization of reflection. See the discussion in Don Ihde, *Hermeneutic Phenomenology: The Philosophy of Paul Ricoeur* (Evanston: Northwestern Univ. Press, 1978), pp. 11ff.

46. Ricoeur, *History and Truth*, p. 206; Kenneth Burke, *Language as Symbolic Action: Essays on Life, Literature, and Method* (Berkeley: Univ. of California Press, 1968), pp. 9–13; Eco, *Theory*, p. 7.

47. Paul Ricoeur, *Freedom and Nature: The Voluntary and the Involuntary*. tr. Erazim V. Kohak (Chicago: Northwestern Univ. Press, 1966), pp. 31–32, 471–72.

48. J. Bronowski, *Science and Human Values*, rev. ed. (New York: Harper, 1965); Michael Polanyi, *Personal Knowledge: Towards a Post-Critical Philosophy* (Chicago: Univ. of Chicago Press, 1962); Bohm, *Wholeness*. For McClintock's views see Evelyn Fox Keller, *A Feeling for the Organism: The Life and Work of Barbara McClintock* (New York: Freeman, 1983).

49. Clark and Holquist, *Mikhail Bakhtin*, pp. 84, 214, 217.

50. Keller, *Feeling*, pp. 200–207.

51. Ricoeur, *History and Truth*, pp. 4–14. This tension is a major theme in Ricoeur's work.

52. John J. McDermott, *The Culture of Experience: Philosophical Essays in the American Grain* (New York: New York Univ. Press, 1976), p. 6.

53. Anthony Giddens, *Profiles and Critiques in Social Theory* (Berkeley: Univ. of California Press, 1982), p. 9.

54. This view of student and teacher as theorists informs the work of Harste and his colleagues in *Literacy Stories and Language Lessons*.

55. Paulo Freire, *Education for Critical Consciousness* (New York: Continuum, 1981).

56. Ira Progoff, "The Humanic Arts: Proposal for a New Degree in the Experiential Study of Man," *Forum for Correspondence and Contact* 1 (1968), 36–43.

57. See chapter 4. See also Louise Wetherbee Phelps, "The Domain of Composition," *Rhetoric Review* 4 (1986), 182–95, and Phelps, "Cross-Sections."

58. T. A. van Dijk and Janos S. Petöfi, "Editorial Introduction," *Text* 1 (1981), 1–3.

59. Susanne K. Langer, *Philosophy in a New Key: A Study in the Symbolism of Reason, Rite, and Art*, 3rd ed. (Cambridge: Harvard Univ. Press, 1963), pp. 79–102.

60. Ricoeur, *History and Truth*, pp. 4–5.

Part Two

The Process of Reconstruction

3

Possibilities for a ~~Post~~-Critical Rhetoric

> Beyond the wastelands of critical thought, we seek to be challenged anew.
>
> PAUL RICOEUR, "The Hermeneutics of Symbols"

> Only dialogue truly communicates.
>
> PAULO FREIRE, *Education for Critical Consciousness*

> Joined together, the great mass of human minds around the earth seem to behave like a coherent, living system. . . . We pass thoughts around, from mind to mind, so compulsively and with such speed that the brains of mankind often appear, functionally, to be undergoing fusion.
>
> LEWIS THOMAS, *The Lives of a Cell*

Recently the question of the future of rhetoric has come into focus against the backdrop of a crisis of consciousness in contemporary thought: a "critical moment" of self-reflection, irony, paradox, and skepticism that brings discourse and indeed the very possibility of communication under a radical critique. At the least, this crisis requires us to rethink the nature of a post-critical rhetoric; to some it may appear to jeopardize the whole enterprise. In this chapter I will attempt to reveal a pattern of reciprocities and paradoxical relationships between rhetoric and the critical dimension of modern thought that emerges with peculiar force and poignancy in the writings of Paul Ricoeur.[1] His articulation and, even more, his enactment of this pattern disclose at least one path by which rhetoric might be recuperated in a post-critical spirit.

The concept of criticism or critique is pervasive in contemporary intellectual life, where it appears not merely as the function of consciousness directed at an object, but as the reflexive action whereby consciousness knows itself. Walter Ong sees this obsession as the latest stage in the evolution of human consciousness, by which the world is more and more deeply interiorized. He points to modern novels as narratives of interior consciousness, and to psychoanalysis and phenomenology as conceptual structures for grasping and articulating consciousness and its substrates.[2] A thematized consciousness is inherently critical, in that it separates its object from the self as subject, and within that space deploys the operations of analysis and judgment. In Ricoeur's terms, it problematizes the given, and thus introduces a mood of distanciation, doubt, and skepticism that we call "ironic."

We can trace this vector of critique through the appearance of terms like "critical consciousness" and "reflection" over a surprising range of disciplinary contexts, where they do not always carry a negative charge. The work of the Brazilian educator Paulo Freire, for example, presents the critical spirit as transformational and humanizing, the necessary condition for both education and freedom. We see in Freire's development of this concept a characteristic movement that he calls "conscientização," which raises consciousness from a state of "naive" immersion in nature and culture to one of "critical transitivity."[3] The critically transitive consciousness interrogates social realities and thus envisions the possibility of change. This pattern of conscientization, which Freire identifies in adult literacy education, repeats itself in disparate accounts of evolving consciousness, both ontogenetic and phylogenetic, including for example the growth of conceptual thought in ancient Greece, the history of Biblical interpretation, and the crisis of relativism experienced by modern adolescents.[4]

The passage from naiveté to critical consciousness, however, may be read not only as an ascent to reason but also pathetically, as a fall from grace. Simultaneous with the removal or distanciation of the human subject from its own experience, reflection recognizes itself and therefore places under critique not only consciousness but reason, knowledge, self-understanding, and even the ego as unity. Hence critical thought constantly emphasizes polarizing concepts of distance, absence, alienation, suspicion, and that which is latent or hidden.

The reciprocity of rhetoric and critical thought begins to emerge when we examine the contexts in which criticism turns on itself, and the terms in which it does so. We need to draw together parallel but often uncoordinated moves in different fields, so as to see the nature of this critique. Essentially it attacks conceptual thought through language, specifically through an interrogation of written language as an instrument of critical consciousness. Its unity is manifested through the widespread deployment of revisionist concepts of writing, reading, textuality, and literacy, especially though not exclusively in critical theory, a genre that cuts across disciplinary boundaries.[5] The effect (not always intended) is to break our naive trust in the bonds between writing and thought, writing and truth, writing and meaning, writing and a reader's understanding. Rhetoric is reconstituted as a broken unity, and must constantly ward off the threats it perceives to the efficacy and even possibility of discourse—metaphorically, the specter of the abyss.

If rhetoric is from one point of view the problem that the critique discovers, from another it is the knife that cuts the bonds. The tradition of rhetoric as style (which is often itself treated as a falling away from the comprehensive ideal of classical rhetoric) is explicitly invoked to demonstrate the positive rhetoricality of all discourse, including scientific and philosophical writings. Hayden White, in essays on history and cultural criticism, formulates this insight lucidly.[6] He shows, first, that consciousness has a tropological or figurative structure captured in the "master tropes" of classical rhetoric—metaphor, metonymy, synecdoche, and irony—as well as in many other fourfold models of consciousness from Vico to Freud and Piaget. In discourse, a tropological or prefigurative move is always necessary to establish or "emplot" a particular mode of constituting and comprehending facts.

Next, White finds in the order of the four master tropes the same pattern of growth already described as conscientization: from the naiveté of metaphor to a self-critical (i.e., ironic) consciousness. He implies that the genuinely critical spirit must always become self-critical, echoing the growth of consciousness itself, so that authentic discourse always tends to reflect metadiscursively on its own logic. But Jonathan Culler points out the problem this presents for any discipline wishing "to claim that its statements are structured by logic, reason, truth, and not by the rhetoric of the language in which they are 'expressed.'"[7] The rhetoricality of writing "infects" realistic discourse and apparently undercuts its capacity to formulate communicable truth.

The pattern I have described is one of crisis for critical thought because the semiotic-rhetorical character of writing appears to undermine if not paralyze our capacity to conduct inquiry and communicate knowledge.[8] It is simultaneously a crisis for rhetoric because the critical moment breaks the unities that rhetoric must presume, at least as a hope, if writers and readers are to see their actions as meaningfully purposeful. One way to do so is to treat the movement from naiveté to criticism as a valid but incomplete pattern that cannot be surpassed but must be recursively enacted. This is the possibility opened up by the oeuvre of Paul Ricoeur.

A remarkable feature of Ricoeur's work is the degree to which it organizes itself around a series of "critical moments" dramatized in a characteristic figure or plot. In each case reflective thought attempts to clarify naive experience but discovers it must pay the cost in a loss of depth or meaning. It is this impasse between clarity and depth that Ricoeur repeatedly resolves through a form of dialectic intended to recuperate a post-critical faith—a capacity to experience meaning that both preserves and cancels the critical attitude. In his later work this effort becomes increasingly preoccupied with language, and especially with written language and its interpretation.

The expressive, virtually poetic force of Ricoeur's language in formulating this pattern, its dramatic quality of tensions and resolutions, suggests that it represents for him what psychologists call a "life theme." According to Mihalyi Csikzentmihalyi and Olga Beattie, a life theme is an existential problem that matters to a person above all else, together with the means he discovers for solving it. The life theme is that person's characteristic way of interpreting and relating to reality.[9] In his lifelong struggle with the crisis of consciousness precipitated by reflection, Ricoeur not only anticipates current formulations of the problem but also, as we will see, makes similar connections between critical thought and rhetoric.

In Ricoeur's scholarship a dialectical habit of thought becomes a mode of being and acting that reveals his commitment to certain essentially rhetorical values. In accounts of Ricoeur as a teacher and of his intellectual development, we catch just a glimpse of the centrality and depth of these values for Ricoeur's life as a scholar-teacher; Mary Gerhart, discussing Ricoeur's concept and practice of praxis as a genre, implies that for him a philosophical or rhetorical theory is to be lived through a certain practice.[10] In *History and Truth* he speaks against the opposition of thought and action: "I believe in the efficacy of reflection because I believe that man's greatness lies in the dialectic of work and the spoken word. Saying and doing, signifying and making are intermingled to such an extent that it is impossible to set up a lasting and deep opposition between 'theoria' and 'praxis.' The word is my kingdom and I am not ashamed of it."[11] This point will help us to understand later why Ricoeur's hermeneutical working method is as important as his ideas in convincing us that a post-critical rhetoric is conceivable.

As much as possible in Ricoeur's own language, then, I want to draw from the body of his work the life theme that repeats itself in so many forms, and that personally enacts the crisis of modern philosophy and discourse. In Ricoeur's thought this crisis has the mythological form of the Fall, distinctively conceptualized by Ricoeur as the Fault (*la faute*), an inherent fallibility or fragility in human nature that underlies the experience of human existence as flawed by evil, misery, and loss. It is this condition that Ricoeur struggles both to understand and to confront at many levels of human experience. At the philosophical level, the myth takes the form in modern culture of an awakening of consciousness in the "first Copernican revolution," wherein reflection calls into question all naive understanding. Ricoeur identifies this capacity for reflection with the word, specifically the "dubitative word," the negative: "The word is critical and makes every position critical. The end of 'naiveté' begins. Naiveté is of the order of 'there is': there are things, there is nature, there is history, there is the law or work, there is the power of those who command. The thing, the act of making and inciting to action is virtually brought into question by the dubitative word" (*HT*, p. 206).[12]

The critical attitude is one of distance, a distance, however, that Ricoeur understands from the beginning as a dispossession of the self from a state of grace, defined in various contexts as (for example) a sense of belonging, immediacy, fullness of meaning, authenticity, affirmation, or faith. In one instance of the pattern, Ricoeur takes as his subject the problem of historical consciousness as posed by Hans-Georg Gadamer, more broadly the dilemma of the human sciences, caught in "the opposition between alienating distanciation and belonging. This opposition . . . establishes an untenable alternative: on the one hand, alienating distanciation is the attitude that renders possible the objectification which reigns in the human sciences; but on the other hand, this distanciation, which is the condition of the scientific status of the sciences, is at the same time the fall that destroys the fundamental and primordial relation whereby we belong and participate in the historical reality which we claim to construct as an object" (*HHS*, p. 131).

Here what is lost is the sense of being situated in human history. Earlier it was the meaningfulness of symbols and myths, which stand against the dubitative word as the "poetic word." In the modern world an alienating consciousness has demythologized symbols, myths, the Word of scripture: the masters of suspicious hermeneutics, Marx, Neitzsche, and Freud, have taught us to distrust the language of poetry, passion, drama, and myth as illusory. Once this has happened, we cannot go home again to the natural attitude of being "lost in the world" (*H*, p. 20). Ricoeur imagines the possibility of an "informed naiveté" (*FP*, p. 496) in which humans can reappropriate experience, meaning, history, understanding, or the self while retaining the values of critical thought: an "irreversible gain of truthfulness, of intellectual honesty, and therefore of objectivity" (*SE*, p. 352). Paradoxically, the hope for this "second naiveté" or "postcritical faith" lies in reflection itself.

Ricoeur says: "the time of restoration is not a different time from that of criticism; we are in every way children of criticism, and we seek to go beyond criticism by means of criticism, by a criticism that is no longer reductive but restorative" (*SE*, p. 350). His initial move is the same as that of other poststructuralists: to turn critical thought back on itself in what he calls the "second Copernican revolution," but in a very different spirit. Like them, he discovers critical thought to be itself naive in its assumption of an ungrounded subjectivity and a transparent language. Philosophy is itself grounded in the prereflective, in concrete human existence and the symbol or poetic word: "all has been said *before* philosophy, by sign and by enigma," and it is the symbol itself that gives rise to thought (*CI*, pp. 296, 288). Nor can we trust in our ability to understand the texts of our culture, however inscribed. Thus Ricoeur faces a second task of restoration—recuperating reflection or critical thought itself, and with it the possibility for a discourse that can both express and be understood. This recognition sets the stage for a dialectic between these two naivetés, whereby they can both limit and validate each other. The key to this project is the notion of "productive distanciation."

Here is the strategy in broad terms. Distanciation becomes productive by a deliberate indwelling of the instrument of critique, making what Ricoeur calls a "wager," engaging in a "believing game" that is identified with the famous hermeneutical circle (*SE*, p. 355).[13] Such an indwelling is by definition naive and participatory, and insofar as it is post-critical (self-aware), it can occur only through a suspension of disbelief canceling that reflexive gaze while preserving it as a future moment. Beginning with the initial naive state of the natural attitude, critical thought discloses the limits of whatever it addresses. In order to critique the naiveté of criticism itself, however, we must reenter the world of enigma, symbol, the fullness of meaning, which becomes our new instrument of critique and allows us in turn to develop the limits of reflection. The wager is that this dialectic will not only reveal limits, but also restore the power and energy of each perspective. Ricoeur explains his bet with respect to the second move in the context of his study of symbol and myth: "[I]f I follow the *indication* of symbolic thought . . . [t]hat wager then becomes the task of *verifying* my wager and saturating it, so to speak, with intelligibility. In return, the task transforms my wager: in betting *on* the significance of the symbolic world, I bet at the same time *that* my wager will be restored to me in power of reflection, in the element of coherent discourse" (*SE*, p. 355).

At a lower level of description Ricoeur plays out this dialectic between opposed schools of thoughts, positions, and concepts, sometimes doubled and redoubled in extremely intricate patterns. In each case one position represents his favored or "weighted focus," and his effort is to engage as fully as possible a "counterfocus" or series of them. Don Ihde, who identified this pattern in Ricoeur's earliest work, remarks that these oppositions all represent some type of objectivism acting as counterfoci to a phenomenological method: he names biology, empirical psychology, and psychoanalysis (more generally, "suspicious hermeneutics"), to which may be added structuralism.[14] Ihde also points to the importance in this dialectic of a "third term" or limit-idea; Ricoeur's method itself is a third way, a path between two naïvetés. As his work evolves, language itself becomes the third term, specifically written language and ultimately an enlarged conception of text that sees culture as symbolic inscription. Interpretation, and I will argue ultimately rhetoric, become the third way.[15]

I should like to consider now the sense in which Ricoeur's thematizing of the critical moment is rhetorical, or becomes so through its dialectical pattern. First, as we see in the work of Hayden White, Jacques Derrida, and other poststructuralists, the modern conception of critical thought, insofar as it directs itself reflexively against knowledge, consciousness, and communication, derives from that tradition in which rhetoric is style. From this tropological point of view realistic discourse, like literature, is undermined by its own awareness of prelogical moves and thus inevitably, as White says, passes from metaphor (naïveté) to irony (self-criticism) in its structure.[16] Despite Ricoeur's rejection of the tradition of rhetoric as figure in *The Rule of Metaphor*, he acknowledges himself "the man of *irony*" (*HT*, p. 206), and understands irony to mean precisely that distanciation which recognizes the grounding of all discourse in metaphor and precritical experience.

Charles Reagan, in his account of Ricoeur's intellectual development, describes the odyssey that takes Ricoeur from a projected phenomenology of the will to a semantics of action via a "detour" through hermeneutics. In a very simple sense this "detour" brings Ricoeur into the field of rhetoric, because he takes the production and comprehension of texts as his subject. His work on interpretation, metaphor, the imagination, and now narrative constitutes a rather comprehensive and rich discourse theory. C. Jan Swearingen's essay on Ricoeur's theory of discourse derives from this work the possibility for a dialogic rhetoric, bringing together two previously antithetical strands in both the hermeneutical and the rhetorical traditions.[17] She is building there on a previous article where she linked irony and dialogue in an unusual synthesis suggested by her examination of Plato's attack on sophistic rhetoric and writing.[18] I will draw on her ideas to present Ricoeur's praxis as a model for rhetoric as an architectonic method.

Modern rhetoric, particularly as seen in composition theory, where it is intimately linked with the teaching of literacy, is to some degree trapped in a sterile antinomy between an attempt to return to the natural attitude, in a naive Romantic rhetoric of expression, and the alternative of a manipulative, instrumental rhetoric that is a corruption of the Aristotelian tradition. Swearingen's subtle discussion of Platonic and sophistic rhetoric suggests a third way. This is the possibility of rendering the ironic gaze benign by doubling it in dialogue, making it the limit concept of a post-critical rhetoric. (I place the term "post-critical" under erasure now to suggest that the critical moment is preserved even as it is canceled by this complex strategy.)

Swearingen argues that such a rhetoric would preserve the dialectical character of viva voce discourse, which is originally guaranteed by a question-answer structure and the give-and-take among multiple speakers. Socrates advocates seeking truth through the interweaving of terms and propositions—the true purpose of philosophical (and what we would now call scientific) discourse.[19] Ricoeur, invoking the Greek ideal of rationality, echoes Socrates: "It is not a question of giving in to some kind of imaginative intuition, but rather of thinking, that is to say, of elaborating concepts that comprehend and make one comprehend, concepts woven together. . . . But at the same time it is a question of transmitting, by means of this rational elaboration, a richness of signification that was already there" (*CI*, p. 296). A second, very powerful metaphor used by Socrates is that of *maieutics* or midwifery, depicting a proper dialectic—and rhetoric—as one in which participants help one another to give birth to new ideas in a situation of mutual trust.

According to Plato and many modern critics, writing threatens this epistemological and communicative power insofar as it enhances the possibilities for a depictive, instrumental rhetoric; a reduction of the intersubjectivity of living thought; and misunderstanding. For the moderns, we have seen, the latter dangers lie in critical thought itself. According to Swearingen's analysis, Plato himself ultimately appreciated this point, "recognized the contingencies and relativisms which result from even a properly dialogical exercise of dialectic."[20] Swearingen pictures Plato's Socrates as adopting exactly the strategy Ricoeur suggests, which is to use irony or critical thought not for dissembling or for purely destructive purposes, but for maieutic ones: "Socratic inquiry 'creates' the alienated individual who is no longer capable of immediate experience or unexamined thought." But in the context of "a maieutic and life-long common life with others engaged in dialogue," the consequence is not alienation, but the possibility of inquiry in the full knowledge that "truth cannot be stated discursively," because knowledge is a process that is "the art of true opinion."[21]

The position attributed here to Plato corresponds exactly to Ricoeur's conception of a "postponed synthesis," which recognizes a limit to human knowledge in the light of a philosophic hope. There is a reciprocal relation between the recognition of finitude and the hope that seeks knowledge and truth, a resolution of conflicts and polarities, while distrusting any such synthesis as incomplete (*HT*, pp. 11–14). In the relation between hope and the human dialogue, Ricoeur affirms "the primacy of *conciliation* over paradox" (*FN*, p. 341). Ricoeur follows his friend Emmanuel Mounier in taking the attitude he calls "'tragic optimism,' that is, the mode of confidence, corrected by the experience of indecisive combat and overshadowed by the possibility of failure" (*HT*, p. 149).

I have been trying to suggest here that the modern crisis of critical consciousness is essentially rhetorical in two senses that Ricoeur clarifies. First, it is formulated in terms of discourse and writing, while the critique asserts that all discourse undermines itself tropologically, that is, rhetorically. Second, Ricoeur himself resolves this crisis, though always in the tentative mode of wager, hope, and postponed synthesis, through a dialectic or hermeneutical circle of belief and doubt that meets the requirements for a "true rhetoric" in the Socratic sense.

Like Socrates, Ricoeur's philosophic words coincide with his work through his dialogic method. In his hermeneutical encounters with other thinkers, positions, and disciplines, Ricoeur demonstrates how a maieutic dialogue can come into being through writing, in a dialectic of productive distanciation and appropriation. But the explosion of knowledge makes such intertextuality problematic. Intellectual work is becoming so fragmented and specialized that communication between disciplines is increasingly difficult; at the same time, the academic is more and more unable to speak eloquently to the layman.[22] Ricoeur's practice addresses the first problem more than the second (though he is sensitive to the latter), by seeking out and attempting to enter into worlds of thought that are alien. He does so in the spirit of *charity* required by

> the modest and uncertain formula that I borrow from Gabriel Marcel: "I *hope* to be *in* the truth." The truth, not only formal and abstract, but actual and concrete, ceases to be asserted in a Promethean act of taking a position on the self by the self and of adequation of the self to the self. The truth is rather the lighted place in which it is possible to continue to live and to think. And to think *with* our very opponents themselves, without allowing the totality which contains us ever to become a knowledge about which we can overestimate ourselves and become arrogant.[23]

The "creative attention"[24] that Ricoeur pays to the texts of his culture offers one model for a critical but affirmative interdisciplinarity. Here a post-critical rhetoric fully reveals its inseparability from critical thought and reflection, becoming the architectonic *method* of the disciplines.

Notes

1. This chapter, in a slightly different form, constituted the "parasitical preface" to *Pre/Text* 4 (1983), *Ricoeur and Rhetoric*, a special issue that I edited. The issue was conceived in part as dramatizing the interpretive, critical, and rhetorical relations among texts and their audiences that are discussed here in the context of Ricoeur's hermeneutical practice.

2. Walter J. Ong, S.J., "Reading, Technology, and Human Consciousness," in *Literacy as a Human Problem*, ed. James C. Raymond (University, AL: Univ. of Alabama Press, 1982), pp. 179–84.

3. Paulo Freire, *Education for Critical Consciousness* (New York: Continuum, 1981), pp. 17–20.

4. See Eric A. Havelock, *Preface to Plato* (Cambridge, MA: Harvard Univ. Press, 1963); Lewis S. Mudge, "Paul Ricoeur on Biblical Interpretation," in Paul Ricoeur, *Essays on Biblical Interpretation* (Philadelphia: Fortress, 1980); and William G. Perry, Jr., *Forms of Intellectual and Ethical Development in the College Years:*

A Scheme (New York: Holt, 1968). Mudge's introduction is particularly instructive if read as a general account of the critical moment as Ricoeur experiences it.

5. The overlapping contexts for these concerns include an interdisciplinary debate about the impact of literacy and schooling on thought; classicists' and cross-cultural studies of emerging literacy; literacy education; reader-response theories; and deconstruction.

6. Hayden White, *Tropics of Discourse: Essays in Cultural Criticism* (Baltimore: Johns Hopkins Univ. Press, 1978), pp. 1–25.

7. Jonathan Culler, *On Deconstructionism: Theory and Criticism after Structuralism* (Ithaca: Cornell Univ. Press, 1982), p. 91.

8. Deconstruction, in particular, generates this anxiety, despite denials of such implications by sympathetic interpreters like Culler and Frank Lentricchia, *After the New Criticism* (Chicago: Univ. of Chicago Press, 1980). See White on "Absurdist criticism" in *Tropics*, pp. 261–82.

9. Mihaly Csikszentmihalyi and Olga V. Beattie, "Life Themes: A Theoretical and Empirical Exploration of their Origins and Effects," *Journal of Humanistic Psychology* 19 (1979), 47–48. See also Howard Gardner's description in *Art, Mind, and Brain: A Cognitive Approach to Creativity* (New York: Basic Books, 1982), pp. 352–57, of how life themes organize the work of creative geniuses.

10. Stuart L. Charmé, "Paul Ricoeur as Teacher: A Reminiscence," *Pre/Text* 4 (1983), 289–94; Charles Reagan, "Hermeneutics and the Semantics of Action," *Pre/Text* 4 (1983), 239–55; and Mary Gerhart, "Genre as Praxis: An Inquiry," *Pre/Text* 4 (1983), 273–88.

11. Paul Ricoeur, *History and Truth*, tr. Charles A. Kelbley (Evanston: Northwestern Univ. Press, 1965), p. 5. See also "Work and the Word" in *History and Truth*, pp. 197–219. In this chapter the works of Paul Ricoeur are cited in the text by abbreviated titles as follows: *CI = The Conflict of Interpretation: Essays in Hermeneutics*, ed. Don Ihde (Evanston: Northwestern Univ. Press, 1974); *FN = Freedom and Nature: The Voluntary and the Involuntary*, tr. Erazim V. Kohak (Evanston: Northwestern Univ. Press, 1966); *FP = Freud and Philosophy: An Essay on Interpretation*, tr. Denis Savage (New Haven: Yale Univ. Press, 1970); *HHS = Hermeneutics and the Human Sciences: Essays on Language, Action and Interpretation*, tr. and ed. with an introduction by John B. Thompson (Cambridge: Cambridge Univ. Press, 1981); *HT = History and Truth*; *H = Husserl: An Analysis of His Phenomenology*, tr. E. G. Ballard and L. E. Embree (Evanston: Northwestern Univ. Press, 1967); *SE = The Symbolism of Evil*, tr. Emerson Buchanan (New York: Harper and Row, 1967).

12. Here, as often, Ricoeur sounds extremely Burkean; cf. Kenneth Burke, *Language as Symbolic Action: Essays on Life, Literature, and Method* (Berkeley: Univ. of California Press, 1968), pp. 9–13. Ricoeur shares with Burke a dialectical habit of mind that leads them to a strikingly similar rhetoric, both in theory and in their scholarly practice.

13. See Peter Elbow, "Preface 4: The Doubting Game and the Believing Game," *Pre/Text* 3 (1982), 339–51.

14. Don Ihde, *Hermeneutic Phenomenology: The Philosophy of Paul Ricoeur* (Evanston: Northwestern Univ. Press, 1978), pp. 14–16. I am indebted to Ihde's illuminating analysis for my understanding of Ricoeur's characteristic method. See also Michel Philibert, "The Philosophic Method of Paul Ricoeur," in *Studies in the Philosophy of Paul Ricoeur*, ed. Charles E. Reagan (Athens, OH: Ohio Univ. Press, 1979), pp. 133–39.

15. See chapter 8.

16. White, *Tropics*, p. 19.

17. C. Jan Swearingen, "Between Intention and Inscription: Toward a Dialogical Rhetoric," *Pre/Text* 4 (1983), 257–71.

18. C. Jan Swearingen, "The Rhetor as Eiron: Plato's Defense of Dialogue," *Pre/Text* 3 (1982), 289–336.

19. Swearingen, "Eiron," pp. 321–22.

20. Ibid., p. 324.

21. Ibid., pp. 326–27.

22. Bill DeLoach makes these points in an open letter to Ricoeur, in "On First Looking into Ricoeur's Interpretation Theory: A Beginner's Guide," *Pre/Text* 4 (1983), 225–36.

23. Paul Ricoeur, "Response to My Friends and Critics," in Reagan, *Studies*, n.p.

24. Philibert, "Philosophic Method," p. 136.

4

Imagining a Psychology
of Composition

Composition is beginning now to reflect more explicitly on a meta-theoretical puzzle that is of critical importance to its identity as a field: what is the nature and significance of its relation to other disciplines? I will approach that issue obliquely, by posing a different kind of question about such relations in a given case. The case is psychology, and the usual question would take this form: what knowledge can psychology contribute to composition? Instead I will ask: How can we imagine, or construct, a psychology of composition?

I will begin by considering the import of this change in the terms of our discussion—in particular, how the concept of a psychology of composition suggests a different interpretation of what it means for composition to be an interdisciplinary field. From this starting point I will explore the character and significance for composition of what we might call "syntopical studies."[1] The second part of the chapter draws on syntopical reading of the psychological literature to lay the foundations for a possible modern psychology of composition.

It is broadly recognized, as reflected in the establishment of multi-disciplinary graduate programs in rhetoric, that research and teaching in composition depend heavily on basic knowledge about language, symbolization, and the human mind, knowledge that is developing rapidly across many fields. But we are rightly worried about how we can handle this knowledge without being overwhelmed by it. Our history as a modern discipline, emerging from a profession that had lost touch with its scholarly roots, makes us peculiarly susceptible to importing information without digesting it, or to ordering our own knowledge in the image of other fields.

One can trace the influence of other disciplines on modern composition scholarship through the common titles and topics that link composition with another field or subfield: linguistics and composition, literature and composition, speech-act theory and composition, psychology and composition, to name a few. That conjunctive pattern is revealing: it suggests a perception of connections that we cannot yet make precise, like the student who joins two sentences with an "and" because he does not quite understand, or know how to express, a more complex relation between their ideas. In some cases, the conjunction here stands for a wistful hope that composition can find in another discipline a primary source of knowledge and a model for research that will clarify its identity as a field. The recent history of the field shows a succession of candidates for this kind of hero worship, a relation that is intense and exclusive, but fickle and subject to disillusionment. Even in more eclectic borrowing, the field has had difficulty defining principles for search, evaluation, acceptance, and integration by which to make such knowledge distinctively its own. Without such principles it is difficult to escape an uncritical, dependent stance toward the disciplines on which composition draws.

In working on a long bibliographical essay on psychological issues in composition, I began to reflect on the terministic screens that pattern our thinking about other disciplines, and to play with the logological implications of transforming them.[2] The catalyst for my thinking was the concept of building a "psychology of composition." The grammar of that phrase—the genitive construction that connotes possession—invites us to think about psychology in terms of a structure intrinsic to composition rather than a collection of scattered ideas borrowed and patched awkwardly into it. Such a structure, specifically rhetorical, could act as a powerful assimilative schema to search out and integrate knowledge relevant to psychological issues in composition, without regard to the boundaries or branches of psychology as an academic discipline. If this is possible for psychology, we can conceive of a spectrum of such perspectives constituting intradisciplinary structures within composition.

If we accept the fact that composition is necessarily an interdisciplinary field (and I do), the question then becomes how to define our task so that composition will be more than a mirror of its sources or models. There seem to be at least two senses in which a field could properly be called "interdisciplinary." In the first case, there is a merger of several fields for the purposes of carrying out specific projects to investigate phenomena so complex that they can be studied only through a multiplication of perspectives. Both the component fields and the merged one are institutionally defined; that is, they achieve status in the academic establishment through journals, professional organizations, and ultimately academic departments or centers.

Teun van Dijk and Janos Petöfi have called this arrangement a "cross-discipline," a nice term because it conveys the fact that the participating disciplines retain much if not all of their identity, even in the training of the new generation of scholars.[3] They were speaking of cognitive science, a blend of psychology, linguistics, artificial intelligence, and (on the fringe) the social sciences and education as well, including some research by compositionists. Other cross-disciplines, whose institutional presence on the contemporary scene I will leave the reader to judge, are rhetoric and semiotics.

While participation in cross-disciplinary research is vital to composition, a discipline must have its own work apart from such greater networks. But the work of composition is itself characteristically and essentially interdisciplinary, in a second sense: it draws much of its knowledge base from other disciplines. I want to argue that this need not be a passively derivative relationship, if it is a constructive, transforming, and recontextualizing operation. Composition may be thought of as interdisciplinary in the same sense that medicine is. A major function of each discipline is syntopical research, which abstracts information from one context, where it may be more or less densely connected to other information, and inserts it in another framework, where it acquires a different or enriched meaning from its new connectedness. Unlike the arts and sciences, for composition and medicine the integrative principle is pragmatic; a professional mission motivates the search for information and directs the effort to make sense of it. In the case of composition this mission, whose scope and depth are only now becoming clear, is to help individuals realize the full dimensions of their powers of literacy.

Consider the concept of a psychology of composition again, now in the light of the purposes of syntopical study. Our aim is, first, to construct a synthesis of knowledge that bears on our mission from a psychological perspective. A psychology of composition represents the intersection of our particular focus—reading and writing in relationship—with a dimension of analysis, whereby human experience and action can be studied on different planes. The psychological plane of analysis in conjunction with the focus on literacy means that a psychology of composition must be concerned with written language as a function of the human mind, and with the ways individuals develop and use this power in their social worlds.

When I first began working with this idea, I asked myself what topics, issues, or areas of composition research would fall within the purview of a psychology of composition. This turned out to be the wrong question. The psychological plane of analysis defines one of a number of possible perspectives on the entire field; one that looks at written language in relation to the mind of an individual, and thus at cognitive constructs and processes, underlying structures, and the growth and development of language and cognition. That focus acts as a kind of searchlight playing over work both inside and outside the discipline. When directed at what I call broadly the psychological literature, which is not limited to the discipline of psychology, it helps us seek out and recognize information that matches our own purposes, to assimilate, connect, and transform that knowledge, and to imagine and weigh the practical consequences of concepts and theories. It also helps solve a problem that faces any generalist: coping with the masses of information that are constantly being generated in other disciplines, often inaccessible, partially unintelligible, incomplete, and essentially limitless. (For the limits of our discipline are not logically but strategically defined: we can legitimately appropriate any knowledge that helps us to understand the complex events connected with writing and reading.)

The deeper commitments and needs of the field tacitly guide our probes when we seek out information from other disciplines in order to construct different perspectives on literacy. Although I cannot analyze these "preintentions" or purposeful anticipations, I think we will see them in operation in the next part of this chapter, where I try to identify a set of themes that emerge from the psychological literature as coherent through the interaction of their salience and our purposes. This same interaction works somehow to make it possible to make sense of that overwhelming mass of data we confront. I think what happens is exactly what goes on whenever human beings deal with the world, which always presents us with an information overload—for example when we learn a language. We sample the information, not so much through conscious selection as through the attentional mechanisms that direct us to what is interesting and useful in our environment. From that information we abstract what we can use, and construct an initially fuzzy holographic picture that is constantly modified by feedback: corrected, refined, detailed, clarified, extended. In constructing such a personal hologram of the psychological literature, I discovered an unexpected pattern of rhetorical themes.

Although I am going to speak of a convergence of views in this literature, what impresses one at first is the divergence and indeed conflict of opinions and emphases about discourse. To begin with, there are the disciplinary orientations, for example those of cognitive psychologists, psycholinguists, sociolinguists, computer scientists, text linguists, and ethnographers of communication, to name a few of those more recently prominent and influential in composition. Then there are the factions within each. Ultimately, however, I began to resolve these conflicts into a very basic issue, really a philosophical one, of the relative weight, power, importance, and indeed reality of the organism and its environment. We may translate this for ourselves into the familiar configuration of relationships between writer, reader, text, and context. These relationships are complicated in the extreme by the shift from physical to symbolic reality, in which notions of both organism and environment take on great ambiguity. Nonetheless, many of the arguments about writing and reading, or about the development of language powers, can be crudely reduced to questions of balance and dominance in organism-environment interactions.

The term "interaction" suggests one way out of this polarity that is increasingly attractive to researchers in the human sciences. This theme is perhaps the most global of those I will identify, and the most various in its meanings and manifestations. I would like to work up to it, as I think these researchers did, by following out the implications of new ideas about the constructive power of the human mind and the primacy of context, themes that may seem at first to be mutually opposed.

The constructive nature of human understanding is an idea so well established as to seem less radical than it is. It is most clearly articulated in the work of the cognitive psychologists who struggled to formulate a view of human understanding different from those of behaviorism and a linguistics of symbol manipulation.[4] They developed a view of the human mind, or more properly of the whole organism, as engaged in an active search for meaning in the world around it. That search is characterized as constructive, in that the organism makes enormous contributions to both perceptual and linguistic meanings through comparable processes of problem solving or thinking. The emphasis in this work is on receptive understanding, where the responsibility of the organism for meaning is less obvious. But the processes they describe—of purposeful attention, hypothesizing, predicting, anticipating, planning, responding to feedback, bringing to bear knowledge in memory—are all common to both language production and language comprehension, so that we find their echoes in our own accounts of writing, and the two activities seem to converge on a view to the effect that, in Anthony Petrosky's words, "understanding is composing."[5]

At the same time there is a very widespread recognition now in the human sciences, familiar to us in composition, that language is a sociocultural phenomenon, and that we cannot understand its psychology except in relation to natural contexts of use. At one level this says that a theory of language has got to be a theory of the mind, specifically of how the mind represents knowledge about the world and brings it to bear on understanding discourse. Cognitive scientists made this discovery when they tried to simulate natural language comprehension on computers: their computers had to be programmed with a model of the world to understand even one sentence. But this cognitive sense of context gets us only so far. As Elinor Ochs points out, it won't do to treat culture as nothing more than a cognitive map in a person's head: we miss too many of the connections and mutual influences between language and the social context.[6]

The corrective for this cognitive bias in language studies is to work toward a more ecologically valid psychology that moves out of the laboratory to examine both linguistic and cognitive processes in the natural settings of everyday use. This theme runs through much contemporary work on the psychology of discourse and cognition in general, moderating the extreme subjectivism of some early constructivist views. Many cognitive scientists are expressing doubts about an approach that treats people strictly as symbol shufflers, and are calling for a contextually richer understanding of human cognition and language use. Here, for example, is Donald Norman, voicing thoughts shared with many colleagues at the founding conference for cognitive science: "The human is a physical symbol system, yes, with a component of pure cognition describable by mechanisms. . . . But the human is more: The human is an animate organism, with a biological basis and an evolutionary and cultural history. Moreover, the human is a social animal, interacting with others, with the environment, and with itself."[7]

An ecological view of language use implies a related thematizing of language as functional in context—that is, as expressive of values and intentions. Through this theme there occurs a reconciliation of constructivism and the primacy of context, which shows them to be two sides of the same coin. Construction of discourse meanings is in the first place possible because of the social acquisition of language, and in the second place always motivated and guided by contextually defined goals. Increasingly, language use is understood to be strategic rather than strictly rule-governed even at the level of cognitive processing, so that, instead of highly general models of "the reading process" or "the writing process," researchers are beginning to look for ways to describe the great flexibility and adaptability of these processes to conditions, situations, and specific tasks.[8]

Finally, let us return to the theme of interactivity, which arises from recognizing the great complexity of symbolic events. In work on coherence and discourse structure I have suggested that composition theory must be built up out of inherently integrative concepts.[9] This line of thought breaks with the componential approach, in which one tries to understand complex phenomena by analyzing them into their elements and studying these in isolation, bracketing the problem of their interrelationships. The interactive approach says that there really are no such components, only the interactivity of the system, which defines functional aspects that tend to change dynamically as the activity evolves.

This concept is a powerful one with a great range of applicability. We see it for example in dialectical or transactional concepts of relations between writer, reader, and text; in speculation about interactions between right and left hemispheres in composing; in acknowledgment of the intersubjective construction of reality through language; in the notion that reading is simultaneously top-down (guided by the comprehender's knowledge) and bottom-up (shaped by the information being picked up from the text). Beyond that, studies of complex human events bring into question the whole notion of separate entities or structures in these interactions. For example, some memory researchers have concluded that memory is not a distinct and separate system at all, but rather an aspect of cognition that is continuous with perception and motor activity.[10] The concept of memorability suggests that this memory function is a product of both environmental and cognitive determinants. Ultimately, an interactive view treats the whole subject-object, organism-environment choice as moot, since the interactions are so extensive that the interacting entities simply become functional components of a greater system, and we cannot think of the skin or the interface of consciousness and world as ultimate barriers. If that seems further than some want to go in the direction of an Eastern cosmology, or the atomic world of the modern physicist, it is not much different from contemporary literary theories that bring writer, reader, and text into the abyss of indeterminacy.

The coherence I find in these themes is not simply an artifact of the compositionist's perspective; others have articulated it eloquently. Collectively these themes express an orientation to the human sciences that has been formulated by social scientists, communication theorists, and linguists, among others, called variously a constructive, transactional, interactive, holistic, or interpretive approach. Their characterizations have much to tell us, as Janet Emig has recognized.[11] But for all of us this cluster of themes is already hauntingly familiar, and indeed that familiarity is what prompts us to recognize and appropriate them. What is happening here is that the complexity of human discourse is forcing the sciences of language and mind toward an increasingly rhetorical perspective that carries for us echoes of what Emig called our tacit tradition[12]—echoes of Kenneth Burke and Michael Polanyi, among others—and that has resonance with much contemporary work in the humanities, especially on textuality and reading. In adopting our own language game, the human sciences not only provide us with the kind of knowledge we need in order to carry out our fundamental mission as a profession, but also give us a new opportunity to make useful and illuminating integrations that can feed back into the work of other disciplines and enter into a larger dialogue about discourse.

Notes

1. The term is suggested by Mortimer Adler's conception of syntopical or comparative reading; see Mortimer J. Adler and Charles Van Doren, *How to Read a Book*, rev. ed. (New York: Simon and Schuster, 1972).

2. Louise Wetherbee Phelps, "Cross-Sections in an Emerging Psychology of Composition," in *Research in Composition and Rhetoric: A Bibliographical Sourcebook*, ed. Michael G. Moran and Ronald F. Lunsford (Westport, CT: Greenwood Press, 1984), pp. 27-69. This bibliographical essay constitutes the syntopical basis for the position set forth here regarding the thematic foundations for a psychology of composition.

3. Teun van Dijk and Janos S. Petöfi, editorial introduction, *Text* 1 (1981), 1-3.

4. See, e.g., *Cognition and the Symbolic Processes*, vol. 1, ed. Walter B. Weimer and David S. Palermo (Hillsdale, NJ: Erlbaum, 1974).

5. Anthony Petrosky, "From Story to Essay: Reading and Writing," *CCC* 33 (1982), 19-36.

6. Elinor Ochs, "Social Foundations of Language," in *New Directions in Discourse Processing*, vol. 2 of *Advances in Discourse Processes*, ed. Roy O. Freedle (Norwood, NJ: Ablex, 1979), pp. 207-21.

7. Donald A. Norman, "Twelve Issues for Cognitive Science," in *Perspectives on Cognitive Science*, ed. Donald A. Norman (Norwood, NJ: Ablex, 1981), p. 266.

8. See, e.g., Ann Matsuhashi, "Explorations in the Real-Time Production of Written Discourse," in *What Writers Know: The Language, Process, and Structure of Written Discourse*, ed. Martin Nystrand (New York: Academic Press, 1982), pp. 269-90. See also studies of metacognition and the deliberate control of mental processes, e.g., John H. Flavell, "Metacognition and Cognitive Monitoring: A New Area of

Cognitive-Developmental Inquiry," *American Psychologist* 34 (1979), 906–11, and Steven R. Yussen, Samuel R. Mathews II, and Elfrieda Hiebert, "Metacognitive Aspects of Reading," in *Reading Expository Material*, ed. Wayne Otto and Sandra White (New York: Academic Press, 1982), pp. 189–218.

9. See chapters 6 and 7.

10. See *Perspectives on Memory Research: Essays in Honor of Uppsala University's 500th Anniversary*, ed. Lars-Göran Nilsson (Hillsdale, NJ: Erlbaum, 1979).

11. Janet Emig, "Inquiry Paradigms and Writing," *CCC* 33 (1982), 64–75.

12. Janet Emig, "The Tacit Tradition: The Inevitability of a Multi-Disciplinary Approach to Writing Research," in *Reinventing the Rhetorical Tradition*, ed. Aviva Freedman and Ian Pringle (Conway, AK: L and S Books, 1980), pp. 9–17.

5

Literacy and the Limits of the Natural Attitude

In the last decade a belief in the naturalness of writing has reemerged as a dominant myth in composition pedagogy, reflecting changing theoretical attitudes toward literacy in the social science disciplines. In many respects this myth violates common sense, which has always distinguished sharply between speech as natural and writing as artifice. Such a view, memorably articulated by Plato as a criticism of literacy, ironically provided a founding premise for the subsequent development of rhetoric as an art of planned discourse. However, the "natural attitude" (as I will call it here) has been a recurrent theme in rhetoric and composition studies at least since the Romantic period, and the remarkable multidisciplinary growth in our understandings of language, writing, cognition, and culture has given it renewed vitality.

In its contemporary form the myth of natural literacy is ontogenetically oriented, deeply bound up with controversies over human nature and questions regarding the relationship between psychobiological development and social learning. In attributing naturalness not only to composing acts but to the process of becoming literate, it offers one interpretation of the reciprocity between human learning and cultural instruction in language. To say "writing and reading are natural" is essentially to say that, given a literate culture, young humans make sense of written language in much the same natural, effortless, and unconscious way as they learn speech. This process is often spoken of as "acquisition" or "development" of literacy abilities so as to distinguish it from formal learning. The culture supports this natural process largely by providing the meaningful contexts and experiences of written language events that stimulate the learner's own construction of the symbolic systems and strategies we call "literacy." Recent cross-cultural evidence shows that children exposed to written language begin reinventing and appropriating the literate codes of their culture long before schooling.[1] Such a conception of literacy learning must, if taken seriously, radicalize the praxis and self-understanding of those disciplines that now claim primary responsibility for teaching writing and reading.

The myth of natural literacy has a powerful emotional appeal and persuasive support in research and theory. But I am disturbed by the implications of accepting it uncritically, without qualification or limit. I see, for example, dangers in regarding the teacher as simply facilitating the activities of a relatively autonomous learner, leaving no creative role for authority, codified knowledge, direction, formal instruction, or curriculum. This position simply reverses the previous one, which pictured an active, powerful, purposeful teacher and a passive learner. We need a more complex, subtle, and variable model of the ways in which teachers and learners negotiate power, creativity, wisdom, purpose, consciousness, and action in their transactions. In this chapter I would like to explore this and other limitations of the natural attitude toward literacy through a sympathetic but critical examination of its premises and consequences. On the one hand, I will give full value to the myth of the natural, while acknowledging the need to gain a richer, more analytical understanding of its meaning and of the tensions inherent in such a position. On the other hand, I will point toward a more enlightened development of that myth's opposites or complements—views that emphasize the cultural elaboration of literacy into the skilled, crafted, artful, self-conscious, and reflexive use of language. Ultimately I want to suggest that Western literacy as a cultural practice has a surplus of meaning not accounted for by the myth of the natural, and that cultural instruction must adapt to the expanding possibilities of this meaning over the course of literacy development.

The "Natural Attitude"

The Phenomenological Concept

I have chosen to anchor my discussion in a phenomenological term—the "natural attitude"—that was originally introduced in a philosophical context remote from pedagogical concerns about literacy. The value of this term for my analysis lies in the complex affective and cognitive meanings it carries over from that context, suggestive not merely of a situation or condition but of a task that faces us. What the phenomenological understanding of the natural attitude captures is the ambivalence and conflict inherent in the human attachment to the natural, which embodies a nostalgia for the immediate that is constantly undercut by the critical, reflective impulse. I wish to confront this problem here not only at the level of literacy itself, but also with respect to the naiveté in our own practice of literacy education.

In phenomenology the concept of the natural attitude refers to the universal human experience of the "life-world" or *Lebenswelt*.[2] As Edmund Husserl defined it, the life-world is the domain of common sense, everyday experience into which we are all born and live prereflectively, before science or philosophy. The distinctive quality of the life-world is to be "pregiven" to consciousness as the natural, inevitable surround of the lived body, taking its situational structure from human activity. From myself as a subject, the life-world stretches out toward the horizon as a realm of perceptual immediacy (fading with distance in time and space). Every object and person in the life-world is endowed with cultural and personal meaning. As David Carr points out in his interpretation of Husserl's concept, that meaning and thus the intersubjective structure of the life-world is essentially practical: "For consciousness at this level, the world is the domain of ends to be attained, projects to be carried out, materials to be used in carrying them out. . . . The orientation of the perceived world around the lived body is a *practical* orientation of movement and accomplishment, not a theoretical orientation. Similarly, culture does not essentially present us with a 'theory' of the world, but envelopes us in a domain articulated according to spheres of action, providing norms and directives for getting around."[3]

What is pregiven is not chosen, but simply there: taken for granted, the tacit ground for all activity and thought, for consciousness itself. This is true even if we accept the developmentalists' view that the life-world in Husserl's sense is only gradually differentiated and integrated by the infant through his own activity and interpersonal transactions. At the first level of meaning, then, the natural attitude is the practical consciousness by means of which all individuals necessarily and unquestioningly dwell in the human world. Their spontaneous and deep identification with the life-world reconstructs at the cultural level the sense of belonging to "nature" that was lost in the Garden of Eden. It is now culture that is "natural." Speech is the paradigm case and probably chief instrument of the emergence of the human child into such a natural participation in her culture. The myth of natural literacy is the claim that written language reenacts this experience at a new level of cultural development.

However, even at the moment of defining and celebrating the natural attitude as participation in the life-world, Husserl problematizes it. For he introduced the concept in relation to the phenomenological "epoche" as an effort to transcend the myth of presence, the naive, unreflective acceptance of the world as given or "on hand" to us. I cannot do justice here to Husserl's philosophical projects or the role of the epoche in them. Roughly, however, the epoche suspends or "brackets" belief in the everyday practical world in order for the philosopher to grasp reflexively the relation between a phenomenal world and subjective consciousness. The epoche does not imply that the phenomenologist can deny or escape from his own groundedness in the life-world. But, Husserl thought, he can transcend the natural attitude and the conditon of human finitude by reflecting on, or thematizing, the subject-object correlation itself.[4]

This project, to correct naiveté through a critical moment that enlarges understanding, was originally conceived in the context of a rigorous philosophical effort to grasp the nature of human experience. But it has an interpretation in the mundane world itself, as a characteristic pattern of human consciousness and culture. At least in contemporary Western society, the human child grows up to a world in which the naturalness of belonging to culture is undermined by alienation, distance, and doubt; adolescence is marked by entrance into the critical moment of reflexivity and questioning. As Paul Ricoeur remarks precisely, for the increase in clarity we call civilized, we pay with a loss of depth.[5] This experience, and the consequent desire to restore lost innocence and faith, finds theoretical expression in the great postmodern debate between positivist natural science and interpretive views of the human sciences, where it is intimately and mysteriously connected to literacy, rhetoric, and writing.

It appears that the natural attitude in literacy pedagogy reflects the desire to recapture and refigure the at-homeness in the cultural world that is associated with speech, which has not only a developmental interpretation (for the growing child) but also a historical one in the oral *paideia*. On the other side we have contemporary scholars claiming literacy as the agent for disembedding consciousness from the life-world context, distancing it from an immediacy often pictured as restrictive and illusory, and empowering critical reflection and subtle thought.[6] The tension between these two dimensions or possibilities in literacy is psychologically real for the teacher, who must resolve them practically in the face of great variability and dynamic change in the consciousness of the young learner. My own experience of that conflict led me to ask the two questions motivating this study. First, in what sense, if at all, does the practice of literacy in my culture exceed the natural or naive participation in language and become self-reflective and critical? And second, insofar as it does, how should cultural instruction respond so as to overcome the naiveté of a natural pedagogy without losing its depth?

The Myth of Natural Literacy: Variation

I want now to consider the natural attitude in a different light, as an expression that at once signifies important agreements and conceals deep differences among the groups that share the myth. Such ambiguity is perhaps a condition for beliefs becoming mythical, and indicates a prescientific and uncritical aspect in the conception of natural literacy as manifested in the theory and praxis of composition as a discipline. Ultimately we will need to sort out the various positions, so as to distinguish and select from their often inconsistent analyses of literacy, cognition, and culture the elements for constructing a more principled, though tentative, practical synthesis.[7] In other words, we must develop our understanding of natural literacy from (in Vygotsky's terms) the level of thinking in complexes or families of ideas to that of concepts.[8] Although that is not my task in this chapter, I do want to give some sense of the conflicts of interpretation in the myth as composition has appropriated it, before I go on to treat it in a more unified fashion.

There seem to be three major variations on the theme of natural literacy in composition, each rooted in separate theoretical sources and generating rather different research programs and pedagogies. I call them the biological, the Romantic, and the contextualist. Although I will orient readers to these interpretations by referring to particular schools and individuals, they actually represent ideal types that do not occur in pure form. When you look carefully at the best work, it is too complex, mixed, and balanced to label easily; but rhetorically it influences opinion toward the ideal type, because the author articulates that strand of his ideas with particular passion, clarity, and vividness.

The biological perspective on the natural takes the human being to be an organism adapted by evolution to an environment that includes language. The child is prepared genetically to learn language, and the process occurs universally, without conscious attention or effort, without deliberate instruction, because of the nature of the brain. Within this frame there are two very different notions of how this result occurs, roughly the innatist or Chomskyan position and the adaptive or constructive position derived from the work of Piaget. In both there is a sense that language unfolds as the child grows, but the first emphasizes structures present in the brain at birth, while the second stresses the processes by which the child forms structures through interactions with the environment. As a corollary, the innatist makes language a highly specific and localized function of the brain, whereas the cognitivist thinks of it as developing from prior action schemas through highly general processes of cognition like differentiation, integration, elaboration, internalization, assimilation, and accommodation.[9] Both believe in an active organism constructing or reinventing the language codes through a process of hypothesis testing—an idea they share with information-processing theorists (who have had more to say about comprehension processes than about learning). All these theoretical perspectives have been extended by analogy and independent evidence to literacy.[10] A more limited but influential contribution to the biological interpretation of the myth exploits research on the different functions of the right and left hemispheres of the brain—for example, Gabrielle Rico's book on *Writing the Natural Way*.[11]

The second, Romantic perspective lingers on in the idea of the natural from earlier periods, notably the 1960s, when it strongly affected composition teaching, although perhaps more in the journals than in the profession as a whole. William Coles, Ken Macrorie, Peter Elbow, and Stephen Tchudi are emblematic figures for this conception of natural literacy, and there are Romantic strains in the work of Donald Murray, Donald Graves, Ann Berthoff, and James Britton's research group, among others. The Romantic ideal type contributes to the myth of natural literacy a set of important concepts: (1) the imaginative and symbolizing faculty as inherent in every human being; (2) the creative process as mysterious and unamenable to rational intervention, systematic control, or formal instruction; (3) the dialectic between writing and thought at the point of utterance or comprehension; and (4) the primacy of the self-expressive function of writing as a means of exploring, defining, and declaring ego while attempting to make sense of personal experience.[12] In this last emphasis a pedagogical Romanticism has been refreshed by its meeting with other views that stress not simply the discovery and articulation of the growing self, but the correlation between that process and constructing knowledge about a broader cultural world through "epistemic writing" or "writing to learn." In some interpretations this process becomes dialogic and thus social, merging with the contextualist view that is coming to dominate a pedagogy of the natural way.[13]

Both the biological and the Romantic approaches focus on the individual and generate extremely child-centered ideas of literacy learning, almost to the exclusion of direct cultural instruction. In contrast, the newly vigorous contextualist or ecological orientation to literacy recognizes that the learner lives in a cultural and specifically linguistic world, and thus highlights the interpersonal dimensions of natural literacy learning. A major sign of this change is the move into classrooms, often in interdisciplinary teams, to study through "naturalistic" methods how children learn to write and read. These studies assume that what makes it natural to learn written language is meaningfulness in the life-world. Again, children appear as active agents of their own learning, but the contextualist emphasizes not constructing codes but participating in literacy events. From these experiences learners acquire the abilities to orchestrate both verbal and nonverbal patterns and cues for purposes of making meaning and relating themselves to their social environment. The reinvention of codes and conventions supports rather than drives these activities.

This approach has been so productive and its research so integrated with classroom practice that its theoretical principles are filtering into pedagogy much more rapidly and easily than usual. A strong connection is building up between the early-literacy studies of such people as Donald Graves, Jerome Harste, and their respective research teams (whose work is often reported in *Language Arts*) and influential pedagogies such as that of the National Writing Project or the Bread Loaf School. Graves, Dixie Goswami, James Britton, Sam Watson, Tilly and John Warnock, and others associated with programs for elementary and secondary schoolteachers have inspired teachers themselves to observe and write about the engaged, self-directed learner appropriating literacy through the transactions of the classroom.[14]

Contextualist interpretations of natural literacy are powerful not only in themselves, as exciting and generative for teaching practice, but in their affinities and connections with the work of other fields. The effort to relate language, cognition, writing, and rhetoric in terms of a contextualist framework finds its echo in every human science, especially of course those of language, literature, psychology, and social practices, but also in history, critical theory, philosophy, and many others. For the first time, and not altogether self-consciously at present, composition finds itself in the mainstream of intellectual thought, contributing its own perspective to theoretical and empirical inquiries of far-reaching import. Not only is it exploiting ideas from these fields—for example, the work of Michael Cole, Elinor Ochs, Shirley Brice Heath, Lev S. Vygotsky and the Russian psychologists, Hayden White, Clifford Geertz, Paul Ricoeur, Jacques Derrida, even Husserl, Heidegger, and Habermas—but it is beginning to draw such figures into dialogue with rhetoric and composition. This fact suggests that the concerns in this discussion may point beyond its critique of literacy education, linking composition to the more fundamental task being pursued across the disciplines, namely, to evaluate and balance interpretive (natural or contextualized) approaches with critical and objectivist understandings of human life and experience.[15]

The Myth of Natural Literacy: Core

Over a range of variation in the myth of natural literacy, there remains an identifiable core—not, as I have pointed out, an entirely unified and rigorous concept, but a complex of overlapping features. I will turn now to characterizing, again through a process of idealization, the fundamental commitments and assumptions of these views as they approach myth. This general picture, which favors the dominant con-textualist interpretation of the myth, sets the stage for examining its limits and gaps.

It is convenient to group the features of the myth into four clusters: concepts about (1) language learning (extended to written language); (2) pedagogy; (3) human nature as manifested in cultural interactions; and (4) literacy practices. Together these concepts reveal that, in the terms of the myth, each person—writer and reader, teacher and learner—acts naively, that is, within the natural attitude, which Ricoeur expresses as "lost and forgotten in the world, lost in the things, lost in the ideas, lost in the plants and animals, lost in others, lost in mathematics. . . . What I call living is hiding myself as naive consciousness within the existence of all things."[16]

According to the ideal of natural literacy, the literate environment is to the learner as the sea to a fish. He is immersed in it both physically, being surrounded by it with his environment saturated by inscriptions in print, handwriting, and other media, and also psychologically, experiencing it as a transparent medium in which to make meaning. As soon as he discovers its semiotic function, writing becomes a tacit instrument for understanding and controlling the life-world, just as speech became gesture and then symbol for the infant. The learner constantly forms and checks hypotheses about language forms, but this is an entirely tacit process not accessible to consciousness and thus impervious to direct instruction. The intentionality of what Glenda Bissex calls "child mind" is not directed toward learning in itself, but toward meanings imbued with purpose in the practical, everyday world.[17]

These fundamental assumptions about learning literacy are summarized by Yetta Goodman in terms of three generalizations:

> Building on the work of Halliday (1975), K. Goodman and I extended to literacy learning the idea that learning language is learning how to mean. The child learns how to mean through written as well as spoken language. Initially, as children interact with literacy events and implements in their culture, they grow curious and form hypotheses about their functions and purposes. They discover, as they are immersed in using written language and watching others use it, that *written language makes sense*. It communicates or says something. As this generalization begins to develop, children also become concerned with the organization of written language in terms of *how it makes sense*. They begin to find stability and order in the form of written language in the everyday context of its functional use. As these two generalizations are developing, children discover that *they can make sense through written language* as they use it themselves. They develop control or ownership of the strategies of comprehension and composition similar to those they have used in oral language.[18]

This is the ideal, sometimes presented in case studies of prodigious or at least successful and confident children who take the initiative in writing and reading from an early age. No one claims that literacy learning proceeds so smoothly and successfully for all children, all the way through school, but theorists say that the processes of attending to the print environment, hypothesizing and testing (unconsciously) the rules and strategies of literacy, and orchestrating cues to make sense of written language are the same in every case. Where such theorists do deviate from the pure myth is by admitting into school literacy, as it develops, self-criticism, attention to convention, and other such aspects of critical consciousness. The logic of the natural attitude precludes metacognition as an element of language acquisition along with any struggle to craft language; thus to the degree that literacy theorists acknowledge these aspects of learning, they pass into the realm of the surplus of meaning.

This picture of literacy (independently supported) parallels in every respect the acquisition of spoken language. It follows that a pedagogy of natural literacy is modeled on the kind of cultural instruction that supports language acquisition in the home. The role of teacher is assimilated to that of mother or caretaker who interacts with the infant in various and rich ways to support the child's own reinvention of language. Direct, formal, conscious instruction plays almost no part in this process. What mothers (and fathers, siblings, and others) do for the child is to provide multiple opportunities for participating actively in language events, to value the child's verbal and nonverbal gestures as signs and to respond to them, and in other ways to make language meaningful, useful, and accessible to the child.[19] Researchers who have conducted literacy studies of young children in the home and preschools describe the effective support of written language in exactly the same terms.[20]

By assimilating the classroom to the home and the teacher to the caretaker, the myth of natural literacy places the teacher in a strange and paradoxical position. The caretaker is pictured as a totally naive representative of her culture who needs no special training or conscious knowledge to provide all that a child needs to learn a native language—namely, dialogue with significant others in practical situations. (Indeed, I sometimes get the feeling from language theorists that they almost morally disapprove of parents who attempt to introduce into this relationship their own critical consciousness of language—for example, in correcting the child's grammar or spelling. In any case, they regard such efforts as completely ineffectual and counterproductive.) If literacy is learned, even in the classroom, in the same way, then teachers must themselves be lost in the natural attitude. At the very least, they must act as if they are; one wonders why they need to know what they are doing. Indeed, how can the teacher simultaneously participate naturally in these interactions and also enact the critical spirit that codifies, rationalizes, and questions a cultural tradition? These paradoxes may account for the ambivalence that has always marked the treatment of theory and research in a natural pedagogy. There is an extraordinary resistance to formal verbalization and abstraction among many superb practitioners and some researchers, and a strain of anti-intellectualism is still potent in the profession. Perhaps these feelings are rooted in the instinct to resist loss of that vital sense of belonging to a culture and language that supports natural literacy.

This analysis is beginning to uncover some of the tensions in the myth of natural literacy and to encounter its limiting assumptions. These become more apparent when we ask what conception of human nature and culture is implied by the transactions just described. Basically, culture here is limited to a benevolent family unit writ large. There is no pain, trauma, separation, or loss in this account of literacy, neither in the experiences of meaning expressed and created through writing, nor in the process of development itself. Underlying the Edenic vision of successful literacy in classroom and homes are some premises that need serious examination.

To begin with, the notion of context is situational and local, not comprehensively cultural. In Urie Bronfenbrenner's discussion of the ecological environment for human development, he pictures a set of nested structures with the family at the center, a "microsystem" of interpersonal relationships. This system is related at the next level to other settings in which the developing person actively participates. At the third level, events not experienced by the individual impinge on her life, and beyond that the environment has a macrosystem level where larger social patterns—religious, political, socioeconomic, and so on—operate.[21] Within the myth of natural literacy the only salient context is the familial, conceived as a supportive interpersonal matrix for literacy experiences and projected into the school setting. Teachers become parental figures and other students siblings. Even the bureaucratic realities of the school do not obtrude; the classroom is a self-contained setting presided over by the (usually female) teacher.

The image of this intimate context is overwhelmingly positive at all levels. First, insofar as the home is invoked through student writings, it appears benevolent and supportive, not the scene of child abuse, divorce, or even childhood jealousies. The personal situations that children write about or write for (as in notes to hang on doors and iceboxes, accounts of their pets) are largely domestic and relatively trivial. In the classroom teachers are, or learn to be, good, caring listeners and respondents respectful of "child mind." The children are active, curious, capable—at their different levels of experience and in individual ways; in social relations they are friendly and mutually helpful. In other words, there is a Romantic presumption of the goodness, intellectual potential, and cooperative instincts inherent in every child, along with an image of culture as a nurturing context for development.

There remains one more cluster of concepts to consider, those pertaining to literacy practices. If we follow through the logic of the speech model (granted, few theorists consistently do so), it implies that literacy as a practice is always lived in the moment. Without critical distance, standards, and conscious attention to language and personal meanings as objects, there can be neither work nor skill in literacy. Engaging in literacy naively, the writer cannot free himself from the immediate present in order to plan, cannot distance himself so as to contemplate and judge his own discourse as a work. Even less can he become conscious of his own development as something that might be worked at and planned, as for example through detaching techniques from their textual contexts in order to study and practice them. Here we seem to be brought to a contradiction in terms, because it is precisely all these potentialities for absence, distance, and deferral in writing that are celebrated as freeing thought from its moorings in the practical world of immediate experience.

I am sure this analysis appears unfair to the superb accounts that various researchers have given us of eager natural literacy in the classrooms and homes observed by them. I am not criticizing these reports, which are undoubtedly impressive and truthful images of certain elements and instances of literacy learning. Their view of child mind constitutes an invaluable corrective to the prevailing notion of a reluctant, passive, ignorant learner. Insofar as they mute other realities, it is partly because of the delicacies of the ethnographic situation, which demand respect for the privacy of individuals and tact in dealing with political and bureaucratic facts. Nonetheless, these accounts are shaped by myth: they are selective in their emphasis, and the kind of cultural world I have depicted is an implicit ideal even when it is not the reality.[22] By abstracting away from these accounts and ignoring the ways in which they qualify the myth, we can see both what is valuable and what is lost in a conception of natural literacy. These losses and their potential for recuperation are the subject of my next section.

Transcending the Myth

Limits of the Natural Attitude

I have tried to purify the myth so as to disclose how its inner logic generates contradictions and inconsistencies in actual practice. Clearly there are realities that constrain the ideal and even bring it into question. More important, developmental forces and the practice of literacy itself simultaneously undermine the natural attitude and create new possibilities.

It is not hard to point out the naivetés in the Edenic account of the home and classroom environments, and the nostalgia for belonging that imbues this picture of a nurturing culture. The harder thing is to question it as ideal or goal. As a basis for pedagogy this model is based on many true and ethical insights, but also on false hopes, because it oversimplifies the complex relations between individuals and culture as expressed and mediated in literacy development. A significant danger lies in the implicit arrogance of trying to create the perfect, controlled environment that excludes or ignores the negatives and complexities in these realities.

Children, and later adults, bring to literacy extremely varied personal experience, often bitter, traumatic, tragic, but also silly, trivial, comic, aggressive, and every other variant of human mood. Sometimes they express these feelings through written language—raising issues of privacy and the uneasy therapeutic role of the teacher—and at other times they resist expressing them. Either way, by their presence or absence these experiences and their legacy can represent a powerful and even terrifying reality in the classroom with which teachers must cope, one that becomes even more sensitive in the socially interactive model of literacy.

A natural pedagogy provides the values, but not the intellectual framework and critical understanding necessary, to work with these realities from day to day. Among other things, it is not designed to cope with the variation in cultural frameworks brought to school in American society. The myth embodies a simplistic and monolithic idea of the ecological context and a correlated notion of literacy as a single practice disseminated throughout the society through the shared "print environment." It is plausible, as Harste, Leichter, and others assert, that one cannot distinguish experiences of literacy acquisition in terms of "class theoretical" factors such as race or socioeconomic status.[23] Instead, they identify the family as the ecological setting whose variant practices and attitudes toward literacy and schooling make the difference for children's success in literacy. However, in some cases of isolation from the mainstream culture, for example geographically in the Piedmont or linguistically and ethnically within a Hispanic subculture, language practices may deviate systematically and radically from those expected in school and the larger society. Children from such environments experience complex and troubling relationships between the different settings of their lives. Assuming that their subcultures are literate in some sense and that the processes of natural literacy do operate, these children nevertheless do not necessarily construct literacy as it is understood and practiced in academic, public, and professional contexts. Under such circumstances what is natural to them in literacy (or speech) may make school seem alien to them and literacy as practiced and taught there appear terrifying and incomprehensible. The myth of natural literacy cannot cope with these facts simply by according value to learners' own literacy or language as indeed "natural" and rational.

In a larger sense—and this is as true for the mainstream child as for those from other settings—the social context is not uniformly benevolent at any level of the ecological environment, including the home and school settings. It is true that we are at home in our world, it does nurture us; but to the same extent—even in the natural attitude— we experience it as oppressive, hostile, opaque, threatening. That is in part because in modern society the life-world is really many worlds; each ecological setting has the capacity to either enhance or inhibit growth, and the relationships among them are constantly changing and creating problems of conflict, transition, and readaptation. Inter-personal relations themselves, even at the level of the dyad—mother and child, teacher and student—can sometimes be destructive. At the other end of the ecological spectrum, the distance and possible aliena-tion between learner and culture increases if we consider the impact of institutions on the individual; school, along with literacy itself, must be first on our list. Literacy has bureaucratic, political, and institu-tional dimensions—sometimes devastating in their oppressive im-pact—that the natural interpretation neglects by treating context as a source of meaning and meanings as a source only of good.

The concept of context as benevolent in a natural pedagogy seems to me also to cultivate an unrealistic idea of the teacher's power to affect the child by creating the nourishing situation. In part this will not work because, as I have suggested, such a microsystem cannot be isolated from the other settings and levels of the ecological system. Besides that, human nature resists the teacher's efforts to create and control a completely positive and supportive atmosphere. While the cooperative model is vital to social development, there are other relations and motives woven into literacy experiences—tensions, hos-tilities, competition, cruelty, and unfairness. The teacher, being human, will share and act out these attitudes in her own behavior— will disappoint, fail, oppress her students, be indifferent, careless, angry, and regretful.

Finally, there is a paradox in the emphasis on ownership of literacy within the myth. Ownership comes easy to the child and is correspondingly easy for the adult to tolerate, given goodwill and ideal circumstances, because children's literacy is generally integrative with respect to the culture. (Ideal circumstances, of course, imply harmony between the child's subculture and mainstream understandings of literacy.) If such a situation does exist, it changes with adolescent and adult literacy, which by definition must come into conflict with the establishment and thus even with literacy itself as an institution. With the onset of reflective thought, the comfortable interpersonal relationships of childhood disintegrate. Peers become alternately in league against tradition and hostile or critical or competitive with one another. Teachers become potential enemies, perhaps the more so if they have taken a maternal, accepting, and encouraging role; now they represent the father, rival and critic, upholder of cultural standards (in the stereotype, at least, of parenthood). It is absolutely essential for the growing person to rebel through and perhaps against literacy as the quintessential representation of all that cultural tradition means in Western society. The learner may be fighting for survival, simultaneously in revolt against his own increasingly critical consciousness and against the forces that both deny it and urge it upon him—the schools.[24] Such a situation presents a complex, sensitive, and little understood dilemma for the teacher through high school and early (or delayed) adult development.

I have been attacking the illusion, in the myth of natural literacy, that culture provides, or that we can create, only positive experiences and social support for literacy development. It is terribly important to get a realistic hold on the limitations of this ideal, even as we may try to achieve it. But now I will go much further and say we would not want to. Literacy takes part of its meaning from its association with the critical transmutation of experience, including bitter experience, into understanding; and much of its power from the struggle to liberate oneself from the institutions and immediate realities of one's culture. Thus, ironically, it is these very realities, so far treated as constraints and obstacles, that are the crucible for shaping the developing critical attitude by which literacy surpasses the natural state.

The Surplus of Meaning

The seeds of the unnatural exist in every child, and every descriptive account informed by the myth of natural literacy has, implicitly or explicitly, recognized them. This is to say that a critical or unnatural literacy is, paradoxically, natural in developmental terms. I am going to examine these potentials in terms of two closely related concepts: the child as craftsman and the rise of critical consciousness. A corollary to the second idea is the struggle for individuation through crises of separation and distance.

The concept of child as craftsman is developed by David Feldman in his book *Beyond Universals in Cognitive Development*.[25] It must be understood in the context of another idea, that of nonuniversal domains of development and achievement. More accurately, Feldman postulates a continuum of domains from universal (for example, cognition as described by Piaget) to unique, the latter referring to creative achievements within domains (pp. 8–9). In between are cultural, discipline-based, and idiosyncratic regions. Spoken language is a universal achievement in every culture: meaning, that is, depends on species-specific abilities of some kind. Every normal human being reaches a high degree of performance without instruction, and the margin of skill beyond this point is fairly limited (for example, in oral storytelling or extemporaneous speeches). Literacy is hard to locate on this continuum (although Feldman places it in the cultural domain). In its relationships to speech, both genetic and parallel, it has universal characteristics, at least according to the recent evidence for natural acquisition in a literate environment. Yet in other respects it seems to lie between the cultural domain (a skill requiring some instruction that all individuals within a culture are expected to acquire) and a discipline-based achievement (one that is mastered by a small elite group). It varies both from one culture to another, and within a given culture where literacy is developed to very sophisticated levels. To exactly the degree that, and in those respects in which, literacy is not universal (i.e., it requires direct instruction, takes conscious effort to learn, attains high levels of skill and art) it surpasses the natural.

Taking literacy to be cultural, in Feldman's terms, implies craftsmanship and a corresponding need for instruction. Literacy involves what Jerome Bruner has called "amplifiers" of human thought and action, in which Feldman includes "all the symbol systems, models, tools, technology, and artifacts as well as the variety of cultural institutions and their products" (p. 14)."[26] These "amplifiers" require cultural techniques for transmitting them, usually through institutions evolved for that purpose. Feldman argues that such instruction should be based on the metaphor of the child as craftsman, understood in a developmental sense.

One of the consequences of postulating nonuniversal development is to shift the stages and sequences from inside the child to the domain itself. That is, qualitative changes in achievement over time are experienced by learners in such domains, but these stages are context-dependent—defined by an ideal sequence of achievement in the domain. This development is specifically the sequential achievement of craft, the mastery of forms, techniques, and strategies as well as (and by means of) metaknowledge about the processes and products of the domain. Learning does exhibit "staginess"—sequencing and hierarchical integration—but learners are not necessarily "in" a given stage in some holistic sense.

There is very good evidence of development toward craft in a number of domains, including literacy. The most suggestive for literacy comes from studies of artistic development, as reported by Howard Gardner.[27] He sees preadolescence as a time in which children need to rapidly learn skills related to achievements in specific intellectual regions (associated with "intelligences" localized in the brain), in order to cope with the adolescent crisis of critical consciousness. Many studies of early literacy (up through grade school) observe— sometimes with amusing dismay—that at certain points in development children pay increasing attention to forms, conventions, skills, and management of their own composing processes.[28] At the adult level, of course, knowledge about literacy is codified in the arts of rhetoric and literary criticism. The problem is to discover exactly how to integrate instruction in such formal modes with the continuing "natural" modes of learning and their contextual support. This is another way to put the crucial question raised by a critical moment, how to restore what Paul Ricoeur calls an "informed" or second naiveté, the depth or immersion in meaning that characterizes the natural attitude.[29]

This brings me to the second potential for surpassing a natural literacy—the rise of critical consciousness. It is possible to polish craft and skills in what might be called conscious, but not self-conscious, work at literacy performances.[30] This is what Gardner reports for artistic development (particularly evident in prodigies), and what researchers in the grade schools report for literacy. Such actions by children represent a movement beyond the pure natural attitude of infancy, in making language an object to talk and think about and manipulate. Children working at literacy in grade school build up a language for talking about writing and practice the application of standards in judging their work against alternatives. In this way they lay the foundation for the true critical literacy of adolescence. This distinction corresponds to that of Piaget between concrete and formal operations, where thought operates first on objects and later on thought itself.

The critical moment punctures the natural attitude in sometimes traumatic ways. At this point the learner becomes self-aware, and reflexively examines the processes and products of her own literacy. It is important that she can now not only attend hypothetically to forms, but separate them from meanings sufficiently to contemplate alternative and possible meanings as distinct from their linguistic expression. In Western schooled literacy, writing in adolescence and adulthood is (ideally) more and more associated with possibility, and thus with distancing from immediate realities and meanings deeply embedded in context.[31]

In this light it appears that the tensions and hostilities earlier viewed as interruptions or violations of the natural immersion in contextual meanings—often blamed on teachers and schooling—are in fact inevitable. They represent the painful separation that learners must achieve not only between themselves and their parents and homes, but between themselves and natural, taken-for-granted meanings. The effort to transcend the natural attitude is a crisis of identity repeating the early individuation of the infant from symbiosis with the mother, and may sometimes exact a high cost in turmoil, disharmony, rebellion, and loss. If written language is initially natural, like speech, as I believe it can be, then it must become unnatural and alien with the onset of critical consciousness, even as it is also a primary agent in that change. Without settling the cause-effect relations between literacy and consciousness or cognition (I think that is the wrong way to put the question anyway), we can say that in our society they are intricately complicated over the later course of intellectual development. At the same time, the difficulty of relinquishing naiveté in literacy, as in other spheres of activity, prefigures the lifelong effort to recover our symbiotic attachment to the life-world. Prodigies in the arts who experience this crisis most acutely—having developed skill and judgment more rapidly than most in preadolescence—feel acutely the loss of what Lorin Hollander called the seamless control (over music) that he felt as a child. It took him from age seventeen to thirty to recover.[32]

The Responsibilities of Reciprocity in Cultural Instruction

The surplus of meaning in Western literacy, which I have explicated in terms of the child as craftsman and the rise of critical consciousness, sets a project with implications for both research and pedagogy. It is necessary to understand both the natural and critical or reflective sides of ourselves, and the ways whereby each enters into literacy. We have begun to characterize both, and much current inquiry centers on their many-faceted and complicated interdependence. But the more clearly we articulate our questions, the more unsatisfactory our present state of understanding is as a basis for practical decision. It is both our blessing and our curse as a praxis discipline that we must decide what to do anyway. It is in this spirit that I want to offer a general principle for cultural instruction, namely that of reciprocity to at least three dimensions of literacy. Although these dimensions have a developmental interpretation, one does not replace another. As in the case of Bruner's succession of representative systems (enactive, iconic, and symbolic) or Piaget's stages, each new dimension incorporates, reinterprets, and advances the previous one, and all continue to be active. In the following matches, cultural instruction should be understood as including every possible institution from home and school to workplace—any setting where literacy undergoes change and growth.

At the first level the natural attitude prevails. Literacy involves biologically based and contextually motivated acquisition, and learners direct their own reinventions of cultural codes. The growing person is deeply embedded in situational matrices, although these are not always benevolently meaningful and supportive. The model for cultural instruction in this mode of literacy is that of interactions within the home, projected into school and other settings. This model might be interestingly modified and expanded by studying Buddhist instruction. The Buddhist master undertakes his teaching in the mode of an informed naiveté, a return to "beginner's mind" that could not have occurred without his first developing his own rational ego—the "monkey mind." He has thus solved (or perhaps enacted) the paradox that I pointed out before, where the teacher has passed into the critical moment yet addresses a pupil who remains naive or tenuously critical. The Buddhist method is significantly nonverbal and nonreflective. It offers the arduous possibility of teaching that recaptures the natural attitude as depth illuminated by reflection.[33]

The second level of literacy is that of craft and skill. Here literacy is a cultural domain verging on a disciplinary one, with a body of codified principles of performance. Mastery involves attention to form and technique as instrumental, and then renaturalization of these as tacit. This level also develops and fine-tunes control of writing processes involving processes of orchestration (partly the management of attention) and strategic choice. The appropriate model for cultural instruction at this level is the workshop in the performance arts, permeated by "shop talk" among professionals, peers, masters, and apprentices. Here performance skill is dynamically observed and codified as part of a tradition that is strongly oral and social; technique is isolated for analysis, practice, and appropriation. Much learning depends on demonstration.

The third level is that of critical consciousness in Paulo Freire's sense.[34] At this level, thought becomes reflexive and brings into question all meaningfulness, including that of literacy itself. Criticism struggles to reconcile its positive values with its negative tendencies toward skepticism and an empty rationalism. The reciprocal method of instruction is Socratic, the dialogic model that Socrates describes in terms of midwifery—aiding new ideas to be born. As C. Jan Swearingen has demonstrated, this model has a built-in irony or reflexivity that through scrupulous use can become productive.[35]

After analysis, the challenge remains: how—in a spirit of hope, if not of innocence—to find, or perhaps merely to seek again and again, that fragile and fleeting balance whereby we can surpass the natural attitude and yet reclaim it?

Notes

1. E.g., Jerome C. Harste, Virginia A. Woodward, and Carolyn L. Burke, *Language Stories & Literacy Lessons* (Portsmouth, NH: Heinemann, 1984); Anne Haas Dyson, "Emerging Alphabetic Literacy in School Contexts: Toward Defining the Gap between School Curriculum and Child Mind," *Written Communication* 1 (1984), 3–55; Emilia Ferreiro and Ana Teberosky, *Literacy before Schooling*, tr. Karen Goodman Castro (Exeter, NH: Heinemann, 1982); and *Awakening to Literacy: The University of Victoria Symposium on Children's Response to a Literate Environment: Literacy before Schooling*, ed. Hillel Goelman, Antoinette A. Oberg, and Frank Smith (Exeter, NH: Heinemann, 1984), cited hereafter as *Awakening*. See also these thoughtful and balanced treatments of writing as natural: Janet Emig, "Non-Magical Thinking: Presenting Writing Developmentally in Schools," in Janet Emig, *The Web of Meaning: Essays on Writing, Teaching, Learning, and Thinking*, ed. Dixie Goswami and Maureen Butler (Montclair, NJ: Boynton/Cook, 1983), pp. 132–34; John Warnock, "The Writing Process," in *Research in Composition and Rhetoric: A Bibliographical Sourcebook*, ed. Michael G. Moran and Ronald F. Lunsford (Westport, CT: Greenwood Press, 1984), pp. 3–26; and William Teale, "Toward a Theory of How Children Learn to Read and Write 'Naturally': An Update," in *Changing Perspectives on Research in Reading/Language Processing and Instruction*, 33rd Yearbook of the National Reading Conference, ed. Jerome A. Niles and Larry A. Harris (Rochester, NY: NRC, 1984), pp. 317–22.

2. Edmund Husserl, *Ideas Pertaining to a Pure Phenomenology and to a Phenomenological Philosophy. First Book: General Introduction to a Pure Phenomenology,* tr. F. Kersten (The Hague: Nijhoff, 1983), part 2, chapter 1, sect. 27–32; and *The Crisis of European Sciences and Transcendental Phenomenology: An Introduction to Phenomenological Philosophy,* tr. David Carr (Evanston: Northwestern Univ. Press, 1970), part 3A, especially section 38.

3. David Carr, "Husserl's Problematic Concept of the Life-World," in *Husserl: Expositions and Appraisals,* ed. Frederick Elliston and Peter McCormick (Notre Dame, IN: Univ. of Notre Dame Press, 1977), p. 211. See also Husserl's concept of the horizon as presented in Cornelius Van Peursen, "The Horizon," also in Elliston and McCormick, pp. 182–201.

4. The idea of transcendence is a controversial aspect of Husserl's phenomenology, and is interpreted variously. Many philosophers oppose or find naive the concept of a transcendental Ego or subject, acting as an absolute ground: e.g., Jacques Derrida, *Speech and Phenomena,* tr. David B. Allison (Evanston, IL: Northwestern Univ. Press, 1973).

5. Paul Ricoeur, *Freedom and Nature: The Voluntary and the Involuntary,* tr. Erazim V. Kohak (Evanston, IL: Northwestern Univ. Press, 1966), p. 15.

6. This issue—the capacity of literacy to disembed—is part of a larger debate about literacy, cognition, and culture wherein fundamentally different disciplinary perspectives are confronting one another. A good sense of the conflict is provided in *Awakening,* especially in the Commentaries by Goelman and Oberg (pp. 201–21). David Olson and Jerome Bruner, with essays in the same volume, are among the prominent theorists who see literacy as emancipating thought from the natural attitude. See also Margaret Donaldson, *Children's Minds* (New York: Norton, 1978). A good bibliography on the subject is Jean Luetkemeyer, Caroline Van Antwerp, and Gloria Kindell, "Bibliography of Spoken and Written Language," in *Coherence in Spoken and Written Discourse,* ed. Deborah Tannen, vol. 12 in *Advances in Discourse Processes,* ed. Roy D. Freedle (Norwood, NJ: Ablex, 1984), pp. 265–81.

7. Cf. the "developmental synthesis" proposed by Robert Cairns in *Social Development: The Origins and Plasticity of Interchanges* (San Francisco: Freeman, 1979), which assesses the contributions of psychobiology, social learning theory, cognitive development, and ethology and evolution to an understanding of social development.

8. Lev S. Vygotsky, *Thought and Language,* tr. and ed. Eugenia Hanfmann and Gertrude Vakar (Cambridge, MA: MIT Press, 1962), pp. 52–81.

9. For a brief statement of the contrast, see Howard Gardner, "Encounter at Royaumont: The Debate between Jean Piaget and Noam Chomsky," *Art, Mind, and Brain: A Cognitive Approach to Creativity* (New York: Basic Books, 1982), pp. 16–26.

10. In addition to research already cited on literacy, e.g., *Awakening,* and Harste, Woodward, and Burke, *Language Stories,* see Stephen Krashen, *Writing: Research, Theory, and Application* (New York: Pergamon, 1984).

11. Gabrielle Rico, *Writing the Natural Way: Using Right-Brain Techniques to Release Your Expressive Powers* (Los Angeles: Tarcher, 1983).

12. Richard Young has characterized the Romantic strain in "current traditional rhetoric" in several essays, for example "Arts, Crafts, Gifts and Knacks: Some Disharmonies in the New Rhetoric," in *Reinventing the Rhetorical Tradition,* ed. Aviva Freedman and Ian Pringle (Conway, AK: L & S Books, 1980), pp. 53–60. His ideas have been developed further by James Berlin, most fully in *Writing Instruction in Nineteenth-Century American Colleges* (Carbondale, IL: Southern Illinois Univ. Press,

1984). However, serious study is just beginning both on current traditional rhetoric itself (in the twentieth century) and on the historical influence of the Romantic tradition on the development of composition teaching. Historians are likely to revise these early and somewhat impressionistic views.

13. On epistemic writing, see Kenneth Dowst, "The Epistemic Approach: Writing, Knowing, and Learning," in *Eight Approaches to Teaching Composition*, ed. Timothy R. Donovan and Ben W. McClelland (Urbana, IL: NCTE, 1980), pp. 65–85. "Writing to learn" is a concept that is being enacted and defined in practice in writing across the curriculum programs, in the National Writing Project (especially by Sam Watson in North Carolina), in the summer program of Bread Loaf School, and in faculty workshops.

14. For example, see *Observing the Language Learner*, ed. Angela Jaggar and M. Trika Smith-Burke (Newark, DE: International Reading Association and NCTE, 1985).

15. See Richard J. Bernstein, *Beyond Objectivism and Relativism: Science, Hermeneutics, and Praxis* (Philadelphia: Univ. of Pennsylvania Press, 1983); and John B. Thompson, *Critical Hermeneutics: A Study in the Thought of Paul Ricoeur and Jurgen Habermas* (Cambridge: Cambridge Univ. Press, 1981).

16. Paul Ricoeur, *Husserl: An Analysis of His Phenomenology*, tr. Edward G. Ballard and Lester E. Embree (Evanston, IL: Northwestern Univ. Press, 1967), p. 20.

17. Glenda L. Bissex, "The Child as Teacher," in *Awakening*, pp. 87–101.

18. Yetta Goodman, "The Development of Initial Literacy," in *Awakening*, pp. 102–9.

19. See Andrew Lock, *The Guided Reinvention of Language* (New York: Academic Press, 1980); and *Developmental Pragmatics*, ed. Elinor Ochs and Bambi B. Schieffelin (New York: Academic Press, 1979).

20. E.g., Denny Taylor, *Family Literacy: Young Children Learning to Read and Write* (Exeter, NH: Heinemann, 1983); Lucy McCormick Calkins, *Lessons from a Child: On the Teaching and Learning of Writing* (Exeter, NH: Heinemann, 1983); and Glenda L. Bissex, *GNYS at WRK: A Child Learns to Write and Read* (Cambridge, MA: Harvard Univ. Press, 1980).

21. Urie Bronfenbrenner, *The Ecology of Human Development: Experiments by Nature and Design* (Cambridge, MA: Harvard Univ. Press, 1979).

22. For a counterexample, see Shirley Brice Heath, *Ways with Words: Language, Life, and Work in Communities and Classrooms* (Cambridge: Cambridge Univ. Press, 1983), a beautifully nuanced and richly detailed ethnographic study of literacy practices in two communities. This work expresses a sophisticated and critical understanding of literacy and culture, not at all naive or mythical in the sense I mean here.

23. Harste, Woodward, and Burke, *Language Stories*, ch. 4, "Race, Sex, Socioeconomic Status & Language"; Hope Jensen Leichter, "Families as Environments for Literacy," in *Awakening*, pp. 38–50. The concept of "class theoretical" terms is that of Kurt Lewin, discussed in Bronfenbrenner, *Ecology*, p. 17.

24. See William G. Perry, Jr. *Forms of Intellectual and Ethical Development in the College Years: A Scheme* (New York: Holt, 1968), for a study of these conflicts in Harvard and Radcliffe students.

25. David Henry Feldman, *Beyond Universals in Cognitive Development* (Norwood, NJ: Ablex, 1980).

26. Jerome Bruner discusses representation systems as technologies in his study *Beyond the Information Given: Studies in the Psychology of Knowing*, ed. Jeremy M. Anglin (New York: Norton, 1973), section 4.

27. Gardner, *Art*, pp. 91–102, 208–17.

28. E.g., Calkins, *Lessons*; Bissex, *GNYS*; Donald H. Graves, *Writing: Teachers and Children at Work* (Exeter, NH: Heinemann, 1983).

29. This is a recurring theme in Ricoeur's work; see chapter 4.

30. Yetta Goodman makes this point in "Development," p. 104.

31. In *Awakening*, see Jerome S. Bruner, "Language, Mind, and Reading," pp. 193–200, and David R. Olson, "'See! Jumping!' Some Oral Language Antecedents of Literacy," pp. 185–92, among many statements of this position, which remains controversial.

32. Lorin Hollander, "Child's Play: Prodigies and Possibilities," *Nova*, PBS, March 16, 1985.

33. See Chögyam Trungpa, *Cutting through Spiritual Materialism*, ed. John Baker and Marvin Casper (Boulder: Shambhala, 1973), and *Meditation in Action* (Boulder: Shambhala, 1969). Trungpa is a Tibetan Buddhist.

34. Paulo Freire, *Education for Critical Consciousness* (New York: Continuum, 1973).

35. C. Jan Swearingen, "The Rhetor as Eiron: Plato's Defense of Dialogue," *Pre/Text* 3 (1982), 289–323.

6

The Dance of Discourse

Since the start of the twentieth century a new physics has radically, deeply, and indelibly changed our beliefs about physical reality and human knowledge of the physical world. Quantum mechanics and relativity describe the universe as a cosmic dance of energy patterns that is understood, and indeed constituted as we know it, through our interaction with it. This new framework for understanding the physical world invites a corresponding revolution in our concept of understanding symbolic realities, specifically the structures of meaning in written discourse. When the modern view of physical reality is extended to the symbolic realities of texts, it transforms the structure of prose into an illusion of the dance of discourse created by our participation in it. In this chapter I seek to develop such a dynamic, relativistic view of discourse structure for composition and suggest its relevance to our models and representations of structure in the teaching of writing.

The issues I address are philosophical, not technical. They generate questions like these: What is being structured in written discourse? From what perspectives do we interpret structure? In what time frames is discourse structure constituted? What roles do we play, as writers and readers, in constituting it? Questions, on the other hand, about how in the instrumental sense—how writers and readers construct or reconstruct specific structures, how texts express and elicit them—are not asked here; they await transformation of the ontological and epistemological framework that organizes research and teaching in the emergent discipline of composition.[1]

A point of entry into any conceptual framework is through its terminology. In Kenneth Burke's formulation any nomenclature, whether deliberately chosen or spontaneous, acts as a "terministic screen" through which reality is selectively perceived. It screens or filters first, by its power to redirect the attention into certain channels rather than others; and more deeply, by defining the range of what is possible and what is problematic.[2] In the case of composition theory, the contemporary scene is dominated by a powerful terministic screen presented as an *antithetical pair* around which value polarizes. This pair, which organizes our perception and conception of discourse structure along with much else, is "process" and "product."

Briefly, "process" refers to writing as a productive activity to which are attached the positive values of speech (as both thought and human action) and art (the creation of a symbol). "Product" characterizes texts as the artifacts or meaningful forms resulting from a writer's composing process. For reasons that will become clear, both the logic of this conception of writing and the historical circumstances in which it was formulated make text as product a reductive concept with highly negative connotations. This characterization of texts places strong constraints on a concept of discourse structure, which must ground itself in ideas of texts and their meanings.

The antithesis in composition between process and product was explicitly formulated as a symbolic weapon in the revolt of the 1960s against a failed teaching tradition. It was intended to make a contrast between a teaching practice preoccupied by textual objects, rules, and conventions, and a projected dynamic pedagogy that would focus on the psychology of writers' composing processes. It succeeded in reversing the value structure of composition pedagogy and, by opening a new field of questions and topics, in reconstituting the field as a research discipline. What it did not do was lay bare the sources of that antithesis in the teaching tradition itself, nor the connections between it and currents of thought in twentieth-century language studies. This fact may help to explain why composition, so long a highly unself-conscious field, remained, until recently, relatively impervious to changes in attitudes toward texts within sister disciplines such as literary theory, and why I have chosen here to invoke modern physics instead as a source of insight about our notions of discourse structure.

One unobserved point within early modern composition theory was that the process/product opposition restates a very general, fundamental polarity between process and structure that underlies the modern study of symbolism in general and language in particular, and has motivated many of its controversies. During most of this century structure was the dominant and favored term in language studies. The polarity received classic expression in two closely related distinctions made by the French linguist Saussure, between *langue* and *parole*, synchrony and diachrony.[3]

In Saussure's vocabulary *langue* is the abstract system of language structure that underlies individual acts of speaking (*parole*). For the purpose of analyzing the relations within this system, the linguist considers it synchronically along the "axis of simultaneities," where all its elements coexist timelessly in a given state. Diachronic analysis deals with the "axis of successions" along which things change over time; thus it is concerned with language history and use. Most of Saussure's influential interpreters have read him as giving not only methodological but ontological priority to structure, thought of as abstract, relatively stable, well-ordered, and self-contained, over process or event, the transient, personally idosyncratic phenomena of actual speech acts. This priority correlates with an emphasis on the synchronic or simultaneous perspective over the linear, temporal, diachronic one.

When these structuralist notions are applied to literature, the text becomes the object of study that corresponds to *langue* and calls for synchronic analysis. The text tends to assimilate to itself the characteristics of language, including structure, autonomy, and inherent, self-contained meaning independent of the particular reader and context. Particularly if it is nonpoetic prose, as in the texts of the composition class, the text appears to be governed and produced by the rules of *langue*.[4] Given such a conception of the text, discourse structure becomes an empirical property of a nonliterary ("expository") text that can be abstracted objectively and reported by readers reliably and consistently, in part because it has been fixed into the text by a writer from a mental or written outline.

In the teaching tradition these objectivist conceptions of text, textuality, meaning, and discourse structure were not well-articulated theoretical constructs. The structuralist influence was not scholarly but cultural (so that the historical variations and subtleties of actual structuralist positions are largely irrelevant to composition). Through composition teachers trained primarily in literature, structuralist ideas filtered indirectly into composition texts and the classroom, where they met and reinforced the still powerful intrinsic formalism of the New Critics. Since they did not come through scholarly channels and were not perceived as fitting into theories, these concepts received little critical attention and were absorbed and used in vague, selective, and contradictory ways. As has been frequently pointed out with respect to the traditional teaching paradigm in composition, such concepts constituted a body of received, tacit wisdom that managed to make overall sense to people in pragmatic terms, partly through sheer familiarity, until the whole was challenged and opened to critical examination in the 1960s. As far as discourse structure is concerned, the prevailing concept of text and its structure was (and is) expressed pragmatically by such notions and practices as outlining, the five-paragraph essay, the classification of paragraph types, the interpretation of all these as rules for creating structure, and the "correcting" of texts by teachers.

Objectivist conceptions of texts and their meanings are now under sharp attack across a broad spectrum of fields concerned with symbols, where movements toward a constructivist, interactionist, context-dependent view of language are gathering force and converging. We may picture these currents of thought in linguistics, literary theory and criticism, cognitive science, philosophy, rhetoric, ethnography of communication, and other human sciences as representing a comprehensive redirection of interest, attention, and value from the structure to the event pole of the polarity, from symbols and symbolic structures in themselves to acts of symbolizing in social contexts. In the case of texts and their interpretation, that shift translates into such ideas and emphases as these (shared to some degree by an astonishingly diverse and multidisciplinary group of thinkers): the reader as constructor, creator, or major contributor to textual meaning; the dissolution of texts as static objects; the principle of the indeterminacy of meaning; the radical dependence of meaning on scene or context; the importance of structures of expectation; notions of implicit dialogue; the significance to understood meaning of what is not there; and the historicality of interpretation.

The reversal of polarity in composition appears to fit neatly into this picture, but in its early development it remained curiously isolated from parallel developments in other fields. The change embodied in the foregrounding of the composing process was experienced within the field as a purely local phenomenon. Numerous descriptions of "paradigm shift" even now make no mention of external influences; the motive for change is located in researchers' and teachers' recognition of discrepancies between actual writing behavior and the recommendations and practices of the textbooks and classroom, along with their dissatisfaction with the progress of research in the field. The egocentricity of a field pulling itself up by its bootstraps, trying to transform a teaching practice into an art and a science of composition, is understandable. It is harder to explain how an objectivist attitude toward texts could survive intact the overthrow of the value system in which it was embedded, or why the dynamics of "process" were not extended to the text and its interpretation as in other disciplines, especially since compositionists are generally aware of this move in such fields as literary theory and reading theory.

Two reasons, at least, suggest themselves: the paradox of the terminological pair, and the strategy of compartmentalization. In a terminological opposition, one pair is defined and given its positive value by contrast to the other, the negative or absence of those values. The second term must be so construed as to play this role with reference to a specific issue or question that the polarity addresses. In composition the polarity of structure and event was framed as a solution to a pedagogical crisis in which the issue was how to teach writing, and success was defined as an individual's ability to produce a good text. In that context the polarity of process and product served to devalue teaching based on judgments of finished texts as compared with teaching aimed at helping students with the task of production. But this opposition was quickly reinterpreted as a description of the psychology of "making" texts in which the composing process acquired intrinsic value. It is this limitation to a psychological framework (as opposed to a transactive one) that locked the compositionists into a conception of text as product. The narrowing of the event of discourse to the writer's process of making a symbol required the made symbol or product as its opposite. To that notion of product were attached all the negative associations of teaching based on texts. Texts became even more quintessentially objects—inanimate, static, self-contained, and rigidly organized—by comparison with the vital, creative, temporal, subjective, fluid, open-ended features of composing.

The strategy of compartmentalization reinforces this paradox. The process/product opposition is itself compartmentalizing, in that it separates the text from the historical process of production, and writing from reading. As a result, theorists can tolerate severe dissonances in their belief systems about texts, structures, writing, and reading—for instance, adopting an objective, empirical approach to the study of discourse structure in student writing and model expository prose; taking a radically subjective point of view in literary criticism; and holding a constructivist position about the psycholinguistics of reading, distributing approaches, techniques, and attitudes acquired from other fields into the appropriate boxes. This compartmentalization has effectively protected a traditional conception of discourse structure from the more dynamic, relativistic views of language put forth in other fields.

It is claimed that the reorientation of composition from product to process effected a paradigmatic change. I do not think so, despite its profound and dramatic impact. The dichotomization of process and product, the psychological, writer-centered interpretation of process, the ironic way these preserve and heighten an objectivist characterization of texts and their structures—all these suggest rather a transitional stage leading to a genuinely new paradigm as yet only dimly perceived. The essence of the underlying paradigm that still controls our view of symbolic realities (especially in practice) rests not in the way the polarity is construed, but in the dualism itself, in the ontological split and its implications for a theory of knowledge or an epistemology of the text. We may recognize the new paradigm when we find it (if that is not a contradiction in terms, since paradigms are made up of precisely those assumptions that remain tacit, unrecognized, and unexamined) by its power to reintegrate texts into a dynamic of discourse.

In this chapter I suggest that one way out of the trap that we created is to recognize our conflicts as a local expression of the confrontation between two epistemologies: on the one hand, the worldview of Western classical science inherited from Newton and Descartes, and on the other, the new physics as it has developed in the twentieth century from relativity theory and quantum theory. Let me expand this comparison briefly.

There are two strands to the notion of objective description arising from the Cartesian division of the world into mind and matter, or subject and object. The more basic, I think, and the less obvious is the immutability of reality in both its subjective and objective aspects. The very possibility of consistent and repeatable observation depends on the conception of both subjects and objects as stable, determinate wholes that do not significantly change over the interval of observation. That is, they are treated for the purposes of description as fixed states rather than dynamic processes. A static perspective on the observer and the observed is closely linked to the second strand of this notion, the absolute ontological independence of objects from the consciousness and situation of individual observers. The ability of the human observer to perceive and describe reality directly and without mediation is taken for granted, as is the observer's accuracy, lack of prejudice, technical skills of observation, and canonical perspective.

These are the same assumptions that underlie the opposition of structure and process in the context of symbolic realities, and that specifically govern the practice in composition of describing the meaning structures of texts. But it is exactly these assumptions that have been shattered by the new physics. From relativity theory and quantum theory emerges a new physics embedded in a radically different metaphysics, which must ultimately transform the understanding of symbolic as well as physical reality. The new metaphysics transcends these dichotomies by merging subject and object, structure and process in a play of energies whose patterns are realized as objects precisely through our temporal interplay with them. I propose to explore the implications of the dynamic, relativistic worldview for a conception of structure as process in written discourse. Throughout my discussion I will be drawing my characterization of this new worldview largely from two lucid books written as introductions for the layman: *The Tao of Physics* by Fritjof Capra, and *The Dancing Wu Li Masters: An Overview of the New Physics* by Gary Zukav. Both authors emphasize the convergence of this view of the universe with that of Eastern mysticism, where the structure of physical reality emerges from a cosmic dance of creation and destruction through the interaction of observer and observed. First, however, I would like to consider how a conception of discourse as dance is motivated from within the field of composition itself.

Problems of Practice

Because composition now draws information constantly from fields where interactionist epistemologies have been and are being articulated, it might be expected to change its outlook on symbolic realities through their influence, despite the retarding forces I have described. I think, however, that this will happen only to the degree that these attitudes or views are perceived as meeting an existing need for reconceptualization. There are indeed powerful internal forces at work in composition studies to motivate a new view of discourse structure. These forces are pragmatic, arising from the strain on composition practice caused by the identification of more and more problems in teaching and analysis that cannot be solved through a traditional conception of discourse structure. As these tensions gradually erode the old paradigm from within, they also functionally anticipate a new one, defined by what it must do and explain. From this point of view modern physics appears as a solution to the problem posed by the inadequacies of the current conception of structure, because its principle of the dance fits the criteria we arrive at empirically for a new one.

To understand the deficiencies of the present view of discourse structure in composition, we must examine how this largely tacit

concept is institutionalized in teaching practice. (The scattered theoretical discussions of form in composition, though interesting and
suggestive, are not at all illuminating about the underlying conceptual
agreements embodied in our use of the term "discourse structure" in
both teaching and research. An example is the debate over paragraph
structure, which never addresses these concerns.[5]) To get at this concept, it is easiest to start by establishing its reference, which can then
become the common ground between the traditional concept and the
revised one I will propose. In philosophical terminology, the reference
of a term is its power to point to some environmental fact in our
common experience. What concrete fact of experience, then, are people pointing to when they "refer" to the structure of a given text?

This is an extraordinarily difficult question to answer. In one
sense, the reference of the term "structure" here *is* the text, as a
symbolic construct that embodies an organized meaning. But people
separate, or abstract, the organization of discourse as meaning from
its specific form as a verbal object, as shown by their ability to restate
or summarize that meaning in different language. In this sense, when
they speak of structure they are referring to a mental experience. To
define the reference of "discourse structure" as the text does not get us
anywhere. How, then, are we going to specify reference to a mental
experience?

Fortunately, the reference of the term "discourse structure" has
objective correlates other than the full text. Not only can people
reconstruct meanings as different full text, but they can represent them
in a special way that highlights structure, which I call making *discourse maps*. The most homely and common example is the traditional Roman numeral outline and its looser variants. If you ask
people to describe (in the sense of *indicate* or *point to*) the structure of
a text, most of them will make a rough outline using some numbered
system with linear order down the page plus indentation. What they
are doing is abstracting the meaning or content of the text and recast-
ing it in a form intended to bring out its principles of organization, its
plot, how it is put together. A discourse map is any representation of
textual meaning that renders the organization (i.e., structure) of the
discourse more vivid to the senses and mind by condensing meaning
elements and arranging them in a spatial array that reveals their
relations. Among the more exotic examples (rarely taught in the
composition classroom, but used frequently by both discourse researchers and ordinary people) are trees, flow graphs, networks, and
matrices.[6]

The common use of some form of traditional outline for nonfiction texts suggests that it is a relatively direct and complete, if not perfect, representation of a mental experience of discourse structure. It thus supplies us with an ostensive definition of structure as a set of features that characterize textual meanings. First, there are three features that are rendered iconically: division into elements, indicated by numbering and lettering; linear order of experience, indicated by numbering and vertical space; and hierarchy, indicated by indentation. The elements are of course specified by condensed language ("topics" or sentences). Relations among the elements, insofar as these cannot be expressed by order or hierarchy, are more or less clearly named; importance, for example, could be expressed by subordination or position in climactic order, whereas contrast, cause-effect, and problem-solution relations would have to be named. (Without modification, traditional outlines cannot express the latter iconically, though other discourse-mapping techniques can.) Finally, the physical boundaries of the outline, often confined to one page, mark off the meaning unit represented there as relatively self-contained and, through its organization, a whole greater than the sum of its parts. Except in its entirety, the outline cannot directly express this integrity of meaning, but often tries to evoke it indirectly by code language highly saturated or resonant with meanings, such as a title, a main-topic phrase, or a thesis statement.

The outline plays an important part in institutionalizing and reinforcing a static model of discourse structure, in which we view meaning as an object contained in the text, accessible to an "objective" description, and capable of spatialization and thus open to simultaneous comprehension of all its parts. This static model represents an interpretation of the features of structure I have described, and of our relation to what is being structured. It is the narrowness of this interpretation that I want to question, not the features themselves, which are stated generally enough to characterize many complex systems. This interpretation is not a direct consequence of the nature of an outline as an icon, that is, a visual scheme, but arises in our use of it. Although the outline as a spatial array does allow static, synchronic interpretation, it also has a linear (vertical) dimension that could represent the reader's time. Outlines and other discourse maps could also be used in sets to represent the development of a meaning structure over the writer's time in composing, or variations in the interpretation of structure according to the perspective of the observer. Indeed, when we actually observe students working on papers in a classroom or a writing lab over an interval of days or weeks, they often produce a series of representations—lists, notes, outlines, drafts—that objectify stages in the evolution of structure toward its characteristic discursive form in the final text. Thus an outline is not inherently incompatible with a dynamic, relativistic concept of discourse structure; it simply reflects our inability to think in such terms within the dominant objective paradigm.

The descriptive inadequacy of a model of discourse structure based on this paradigm can easily be observed in a classroom setting because of the problems it creates in teaching writing. I have already implied one, its inability to account for the evolution of structure through what I like to call "shadow texts": all the various pre/textual and textual writings that lead up to a finished text, especially when the composing act is extended. The static model is functionally ahistorical because it applies only to full, final texts. In addition, the model does not recognize fragmentary or partial structure where meanings have acquired only some of the structural features of discourse and may lack others, such as order; so it cannot handle pre/textual structure even if we try to apply it historically.

There is a corresponding weakness in a static model with respect to reading: its inability to account for the construing of structure in the reader's mind over time. There are two kinds of "time" here during which reading is experienced as an event, that is, as a series of cognitive acts felt as responses to another person's speech act. The first is the time of a single reading or "read-through" from beginning to end. This time and what happens during it are under intensive investigation by scientists interested in the process of language comprehension. The second kind of time, which has received less attention, is the span during which a reader peruses a text more than once, often in separate time periods, and perhaps with aids such as note taking, intensive study of some sections, and so on. Experience of the second kind of time leads readers toward a more synchronic grasp of meaning, with all its elements and relations experienced simultaneously. Both these dimensions are necessary to understanding the processes by which readers comprehend, remember meanings, and perform thought operations such as comparison and criticism on the meaning structures of texts.

The inability to cope with structure as it develops over these different time frames is one aspect of the most profound defect in a static model of written discourse structure. This is the fact that it cannot connect text as a symbolic object to the event of discourse.

Written discourse is patently a communication transaction involving experiences by writer and readers that are life events for both. When the text is detached both from composing acts and from correlative reading acts and is transformed into an autonomous, context-free object in which meaning has somehow been fixed as "content," there is no way to explain its participation as a mediating element in the felt event of communication initiated by the writer and consummated uniquely by each successful reading act. The text and the acts of the discourse event become ontologically incompatible within a static concept of discourse structure.

Finally, a static model is unable to account for simultaneously valid interpretations of what is being structured, which would be experienced by a single writer or reader as alternating perspectives. There seem to be several ways to "see" the meaning of a text: for example, one might take a particular text rhetorically (pragmatically) as a series of logical and emotional appeals, or semantically as a set of assertions. Many factors determine a choice of perspective, among them motive, immediate situational context, cultural setting, stage in the writing or reading process, and knowledge and beliefs of the observer. But the event-nature of discourse makes certain perspectives more immediate or natural, directing our energies into one or another channel of interpretation.

The needs discovered in teaching based on the current model lead us to state the following criteria for a new conception of structure in written discourse. First, it must be *dynamic*, accounting for change and development in a structure over time, both as it is composed and as it is read. Second, it must be *relativistic* or *perspectival*, allowing interpretation to vary with alternate perspectives or gestalts of meaning according to contextual factors. Third, it must *account for the constitution or reconstitution of structure* as a process in which the observer plays an interactive role as participant in a communication event. The next section will consider the correspondence of these criteria to the principles of modern physics.

The Worldview of the New Physics

As the demands for a new concept of structure originally develop in relation to practical tasks, they present themselves as separate and independent problems. If we solve them in any sense, our solutions are ad hoc and incoherent because we lack the philosophical framework to connect them.[7] Thus we may argue in one context for examining and teaching discourse structure over composing time, and in another for the possibility of semantic or pragmatic perspectives on what is being structured, and in yet another for the mediating function of the text, without ever exploring the logical and psychological interdependence of these ideas. The view of knowledge and reality expressed by modern physics (which corresponds to that of Eastern philosophies) gives coherence to these disconnected observations and conclusions about structure by giving us an epistemology in which two principles are organically related. The first is the basic event-nature of the universe in which objects (as structures or forms) are constituted interactively from the energy of flux (i.e., structure *is* process). The second principle is the identity of the dancer with the dance: the significance of perspective to all knowledge, and thus the participation of the observer in the reality observed. These principles correspond almost exactly to the criteria for the concept of discourse structure that are empirically motivated by composition practice, and lead us independently to a dynamic, relativistic view of discourse, its structure, and our knowledge of these as writers and readers.

No matter where we start in the new physics, it leads us (as Gary Zukav puts it) back to ourselves.[8] A number of independent discoveries converge to emphasize the creative role of human consciousness in constituting reality as the phenomenal world of everyday experience and the more sophisticated perceptual world of the scientist. Among the most important are relativity theory and, in quantum theory, Bohr's principle of complementarity (an aspect of the Copenhagen interpretation of quantum mechanics) and Heisenberg's uncertainty principle. Although I share the ignorance of most nonphysicists about these concepts, with the help of Capra and Zukav I think we can understand how radically such notions have changed scientists' views about our knowledge of reality.

Each of these ideas or theories recognizes in a different way the significance of perspective to understanding. From there it is a short step to seeing observers first as participants in the reality they observe and then as creators of it. (The process is not solipsistic but intersubjective: that is, the world as we know it is a collective creation of human consciousness, not a dream of the individual.) Einstein was the first to radically undermine the Cartesian-Newtonian paradigm. His relativity theory showed that the geometry of space and time is not inherent in nature but a construct of the human mind. Einstein discovered that all measurements of time and space depend on the observer's frame of reference—that is, they are relative rather than absolute. Events appear different to observers in different coordinate systems. Zukav tells us:

> Einstein's revolutionary insight was that events which are simultaneous for one observer may occur at different times for another observer depending upon their relative motion. Put another way, two events, one of which occurs before the other as seen from the frame of reference of one observer, may occur at the same time when seen from the frame of reference of another observer. . . . In other words, "sooner," "later," and "simultaneous" are local terms. They have no meaning in the universe at large unless they are tied down to a specific frame of reference.[9]

Since there is no privileged (motionless) frame of reference known to us, the relativity of measurements means that both space and time themselves are relative concepts rather than absolute properties of reality, "merely elements of the language a particular observer uses for his description of the phenomena."[10] Nor are space and time independent, as in the Newtonian model; they form the four-dimensional continuum of space-time.

Although in a relativistic framework space-time measurements, and thus knowledge of an object, are dependent on the point of view of the observer, this is not quite the same as saying that the observer constitutes the object. Quantum theory takes us this further step, blurring the ontological distinction between subject and object. The initial conditions postulated in quantum theory may seem at first to maintain the distinction, for the theory begins by dividing the physical world into the observed system and the observing system.[11] (The observing system includes not only the scientist doing the experiment, but the entire physical context of the observed system.) Quantum theory describes the observed systems in terms of probabilities, or tendencies for subatomic particles to exist or atomic events to occur. But these tendencies are actualized by the process of observation: in other words, the observer actually constitutes the observed reality by his interaction with it.

Capra makes the following analysis of observation in atomic physics.[12] The process of observation involves first isolating a particle by means of the preparation process and allowing it to travel unobserved (thus undisturbed by processes of preparation or measurement) over some physical distance, where it is then observed through the process of measurement. As Capra points out, this analysis makes the particle an artifact of the observation process: "the particle constitutes an intermediate system connecting the processes of A and B and has meaning only in this context: not as an isolated entity, but as an interconnection between the processes of preparation and measurement" (p. 135). Since one can only approximate the "isolation" of the particle (from the rest of the universe!) in the interval between preparation and measurement, the "particle" itself as a distinct physical entity is an idealization or abstraction from a seamless unity. Zukav calls it a "correlation": "All that exists by itself is an unbroken wholeness that presents itself to us as webs (more patterns) of relations. Individual entities are idealizations which are correlations made by us" (pp. 95–96).

The concept that particles are correlations created as objects through the process of observation is only one of several features of quantum theory that undermine the Cartesian split between objective, independent reality and an observing subject. The Heisenberg uncertainty principle describes the limits of our possible knowledge about subatomic nature. Heisenberg showed that we cannot in principle know at the same time both the position and momentum of an individual subatomic particle such as an electron, because in trying to measure its properties we change them. (We can locate or indirectly "see" an electron using gamma rays, but the energy of gamma rays knocks the electron out of orbit and changes its momentum unpredictably. Less energetic rays, as for example light, have too long a wave length to "see" such a small thing as an electron.[13]) Furthermore, as Zukav points out, since particles are *defined* in terms of their position and momentum, we can never see them as they "really are" but only as we choose to see them (p. 135).

Bohr's principle of complementarity deals with the problem of perspective in yet a different way. He formulated this principle to explain the wave-particle duality of light, which later was discovered to apply literally to all physical phenomena. Light exhibits wavelike properties in some contexts and particlelike behavior in others. This fact presents the quantum paradox, since these behaviors or properties are mutually exclusive: something cannot be both wavelike and particlelike at the same time. Essentially, Bohr resolved this paradox by accepting it. He said these contradictory views are both right, and both necessary for a complete understanding of the phenomenon of light. Since we cannot understand light both ways simultaneously, the property that light reveals is decided by our choice of experiment. This means, however, that we are not observing properties of light itself, but of our interaction with light. Since light is constituted through our observations of it, its reality is dependent on such interactions with human consciousness (and for that matter, we ourselves exist by virtue of these interactions) (Zukav, pp. 116–18).

Although there are disagreements among physicists over the philosophical interpretation of quantum theory, the common element in such interpretations is an interactive conception of the relation between ourselves and reality. In a world where we ourselves are integral elements in a web of energy patterns, suggests physicist John Wheeler, there is no such thing as an independent observer:

> Nothing is more important about the quantum principle than this, that it destroys the concept of the world as "sitting out there," with the observer safely separated from it by a 20 centimeter slab of plate glass. Even to observe so miniscule an object as an electron, he must shatter the glass. He must reach in. He must install his chosen measuring equipment. It is up to him to decide whether he shall measure position or momentum. To install the equipment to measure the one prevents and excludes his installing the equipment to measure the other. More-over, the measurement changes the state of the electron. The universe will never afterwards be the same. To describe what has happened, one has to cross out that old word "observer" and put in its place the new word "participator." In some strange sense the universe is a "participa-tory" universe.[14]

The redefinition of the observer as participant in a cosmic web of patterns is closely connected to a redefinition of reality as basically event (temporal flux or dance) and only derivatively—in transient illusions—as object or state. The connection emerges with particular clarity in S-matrix theory, the most successful attempt so far to combine quantum theory and relativity theory in a quantum-relativis-tic description of subatomic particles. S-matrix theory applies to hadrons, which are particles held together by strong interactions (the nuclear force binding the nucleus). According to Capra:

> The important new concept in S-matrix theory is the shift of emphasis from objects to events; its basic concern is not with the particles, but with their reactions. Such a shift from objects to events is required both by quantum theory and by relativity theory. On the one hand, quantum theory has made it clear that a subatomic particle can only be under-stood as a manifestation of the interaction between various processes of

measurement. It is not an isolated object but rather an occurrence, or event, which interconnects other events in a particular way. . . . Relativity theory, on the other hand, has forced us to conceive of particles in terms of space-time: as four-dimensional patterns, as processes rather than objects. The S-matrix approach combines both of these viewpoints. (p. 264)

In S-matrix theory an individual hadron (particle) is defined as a transitory state in a network of reactions, a local condensation or concentration of a quantum field. According to Capra, "the structure of a hadron . . . is not understood as a definite arrangement of constituent parts, but is given by all sets of particles which may interact with one another to form the hadron under consideration" (p. 266). Structure or form in the physically experienced world is thus defined dynamically as the tendency or probability for certain reactions to occur, whereby the energy of the atomic patterns manifests itself as mass, or particles. "Subatomic particles are dynamic patterns which have a space aspect and a time aspect. Their space aspect makes them appear as objects with a certain mass, their time aspect as processes involving the equivalent energy" (p. 203). These tendencies are governed by conservation laws that allow energy to flow only through certain reaction channels, corresponding to quantum numbers. Thus structure does not emerge arbitrarily from the matrix of the dancing energy patterns, even though it is defined in terms of processes rather than stable objects.

Both Zukav and Capra frequently use the metaphor of a cosmic dance, drawn from Hindu mythology, to emphasize that the universe as described by modern physics is in essence event, or "patterns of organic energy," as *Wu Li* (the Chinese word for physics) is translated. Structure as an aspect of processes is the orderliness of the cosmic dance; as an aspect of objects it is constituted by the intentionality of human consciousness, simultaneously directed toward and participating in this dance. Capra paints the following picture of reality as a Heraclitan flux, undergoing constant movement, change, and transformation:

The exploration of the subatomic world in the twentieth century has revealed the intrinsically dynamic nature of matter. It has shown that the constituents of atoms, the subatomic particles, are dynamic patterns which do not exist as isolated entities, but as integral parts of an inseparable network of interactions. These interactions involve a ceaseless flow of energy manifesting itself as the exchange of particles; a dynamic interplay in which particles are created and destroyed without end in a continual variation of energy patterns. The particle interactions give rise to the stable structures which build up the material world, which again do not remain static, but oscillate in rhythmic movements. The whole universe is thus engaged in endless motion and activity; in a continual cosmic dance of energy. (p. 225)

In the next section I will describe a dynamic, relativistic view of discourse structure in accord with both the needs demonstrated by teaching practice in composition and the epistemological principles laid down in the new physics. The fundamental reality we will be dealing with is written discourse as a communication event, the dance of discourse. Discourse structure will be treated as an organization of this experience that may be interpreted by participants from various perspectives, called gestalts. Observers trying to describe structure (e.g., discourse analysts or teacher-editors) are always necessarily participants in the communication event. As event, structure develops within a time frame. Because of the nature of inscription, which separates discourse participants in time-space, we will take into account various experiential times: two historical times, those of the full writing and reading acts, which may involve repeated passes through a text and its pre/texts; and the virtual time associated with the speech act performed by the text and experienced in any pass through it.

Structure as Process

The basic premise for the conception of discourse structure to be considered now is that all discourse, spoken or written, is an event in the life processes of individuals. In Paul Ricoeur's words, "discourse has an *act* as its mode of presence."[15] The minimal speech event incorporates two reciprocal acts, an overt productive act by a speaker and a covert receptive act by one or more listeners. In writing, this speech event is somehow inscribed in a text. Let us consider now exactly what this premise means, drawing both on Ricoeur's rich work in hermeneutics, or theory of interpretation, and on speech-act theory as developed by John Searle and others from the work of J. L. Austin.

Ricoeur's characterization of discourse as event is made in the context of his effort to resolve dialectically the structure/process polarity as posed by structural linguistics. He thus develops his definition in terms of Saussure's contrast between discourse as *parole*, or individual act of speaking, and *langue*, language as system.[16] Discourse as event differs from language as system in a number of important traits. First, speech acts are actual, therefore temporal, whereas systems of signs are virtual, therefore atemporal. Second, they are creative (always producing new sentences), therefore infinite, whereas the language system is a finite, closed set of signs. Third, discourse as event has reference both to the world and to the self, that is, to the participants in the event, their discourse acts, and their immediate situational context. Signs considered within the semiotic system (i.e., not in use) do not refer or self-refer; rather, they have a differential value, being formally defined by their difference, their opposition to other units in the system. In Ricoeur's view, these characteristics of discourse as event give it an ontological priority over the system.

Inscription does not change the fact that discourse is an event—it still involves two or more individuals performing reciprocal, interdependent acts in a real world. But it does greatly change the way all these traits of speech and events are realized. Most of the differences arise from the separation of the two component acts of the discourse event in space-time, which is made possible by the mediating function of the inscribed symbols. Structural features laid down in the text must organize the dance of cognitive energies between writer and reader so as to constitute the complete discourse event.

One major effect of inscription is to divide and complicate the simple time frame that in speech is shared by speaker and listener. The productive and the receptive acts acquire the potential to be greatly stretched out—over days, weeks, or more. In the case of writing, structure takes on a historical dimension through its gradual evolution (sometimes radical transformation) over composing time. It is often possible to actually observe the life history of a discourse structure and to study the forces shaping it as it passes through pre/textual representations, drafts, and revisions. Ironically, the drawing out of reading time through rereading and study (that is, repetition) has the opposite effect of making possible a synchronic understanding of the text as a simultaneous network of elements and relations—a meaning-object.

Distinct from the historical times of the actual, indefinitely prolonged writing and reading activities is an internal discourse time frame in which the speech act is performed and taken up. This time frame is virtual in the discourse and is actualized uniquely by each reader. To understand what this virtuality means, we must consider what happens when a speech act is inscribed in the text. The writer composes a speech act *as* text, which means that she invests in the text her own power to perform a speech act. To do so she creates a persona, a speaker-in-the-text, who performs a speech act invented and authorized by herself and directed toward imagined readers. The time frame of this speech act, though lived by the writer in any sustained thinking or writing through it, is shaped to fit the cognitive processes of the anticipated comprehender. The virtual speaker and act, including its time frame, must be activated by the reader's comprehension in order to consummate the speech event.

The complexities of the viritual speech act and the reciprocal reader's act of comprehension are crucial in determining the possible interpretations of discourse structure. The virtual speech act created by a writer (as distinct from the writer's act of composing) has two dimensions, which I will call *conceptual* and *rhetorical*. These are not distinct acts, but aspects of one act that I am abstracting for purposes of discussion. They correspond roughly to the terms "referential" (sometimes "semantic") and "pragmatic" respectively, used by many linguists and philosophers to describe two major functions of language; and also to John Searle's distinction, with respect to speech acts at the sentence level, between a propositional act (what I say) and an illucutionary act (what I do in saying).[17] The conceptual or reflective act, as a function of the whole discourse, is a train of thought that progressively develops a conception of the world. Such an act of thought must be directed at, or operate upon, something construed as an object. The object in this case is a selected set of facts of experience treated in the discourse as given. In nonfiction discourse the speech act operating on this act progressively produces an interpreted object that is identified with the real world, of which interlocutors are presumed to share an overlapping experience confirmed by a common language. In its subjective aspect, we may call this interpretation, in Kenneth Boulding's term, an *image* of the world, meaning that it is the picture of the world (knowledge, beliefs, attitudes) held by the writer as an individual.[18]

In the rhetorical function of the discourse act, a writer addresses this reflective train of thought (and the conception of the world it produces) to an audience, giving the whole conceptual act a certain communicative (or illocutionary) point and force. In this aspect the discourse is an investment of self into a conception, a commitment to it in social terms and for social purposes; it invites the reader to take up this commitment as intended.

The reader's act has two aspects also, but only one is fully inscribed and therefore significantly structured by the text. This is what I will call the *allocutionary* act, adopting a term used somewhat ambiguously by Ricoeur.[19] By this I mean what Austin calls "uptake"—the reader's comprehension of the speech act as intended in its conceptual and rhetorical dimensions, which should ideally correspond exactly to that speech act as laid down in the text. Contemporary research on language comprehension, which studies this receptive act under the name "discourse processing," shows it to be enormously complex, constructive, and inferential, though closely guided by the text. Terry Winograd, an artificial intelligence specialist interested in modeling language use on computers, describes the text from this point of view as "a concrete trace" of the reader's comprehension processes. "In language . . . a comprehender begins with a perceptual object that was designed with the explicit intent that someone would analyze it. The speaker designs a sentence anticipating how the hearer will interpret it, and the hearer interprets it in the light of hypotheses about the intent of the speaker."[20]

The allocutionary act, or processing level of the reader's act, contrasts to the *perlocutionary* act in the degree to which it is a structured part of the discourse event as mediated by the text. The perlocutionary act, as I define it, is that aspect of a reader's response that escapes detailed inscription: it is invited, stimulated, or opened up by the text, but not closely controlled by it. For example, it includes sustained emotional effects and their consequences in (the reader's) action; the logical extension of an argument or world beyond what is articulated in the text; or comparison and evaluation. Perlocutionary effects in this sense belong broadly to the sphere called "rhetoric," where expression and comprehension expand into a dialogue between reader and text that is only vaguely anticipated in the writer's original intention.

Ricoeur gives an interesting sketch of the ways different aspects of speech events are inscribed, and how fully. He concludes that the propositional act is quite fully exteriorized in the sentence, through the grammar of the language. The illocutionary act in speech depends somewhat more on gesture and prosody, but it can also be fixed in writing through grammatical paradigms, as can the interlocutors themselves (through self-reference) and their immediate contexts of writing, speaking, and reading, within situations and worlds. (These are expressed through deictic features that point to the environment: e.g., tense, definite articles, demonstrative pronouns. For example, "I" as both writer and projected speaker of a text can speak of "you" the reader, of "now" and "later" in the discourse time, of "this" or "that" which I just spoke of.) However, Ricoeur says:

Without a doubt we must concede that the perlocutionary act is the least inscribable aspect of discourse and that by preference it characterizes spoken language. But the perlocutionary action is precisely what is the least discourse in discourse. It is the discourse as stimulus. It acts, not by my interlocutor's recognition of my intention, but sort of energetically, by direct influence upon the emotions and the affective dispositions. Thus the propositional act, the illocutionary force, and the perlocutionary action are apt, in a decreasing order, for intentional exteriorization which makes inscription in writing possible.[21]

Not all, then, of the actual experiences of the discourse event by writers and readers can be inscribed. What is inscribed, and therefore strongly structured through the text, are the essential aspects of the discourse as communication. The general form of this structure has been described earlier as a set of structural features (division into elements, order, hierarchy, etc.). The question, then, is how these features apply to or organize the discourse event as experienced by writers and readers. Another way to ask the question is this: how does the nature of the inscribed discourse event determine in what ways structural features are interpreted to form wholes? I suggest that from this description of event we can derive certain gestalts, or perspectives on structure, that are natural for writers and readers to take. These are not different readings of the textual meaning in the sense that literary critics may disagree over the character of Hamlet. Rather, they are alternate complementary views of the same structural features that may be taken by the same or different readers, views strongly associated with context and purpose. These perspectives allow us to understand the same structure as dynamic process or static object, act (pragmatic) or world (referential) or image (belief set), meaning or language, just as the wave-particle duality allows us to understand light in two complementary aspects.

The notion of gestalts as perspectives on structure was introduced in the context of linguistic analysis by George Lakoff, to solve a problem presented by the description of sentence structure in terms of transformational derivations.[22] It has been established that transformational derivations do not accurately describe the way people actually construct (or comprehend) sentences in real time. They are an attempt to account for conflicting or at least different interpretations of the structure of a sentence, interpretations that we clearly need to make in order to understand sentences. The metaphor of depth or levels is used to account for such conflicts, and these levels are projected onto stages in an ordered derivation, with the deepest level corresponding to the earliest stage. Regardless of linguists' protests that they do not mean derivations to describe performance, the term itself clearly forces us to think of different systems of information as structural alternatives that replace one another in linear succession. What this means, says Lakoff, is that, with respect to the structural features of sentences, "[g]enerative grammar does not allow for apparently conflicting analyses both to be right from different viewpoints."[23] He thus suggests eliminating derivations in favor of describing sentences in terms of the intersection of simultaneous gestalts, by means of which sentences can interrelate different kinds of information. (I would add that, though gestalts are simultaneous in one sense, only one can be focal for a given person at a given time while writing or reading; the others function tacitly.)

This proposal makes a great deal of sense in the linguistic context, but may not mean much to someone who is not familiar with the various linguistic perspectives Lakoff gives as examples of possible gestalts (e.g., GRAMMATICAL, UNDERSTOOD ROLE, PHONOLOGICAL).[24] Without that knowledge, perhaps even with it, the whole idea seems highly abstract and vague, and the analogy with discourse structure hard to make. In general, though we are very familiar with the notion of multiple perspectives on phenomena in everyday life, it seems much harder to apply this idea to a symbolic reality like the structure of meanings in a text. For this reason, it may help to consider a simpler, physical case of multiple viewpoints, namely the visual perception of multistable phenomena, where abstract line drawings can be perceived in two or more variations. These have been discussed from a phenomenological point of view by Don Ihde in his book *Experimental Phenomenology*.[25]

When people first look at an abstract line drawing such as the famous Necker cube, they "see" the drawing immediately in one or another variation (see Figure 2). The drawing appears to them *as* this or that. This appearance is a gestalt, in which the lines structure a particular whole. In the case of the Necker cube, there seem to be two natural perspectives, each producing a different visual interpretation. Ihde calls them the rearward and the forward three-dimensional aspects or gestalts. In one we see from above, looking down on the top of a box projecting toward us from right (back) to left (front). In the second we see from below the bottom of a box projecting toward us from left (back) to right (front). These gestalts are mutually exclusive interpretations of the lines as structuring one or another whole—let us

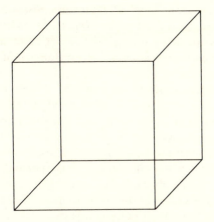

Figure 2. Necker cube.

say Box 1 or Box 2. However, it is relatively easy to shift from one perspective to another. Most people do so spontaneously and can easily learn to do so at will.

Deliberately seeing the cube two ways, and moving back and forth between them, takes the viewer from literal-mindedness, in which he sees reality as having only one ("normal") aspect, toward polymorphic-mindedness, the ability to fluently shift perspectives on reality. Ihde shows that, by practice in phenomenological methods of deconstruction and reconstruction, viewers can greatly expand the number of variations they see in a multistable figure.[26] These variants are not limitless or idiosyncratic to the viewer; they are systematic topographical possibilities that follow from the essential nature or givenness of the phenomenon.

A perceptual gestalt is from the point of view of the perceiver a comprehensive interpretation of the object that excludes other, simultaneously focal understandings of its structure. Anything that does not fit this interpretation (e.g., an unmotivated line in the Necker cube) becomes a nonstructural detail that fades into the background like static in a radio broadcast or a stray pencil mark on a typed page. But the experience of polymorphic variation instructs us that any spontaneous perceptual gestalt represents only one mode of presence of the object. When gestalts lose their sedimented perceptual inevitability, they come to be felt as complementary ontological possibilities in the figure corresponding to epistemological possibilities in our minds. These simultaneous possibilities for gestalts can be projected into time as alternate realities, each acquiring greater richness and depth through the viewer's tacit awareness of the others. We have arrived by another path at Bohr's principle of complementarity.

In the deliberately simplified example of abstract figures, naive seeing produces a very limited set of "natural" gestalts (in the case of the Necker cube, two). It is not so easy to identify certain gestalts as natural for viewing texts—"natural" in the sense of being spontaneously taken up by the discourser without effort or will. For one thing, with texts we are not talking about a single person's private mental experience of seeing an object, but about a highly complex social event involving two participants whose activities mutually define, determine, and affect each other. Inscription complicates the matter further by creating roles for real participants to play (and exchange), and by opening the abstract event laid down in the text to unknown numbers of reading partners. Furthermore, the experience of a discourse event through the mediating text changes its condition from spontaneity to deliberation, making possible planning for the writer and repeated readings and study for the reader. Under these conditions a discourser may take up gestalts purposefully; even if he does not, there is no reason to suppose that an initial gestalt will endure or even dominate the whole experience of writing or reading.

On the other hand, there is not unlimited or arbitrary variability to interpretations of written discourse as structured, any more than with the line figure. Gestalts flow first from the basic nature of written discourse as human event, specifically one in which symbols are instrumental to human transactions. Any analysis of symbolic action, such as Kenneth Burke's pentad, the communication triangle, or Roman Jakobson's analysis of discourse functions, yields essentially the same elements, presumably reflecting basic structures in human consciousness of events: participants, their roles, their actions, objects and instrumentalities, and situational context or background for the event. (Grammar reveals the same underlying structures.)

Gestalts of discourse structure arise through the foregrounding or focusing of attention by participants on one or another of these basic elements in discourse events under the special conditions of inscription. For example, following my own analysis of the inscribed discourse event, I could develop at least these ways of experiencing the text (each open to both participants):

1. The text as a *voice* enacting a symbolic action on behalf of a writer.
2. The text as a *world*, accepted as corresponding to the "real world" the discourser knows and believes in.
3. The text as an *image* or set of beliefs held by the speaker about a common world, to be weighed against those of others.
4. The text as a *trace* of the process of comprehension, a set of clues corresponding to a planned sequence of cognitive events.
5. The text as a *conventionalized discourse situation* with a historically sedimented generic structure (reflecting frames for understanding types of speech events).
6. The text as a *linguistic object* obeying rules of a grammar, conventions for inscription, customs of usage.

The text may be said to structure each of these experiences or gestalts through its cues to structural features like global conception, division, ordering, hierarchy, and internal relationships among ideas.

These gestalts represent broad channels along which attention naturally flows to constitute structure, though they are not equally salient under all circumstances for all participants. They can be observed in practice: for example, in the way outlines are filled in with topics and sentences, the terms in which writers and readers talk about and edit drafts in classroom workshops, and the way people summarize texts such as news articles to one another in everyday conversation. But at the same time gestalts can be multiplied indefinitely by abstracting elements differently from the event matrix as well as by narrowing the field of view. Discourse structure emerges from the dance of discourse as one thing or another—the progress of a metaphor, the clashing of positive and negative lines of force, alternating voices in a conversation—by virtue of the attention of the dancer. Like other aspects of cognitive processing, the attention of the reader is subject to textual cuing; but it is too volatile and too fluid over a period of time to be consistently controlled. And both writers' and readers' attention follows naturally the course set by their purposes, even if they do not deliberately take up different gestalts.

In the natural attitude, a discourser grasps symbols as meaning, and it requires a special and "unnatural" effort in speech to concentrate on symbols for their own sake, though we do this often enough (e.g., noticing a grammatical slip in someone's speech, or hearing an unintentional pun). But it is natural in written discourse to alienate oneself or, in Ricoeur's term, to distanciate oneself from the event to consider the textual object instrumentally and perhaps analytically, because one of the functions of inscription is to permit objectification of the event in various aspects for different purposes, especially those related to the possibility of craft and skill in writing and reading. In fact, this objectification can apply to the "meaning" in event (i.e., what is done, what is said, what is felt) as well as to the text as a linguistic artifact, an instrument of conception and communication.

Structural gestalts are not, then, abstract entities residing in texts, but correlations made by us, just as are subatomic particles. They are experientially a function of attention or focus as the mind plays over the empirical possibilities afforded by the text (perhaps deliberately inscribed by the writer) and its situational context. Since human attention fluctuates constantly over any period of lived time, and writing and reading take real time, it follows that any discourse gestalt, or more accurately the text understood through a gestalt, is properly described as transient and illusory, like the correlations of the physical that momentarily realize energy as mass, or particles. It is likely that discoursers drift in and out of structural gestalts in the course of composing and interpreting texts, to a considerable degree without conscious control or volition. We need to explore deeply, through such methods as phenomenological inquiry and protocol analysis, exactly how changing interpretations of structure come into being and what their function is in the craft of writing or careful reading, especially within the composing acts of the classroom, which involve the interactions of student writers, peer editors, and teachers.

This chapter performs a polymorphic variation at a higher level than those we might ask of student writers and readers or even of teachers looking at particular texts. It asks that we as a profession step back from and deconstruct our sedimented conception of discourse structure in order to carry out a reconstruction. In that reconstruction, discourse is essentially dance, event, or pattern of symbolic energies in which the discourser participates, ordered or structured with the aid of cues laid down by the writer in the text for himself and the reader. The aspects in which this structure and what is structured appear to us are a function of how we relate ourselves to the event as we experience it and contemplate our experiences through objectification.

I do not intend to take up at any length the implications for either research or teaching practice of such a dynamic, relativistic view of structure. Many such implications are implicit in my discussion of problems of practice in the old paradigm, which defined what a new conception of discourse structure must do or explain. For example, it is now possible to treat the entire set of inscriptions preceding a final text as the same object (or event) in different stages of its history. Such a view calls among other things for the diversification of techniques for discourse mapping to fit the needs of both writers and readers (especially critical readers such as student writers, peer editors, and teachers) during composing. Indeed, competing descriptions of structure, which are usually closely associated with a representational scheme (for instance, the cube suggested by Ellen Nold and Brent Davis for analyzing paragraphs),[27] can now be seen as complementary, correlating to one or another focus suitable for some purpose and stage in writing and reading activities or in subsequent analysis. Other research tasks and teaching strategies are suggested by the concept of gestalts and the question of their function to writers and readers. Surely it would behoove teachers to develop, and learn to teach, techniques for systematic free variation of perspectives that could be selectively taken up during composing and editing by themselves and others working with student writers on pre/texts and texts. For example, the gestalt that sees a text as a trace of reading processes is a useful perspective for discussing and evaluating transitional cues in drafts.

In the end, though, it is emphatically not the purpose of this discussion to prescribe practice or even give advice, but to change conceptions, from which changes in attitude necessarily follow, and hence changes in ways of understanding and acting in situations. If some of us have professed something like a dynamic, relativistic view of structure, or at least have been quick to repudiate a static one, few if any composition professionals have really believed it enough to act on it. (Imagine a teacher picking up a student theme—not a literary text—and reading it with a consciousness of her role as participant in a dance of symbolic energies that the text attempts to structure, or treating a scribbled list as the first manifestation of an emerging structure to be realized as a future text.) If we do come to take seriously an interactive view of written discourse and its structure, composition teaching and research will operate in a new world as unstable and exciting as that of early twentieth-century physics, which Zukav describes as "a picture of chaos beneath order" (p. 213), and of which Heisenberg wrote, "the demand for change in the thought pattern may engender the feeling that the ground is to be pulled from under one's feet."[28]

Notes

1. I have avoided the term "rhetoric" here because I am specifically concerned with concepts that have characterized the teaching of nonfiction writing in American universities, as expressed in school textbooks and pedagogical practices. For this, "rhetoric" is too inclusive a term, though we might speak more narrowly of something like a "compositional rhetoric": that is, the theory of communication through written symbols that was implicit in earlier composition teaching and is now being explicitly formulated and revised in theoretical studies and empirical research.

2. Kenneth Burke, "Terministic Screens," *Language as Symbolic Action: Essays on Life, Literature, and Method* (Berkeley: Univ. of California Press, 1968), pp. 44–62.

3. Ferdinand de Saussure, *Course in General Linguistics*, tr. Wade Baskin, ed. Charles Bally and Albert Sechehaye in collaboration with Albert Riedlinger (New York: McGraw-Hill, 1959).

4. See Mary Louise Pratt's discussion of this illegitimate metaphor in *Toward a Speech Act Theory of Literary Discourse* (Bloomington, IN: Indiana Univ. Press, 1977), pp. 3–37.

5. See the bibliographical essay on "Structure and Form in Non-Fiction Prose" by Richard Larson, in *Teaching Composition: Ten Bibliographical Essays*, ed. Gary Tate (Fort Worth: Texas Christian Univ., 1976), pp. 45–71.

6. See Thomas G. Sticht, "Comprehending Reading at Work," in *Cognitive Processes in Comprehension*, ed. Marcel Adam Just and Patricia A. Carpenter (Hillsdale, NJ: Erlbaum, 1977), pp. 221–46, for a study of representational schemes used in solving logical problems.

7. I am speaking here from practical experience, having worked for some years to develop a dynamic model of discourse structure for teaching. Although I arrived at most of the principles described here, I could not make them coherent with one another until my reading about modern physics provided an overall principle of integration, symbolized here by the metaphor of the dance.

8. Gary Zukav, *The Dancing Wu Li Masters: An Overview of the New Physics* (New York: William Morrow, 1979), p. 136.

9. Zukav, *Dancing*, p. 168.

10. Fritjof Capra, *The Tao of Physics: An Exploration of the Parallels between Modern Physics and Eastern Mysticism* (Boulder: Shambhala, 1975), p. 63.

11. Zukav, *Dancing*, p. 93.

12. Capra, *Tao*, pp. 134–37. This is the Copenhagen interpretation of quantum mechanics, which is not accepted by all physicists. However, other interpretations are even wilder and farther from common sense, and all agree on the creative role of the observer. See Zukav's discussion of these philosophical issues with respect to the actualizing of the Schroedinger Wave Equation, *Dancing*, pp. 96–110.

13. Zukav, *Dancing*, pp. 133–34.

14. J. A. Wheeler, in *The Physicist's Conception of Nature*, ed. J. Mehra (Dordrecht, Holland: Reidel, 1973), p. 244, quoted in Capra, *Tao*, p. 141.

15. Paul Ricoeur, "Structure, Word, Event," tr. Robert Sweeney, in *The Philosophy of Paul Ricoeur: An Anthology of His Work*, ed. Charles E. Reagan and David Steward (Boston: Beacon Press, 1978), p. 114.

16. In addition to "Structure, Word, Event," see Ricoeur's "Creativity in Language," tr. David Pellauer, *Philosophy Today* 17 (1973), 129–41; and his *Interpretation Theory: Discourse and the Surplus of Meaning* (Fort Worth: Texas Christian Univ.

Press, 1976). Primary sources for speech-act theory are J. L. Austin, *How to Do Things with Words* (Cambridge: Harvard Univ. Press, 1962), and John R. Searle, *Speech Acts: An Essay in the Philosophy of Language* (Cambridge: Cambridge Univ. Press, 1969).

17. Searle, *Speech Acts*, pp. 22–30. Austin originally established this distinction in slightly different terms and without the very general application that Searle and later theorists give it.

18. Kenneth Boulding, *The Image* (1956: rpt. Ann Arbor: Univ. of Michigan Press, Ann Arbor Paperbacks, 1961).

19. Ricoeur, *Interpretation Theory*, p. 14. The usage of terms in speech-act theory and its applications varies idiosyncratically and confusingly from one author to the next. I am departing from classical speech-act theory in attributing some components of the total speech event (which there are considered part of the speaker's act) to the reader. In this respect I agree with W. Ross Winterowd's analysis of speech acts in Dorothy Augustine and W. Ross Winterowd, "Intention and Response: Speech Acts and the Sources of Composition," in *Convergences: Transactions in Reading and Writing*, ed. Bruce T. Petersen (Urbana, IL: NCTE, 1986), pp. 127–48. But our terminology is different; what he calls perlocutionary act I have called allocutionary, in order to preserve Austin's original sense of perlocution as the consequences following from consummation of intention in the reception of a speech act.

20. Terry Winograd, "A Framework for Understanding Discourse," in *Cognitive Processes in Comprehension*, p. 67.

21. Ricoeur, "The Hermeneutical Function of Distanciation," *Philosophy Today* 17 (1973), 132–33.

22. George Lakoff, "Linguistic Gestalts," *Papers from the 13th Regional Meeting*, Chicago Linguistic Society (1977), pp. 236–87.

23. Ibid., p. 246.

24. Ibid., p. 263.

25. Don Ihde, *Experimental Phenomenology: An Introduction* (New York: Putnam, Capricorn Books, 1977).

26. With effort I have achieved twenty-nine variations of the Necker cube, five of them suggested by Ihde. Here they are: Box 1, forward (1); Box 2, rearward (2); an insect centered on a hexagonal two-dimensional surface (3); a cut gem seen (4) from outside and above looking down on its facets, and (5) from inside below looking up at them; a table positioned on a square floor from twelve different angles, six forward and six rearward (6–17); two open books facing each other and touching edges, from eight angles (18–25); a three-dimensional stick man (26) and three two-dimensional stickmen with arms and legs in different positions (27–29).

27. Ellen W. Nold and Brent E. Davis, "The Discourse Matrix," *CCC* 31 (1980), 141–52.

28. Werner Heisenberg, *Across the Frontiers* (New York: Harper, 1974), p. 162, quoted in Zukav, *Dancing*, p. 211.

7

Dialectics of Coherence

In *Philosophy in a New Key* Susanne Langer writes of the great generative ideas that periodically arise to transform our intellectual enterprises by changing the very terms in which we frame our questions and conceive our purposes. When one of these concepts bursts into consciousness, we cannot at first view it critically, because it is the nature of a key change to possess us with its compelling new vision of the world. For some time afterward we are absorbed in exploiting the energizing, fertilizing power of the new idea, which seems limitless in its implications and applications. Only later, as a paradigm matures, can we begin to refine and correct its key concept and to achieve the critical distance necessary to recognize its bounds.

We are approaching this moment in composition, which has taken process as its generative theme since the early 1970s. By keying composition studies to writers' thought processes and the relations between cognition and language, this theme has restored to the field what was lost with the decline of rhetoric: a genuinely rich, humanly significant, and inexhaustible object of inquiry. In the next stage of our development as a discipline, we need to take up a more critical attitude toward process theory, to probe its limits and to articulate and address some of the conceptual problems it leaves unresolved. I would like to make a contribution to that work in this chapter.

My starting point is the difficulty of handling textual issues—for example, matters of style or discourse form—within the process framework. That framework has no principled way to account for the role of texts in discourse events, because it was constituted initially by a contrastive opposition between composing (dynamic process) and texts (inert product). Texts were therefore rejected as proper objects of inquiry in composition. I suggest we might resolve this problem and work toward a more comprehensive theory of discourse by developing concepts on the principle of integrating text and process at all levels of analysis. This project depends on transforming a polarity of two terms—process and product—into a dialectic between two processes of constructing meaning, writing and reading, with texts becoming the third or mediating term. I will explore this dialectic and adumbrate an integrative theory of discourse through an analysis of the concept of coherence, focusing on these relationships from the reader's perspective.

Although the composing process has been the dominant theme of writing research since the decisive turn away from the text-centered traditional paradigm, it is not the only one. Paradoxically, work focused on texts has been a strong countertheme, feeding on the explosive growth of inquiries into text, textuality, and reading in other disciplines. Discourse analysis, evaluation, studies of syntax and readability, theoretical work concerned with coherence and macrostructures of discourse—all these develop knowledge about texts or take texts as their primary data. This fact presents a crucial problem for composition: where do texts and textual studies fit into a framework for research and teaching that is keyed to process?

The process view is of course pluralistic, and does not impose an attitude toward texts or even express a consistent conception of them. What I call "process theory" is not really a theory at all, but the common ground among many theories and practices that encompasses highly diverse and frequently conflicting emphases, beliefs, values, and treatment of texts.[1] My question, however, does not concern the rich variety of what people know, say, and do with texts in their research and teaching, but the flexibility and power of the process framework itself to articulate those intuitions and experiences. At issue is the conceptual reach or stretch of the language of process.

I have argued elsewhere that we have in the process paradigm what Kenneth Burke calls a "logological" problem, a consequence of the terms in which the key concept was originally framed.[2] To assert the centrality of writing acts against the apotheosis of textual objects in the teaching tradition, composition created a vocabulary of discontinuity, emphasizing distinctions and oppositions over connections. This is of course the language of "process" versus "product," a legacy that deeply influences the modern history of the discipline. Its inherently polarizing thrust tends to exclude texts from the sphere of process by reducing them to traces of the writer's cognitive activity. As a consequence, our understandings of text and process are developing independently, through separate lines of investigation. Until we find a way to put them together, it will be difficult to give full value to the dynamic role that texts play in discourse events, or more broadly to do justice to our intuitive knowledge of the dialectics of written discourse.

The method of integration I propose to try out here starts at an intermediate level of analysis, with terms that abstract a significant dimension of discourse experience. Most such concepts—invention, form, style, plan, and coherence, for example—are richly developed at more specific levels, through both the rhetorical tradition and contemporary scholarship. Each term tends to be associated with a particular perspective on discourse: invention and plan with composing process, for instance, and form, style, and coherence with texts. My project would formulate each of these concepts from the beginning in terms of relationships between process and text, or more comprehensively as a nexus of connections among writers, readers, text, and scene, subject to different interpretations depending on point of view. The idea would be to build up a unified theory of composition from already integrated concepts, instead of trying to reconcile separate theories of composing, reading, texts, and social action in context.

The catalyst for this effort is a deceptively simple step: to extend the dynamic of meaning construction from the composing process to the interpretive acts of readers. What this means is that the process/ product relations change and each acquires new reference. Before, "process" referred to the writer's act of composing written thought, and "product" to the text encapsulating that meaning. Now, the overarching "process" is the cooperative enterprise whereby writers and readers construct meanings together, through the dialectic tension between their interactive and interdependent processes. The text is the mediating instrument for that joint effort, whose product is the set of meanings so constructed and attributed by readers to a writer and a text. In this view the composing and reading processes are no longer distinct. The reader's perspective is bound up in the writing process itself, because writers read their own drafts and fictionalize or solicit an audience for them; on the other hand, intended meanings are fully realized only through a reader's comprehension.

This move has momentous consequences, because it changes the root metaphor of composition from that of creation to one of symbolic interaction. It is not simply a question of taking into account the rhetorical motives and functions of writing as social action, but of recognizing that written thought—thought that emerges through writing into situational contexts—is radically social and intersubjective through its very constitution as a discourse. The metaphor of writing as creating an autonomous meaning-object focuses attention on the subjectivity of the writer and handles the social nature of language largely as a property of the finished object to affect an audience. The new metaphor leads us to ask how texts effect the joint construction of meaning as a basis for complex negotiations between discoursers over attitude, belief, and action in the world. This metaphoric shift toward a more intersubjective and deeply contextualized view of written language is, I think, the point of convergence toward which much important work in the profession is moving, from very different initial perspectives, sources, and modes of inquiry.[3] In this discussion it opens the way to examining coherence along the axis of the relationship between readers and texts.

My goals here are limited in important respects. First, my mode of inquiry is conceptual analysis, which means that I am primarily concerned with articulating a working vocabulary in which to formulate questions and carry out observations.[4] This emphasis reflects my belief that philosophical work of this kind is important in laying a foundation for studying actual processes of coherent discourse in context, not only in formal research but, perhaps more importantly, in the classroom, where the practical implications must be worked out directly. Second, my analysis focuses on the interactions between readers and texts as the dynamic that defines coherence. That term is commonly used to render a judgment made in relation to the consummated discourse event. But the phenomenon of coherence encompasses the entire evolution of the relationships among writer, readers, world, and text throughout the event. By taking up a reader's perspective on coherence we form a gestalt of these relations that is full and meaningful in itself, but radically incomplete without the writer's view. I leave that dimension of a theory of coherence for future consideration.

In composition pedagogy, coherence is traditionally a quality attributed (or denied) by readers to texts. But modern views of reading deriving from both cognitive science and literary theory displace coherence from the text to readers' thought processes and experiences of meaning. The paradox arises when we accept both accounts of coherence as true. To relate these two interpretations intelligibly, I will need to explore the modern views of reading and their roots in an interpretive view of human understanding. My analysis will proceed in steps from the interpretive position in general to an interactive theory of reading, and then will move to a dialectical conception of coherence worked out in a series of complementary conceptual pairs: coherence and cohesion, design and flow, transition and motif.

Making Sense of Texts: An Interpretive Synthesis

Compositionists are more or less knowledgeable about a range of text comprehension theories—psychological, literary, hermeneutical. But the potential unity of these theories is hidden by their dramatic differences, especially since few composition theorists know them all equally well. Instead of undertaking a comparison of reading theories designed to penetrate these differences and draw out their deeper affinities, I would like to take a more direct path to a synthesis. A view of understanding as constructive or interpretive has recently emerged within the human sciences as a powerful heuristic for studying knowledge and action, especially where these are symbolically mediated.[5] This view takes radically different forms, depending on the disciplinary matrix in which it arises, but it can be abstracted as a cluster of themes that, singly and together, color much current thinking about language and cognition, including studies of reading and text interpretation. Indeed, the notion of "reading a text" functions for many disciplines as a paradigmatic case of human understanding.

For this reason it is possible to generate a sketch of the nature of text comprehension directly from a constructive account of understanding, provided we are satisfied to keep both of them highly general. My purpose is not to offer a detailed or complete description of reading processes, but to develop a working model of the interactions between texts and readers as the basis for an integrative concept of coherence.

The interpretive-constructivist position concerns itself primarily with the human experience of meaning, or of the world as meaningful. Its first premise is that knowledge of the world is never decontextualized, brute data, but is always relational. More specifically, entities and events are grasped by reference to human situations in which they participate, actually or hypothetically. Hubert Dreyfus calls this aspect of understanding the "field-structure" of experience, by which "the human world . . . is prestructured in terms of human purposes and concerns in such a way that what counts as an object or is significant about an object already is a function of, or embodies, that concern."[6] Similarly, psychologists John Bransford and Nancy McCarrell, speaking of perception, say that "significances are a joint function of the meanings of entities and the particular contexts in which they occur."[7] Currently available information about the occurrence and relation of entities acts as a set of conditions or constraints for building or updating a perceptual model. It is the contextually based general knowledge of interpreters that allows them to recognize or hypothesize a world that makes sense of the possibilities inherent in these cues. Understanding, then, consists of making situational sense of novel information, guided by purposes and goals within a matrix of human activity or praxis.[8]

Shifting focus from the meaningfulness of the world to the ways in which individuals appropriate it, we can draw on the work of cognitive scientists who seek to specify the way that context, in the form of situational experience and abstractions from it, becomes the subjective ground for agents to actively construct meanings from new experiences. Psychologists have somewhat belatedly discovered that so-called receptive cognitive activities like perception and language comprehension are actually complex problem-solving activities in which interpreters make significant contributions to the meanings they construe. Efforts to specify and support this idea have concentrated on defining the role in human cognition of organizing structures called *schemas*—abstract conceptual structures that organize prototypical knowledge about the world so we can bring it to bear in perception, comprehension, thought, and bodily action. Schemas generate what Teun van Dijk calls "macrostructures," which are the specific content structures of particular actions, events, or discourses.[9] They are the cognitive tools by which people build up models of situations and the entities that enter into them. Among their important functions, they enable us to generate conjectural wholes from insufficient detail and to enrich comprehension far beyond the information given.

A relational conception of meaning implies holism, a concept familiar from such varied contexts as structuralism and semiotics, phenomenology (the "hermeneutical circle"), and cognitive approaches that treat the mind as a cybernetic-like system. In the interpretive position holism implies not only an internal structural principle but also the reference of such systems to larger fields, ultimately to the context of cultural practices and their meanings. Although some versions of holism emphasize stasis or synchrony, it is now recognized that understanding is dynamic, since both the organism and the environment continually evolve and interact. Of particular importance for a consideration of coherence is the fact that memory itself grows and changes. Individual, episodic memories for events and facts are now thought to be constantly reconstructed both in retention and in specific acts of remembering.[10] Cognitive structures develop constantly through their interaction with experience, undergoing what Heinz Werner called "increasing differentiation, articulation, and hierarchic integration."[11]

So far I have described understanding in the interpretive view as deeply scenic and pragmatic, actively constructive, holistic, structured, and dynamic. All these together imply one more feature of central importance to a view of written language and coherence: understanding develops interactively and intersubjectively. This point does not deny the subjectivity of cognitive schemas, which in some perhaps unknowable sense are unique to each individual. But the other side of this subjectivity is the cultural basis for schemas, which are interpersonally constructed and socially shared ideas of possible or typical objects, facts, and situations. Such shared experiential frames make it possible to comprehend action in terms of typical situations, goals, and plans within a culture; or to comprehend stories in terms of those action schemas plus structures that we call genre and convention. Language itself is the greatest schema in a culture, displaying a nature at once subjective and intersubjective.

This chapter began by proposing that we need to develop an integrative approach to the analysis of written language that would recognize the intersubjective source of meanings in texts, to be illustrated here through the concept of coherence. The claim that discourse meanings come into being intersubjectively has a special status in the phenomenological version of the constructive position, through its relation to the concept of understanding itself. Interpretive views at their most radical become reflexive, arguing that the researcher's own understanding arises through an interaction between the process of observation and the properties or characteristics of the world observed. If what is being observed is the human world, permeated with symbolic meaning, this interaction is discursive and hermeneutical in character—as are (the argument goes) the human sciences themselves. Thus Charles Taylor describes social reality as a sphere of communal, experiential meanings, constituted and expressed largely through language. And the model for studying such meanings—the reading of a text—itself consists of the joint creation of meanings by author and interpreter.[12]

The model of reading that I will now present translates the interpretive-constructive view into six generalizations. By and large, the model pictures texts as cuing systems designed by writers to shape constructive cognitive activity (and response) by readers.[13] In other words, a text functions like a play script to evoke performances from its readers that are both bound and free, receptive and interpretive. The ability for texts to express meaning presupposes a framework of shared conventions (linguistic and generic) and a common perceptual and social world about which writers and readers have overlapping knowledge and points of view. The transaction itself, of course, depends on the skilled action of both participants. Writers coordinate the complex cognitive-social-linguistic actions of composing, and readers contribute the equally complex actions of comprehension, merging into deeper kinds of appropriation and negotiation. The focus of these generalizations is on readers and their actions. The first two characterize readers in terms of what they bring to texts; the rest concern the reader's task.

1. Readers bring to texts various kinds of knowledge, beliefs, and values on the one hand, and know-how—the skills of reading—on the other.
2. Readers inhabit ongoing situations relevant to their readings, from which they approach texts with a purpose or set of purposes.

Some psychologists make the mistake of treating all reading as the same kind of task, essentially assuming that the purpose of the reader is to learn the text (thus "comprehension" measures memory for the text). Discourse analysts tend to believe that "purpose" is an inherent property of a text, rather than a reader's choice that the text may invite and constrain, but not determine. One important consequence for coherence is that one cannot necessarily assume that readers aim for coherent experiences of all texts, in the sense defined below.

3. Assuming the basic goal of comprehension, the reader's primary task is to make global sense of a text by constructing situational models of its content. Readers must grasp both the referential situation, the world a text describes or points to, and the rhetorical or communicative situation in which they are participating.
4. Situational models are realized as global structures of meaning (macrostructures) that holistically define, interpret, and integrate local structures (microstructures) as their component meanings.

Everyone who studies written discourse distinguishes between the higher, more global levels of structure—the topics, themes, and ideas dominating paragraphs and longer stretches of text; and the lower or local levels—meanings derived from phrases and sentences. Evidence suggests that readers do construct representations of texts that are structured in the same sense as other cognitive schemes—that is, these representations have holistic integrity, differentiated elements, and complex relations. When memory for text is tested under the special conditions of lab settings, people tend to remember a mental representation of the gist of the text, abstracted from its original expression in particular sentences, and remember the higher or "macrolevels" of structure better than the "microlevel," the details.[14]

This is not to say, however, that readers create for every text, as they read, a complete, full, accurate, and logically structured representation of its content. The concept of reading as the building of a macrostructure is conceptually useful rather than empirically predictive, as some researchers assume. They forget both the field structure of human action and the highly skilled nature of reading. The first ensures that people will build representations of textual meaning to fit their purposes, following a general principle of economy of effort. Much reading simply updates existing knowledge directly, rather than resulting in a discrete memory of the meaning and structure of a particular text (think of reading a newspaper). In addition, the skilled nature of reading and its dependence on existing knowledge means that the ability to construct an accurate and complete representation of discourse meaning will vary from one individual to another, and for the same person with different texts and conditions. Finally, coherent experiences—ongoing comprehension—of texts cannot be equated with memory for macrostructure, or a single reading of any text would be equivalent to learning it. It is wiser, therefore, to think of text comprehension as a range of experiences wherein readers build situational models stimulated by a text and incorporating at least some of its structure.

In its ideal rather than empirical sense, then, macrostructure refers here to the patterning of discourse content through genre, topic, the differentiation of elements, order, hierarchy, connection, repetition, opposition, and other structuring principles. Much of such patterning is appositional, as literary theorists have exhaustively demonstrated. (For example, texts can pattern complex attitudes and values through images, or kinesthetic and emotional experience through rhythm.) As we will see later, all systems of language, not just syntactic structures, cue the elements and integration of textual macrostructures, which are not simply propositional. For these reasons, representations such as outlines, trees, clusters, and other maps of discourse each capture a significant part, but not all of what a person may comprehend as the "macrostructure"

—a complex of interlocking patterns of meaning in written discourse.

5. Readers comprehend texts through progressive integration, projecting an anticipatory holistic structure that they continually reform, clarify, enrich, and fill in to whatever degree fits their goals and capabilities. At the same time they abstract and simplify this structure in retrospect, both as they read through the text and later in rereading and memory.

In other words, integration both precedes actual text processing and follows it, in restructuring that may continue indefinitely. Such reorganization and reintegration may apply directly to the text (as it is reread and studied); or to the memory of the text, preserved as a relatively independent unit of meaning (e.g., a famous poem); or to the information (ideas, values, scenes, etc.) derived from the text and assimilated to existing schemas of the world.

6. No matter how extensive their effort and constructive contribution, readers ascribe the integrated meanings derived in reading to the text that cues them, and beyond that to the writer who composed them, so long as they feel they can correlate such meanings globally with a writer's intention.

Ordinary readers (unlike certain critics taking a deliberately "unnatural" reading stance) hold steadfastly to their receptive orientation toward textual meanings, even though they may become self-conscious of the remarkable cognitive effort that goes into understanding, and even in the face of conflicts and difficulties in interpretation. That is perhaps the basic paradox that underlies written discourse: as an interpretive process, reading ascribes meaning to symbols and their creators, even though meaning arises most directly from the reader's own actions. Readers feel themselves to be the performer of meanings intended by another. This intention may be displaced from the author to the text (or its virtual speaker), especially as the discoursers grow remote from one another in time and space, but it remains fundamental to the experience of written symbols as meaning and as event.[15] Comprehension projects meaning back onto the text, where readers can objectify and contemplate it as content, message, information, event, and structure. In this lability of meaning as it wavers between experience and object, at once belonging to writer, reader, and symbol, we can now capture the paradoxes of coherence and define an integrative concept.

Paradoxes of Coherence

Coherence

Let us begin by describing achieved coherence in writing provisionally as *the experience of meaningfulness correlated with successful integration during reading, which the reader projects back onto the text as a quality of wholeness in its meanings.* Here immediately is the paradox: coherence is at once subjective and objective, receptive and productive, mental and textual, experience and object, process and product. But an interactive theory of discourse allows us to state these relationships intelligibly. Coherence belongs to both writer and reader as their joint product through complementary actions. It has its origin in the writer's intention as it has emerged through the course of a writing process and issued in a text; it has its realization in the reader's cognitive activity, both bound and free; it has its sources and materials in the knowledge and feelings of both writer and reader, scenically based; and it has its instrument in the mediating symbol. Since we are concerned here with judgments of coherence and thus the reader's perspective, we pick up this interaction at the point of realization. Here coherence is a relationship between the symbolic guidelines representing the writer's intentions for global meaning and the reader's ability to interpret and successfully integrate a set of component meanings: a relationship that takes form as the attribution of intention to that integration or wholeness.

To return to our definition, then, and rephrase it perhaps awkwardly but more precisely:

> Coherence is a property of intentional global relatedness that readers ascribe to textual meanings when they are able to integrate a satisfying macrostructure for a text in a way that they feel to be directly responsive to and closely guided by multiple, consistent integrational cues. As a result they perceive their own integration as strongly correlated with the intentions of a writer.

The term "satisfactory macrostructure" is deliberately vague. It suggests that readers will vary greatly in what they deem satisfying integrations, according to their expectations, goals, skills, and the individual text and context. In this sense, coherence can never be an abstract structural property of a text, but is an individual judgment characterizing the very personal relationships between a text and its readers. But skilled readers can agree on judgments of coherence because (and when) they share not only a relatively objective and fixed verbal symbol on one side of the relationship, but also, on the other side, knowledge or similar beliefs about the world, a common language and set of discourse conventions, overlapping personal and cultural contexts, and typically human cognitive processes.

This relational definition of coherence has so far addressed the paradoxes of location, possession, and source: where does coherence lie, to whom or what does it belong, who or what creates it? Now let us turn to another paradox of coherence, its nature as event and object. I will explain this paradox by distinguishing between dynamic and static views of coherence emerging from different moments or phases of reading. These are called *flow* and *design*.

Flow and Design

Often when we want to praise a text as coherent, we say "it really flows." Language requires me to name this perspective on coherence with the noun "flow," but it is almost always used as a verb. That is because it refers to something the skilled reader does and experiences the text as doing—moving through the text as if carried on a swiftly moving current from one place or time to another. At other times we talk about coherence as organization, structure, or "design," symbolized by the possibility of representing meaning on the page as an icon. Here the metaphor takes form as an image laying out all the components or parts for the eye to grasp simultaneously, in terms of their spatial relations in the figure: as an outline, a cluster or network, a tree diagram, or a matrix.

Why are there these two ways of talking about coherence? The answer is that different "moments" in the reading process give rise to distinctly different modes of experiencing its global meaning, which we might call coherence as energy (integration in process) and coherence as matter (the integrated structure objectified in retrospect). Let me explore briefly the character of each perspective as related to these two moments in reading: (1) the first read-through of a text from start to finish (and to a lesser degree, later read-throughs); and (2) the retrospective reconstituting and re-viewing of the initial interpretation.

Flow, the sense of coherence as energy or process, is the felt power to integrate that fills readers as they move through a text, successfully making sense of it. The first read-through is most purely flow because the reader is trying to integrate on the basis of a still shadowy, tentative projection of possible structure, and is coping with a great flood of genuinely new information (at least with respect to the discourse). Later read-throughs can only partially recapture this experience, with all its emotional flavor of surprise, satisfaction, and so on, while they are enriched by a background of fulfilled expectations and the network of cross-connections already established.

The power to integrate progressively is very much tied to time, in two senses. The process takes place in real time, which subjects readers to a number of cognitive and contextual limitations (for example, fatigue and interruption). The reader also participates in a virtual discourse time that (ideally) carries him or her forward on a moving point of focused attention, alternately looking backward to the text's "past" and ahead to its "future." This virtual time is often inscribed in the discourse through such phrases as "earlier," "soon," or "for the moment," referring to the discourse as action.

In this phase of reading, attention is quite localized much of the time, while direction, order, linearity, and connections between consecutive items preoccupy the reader. Cues such as transitional words and phrases, which help readers pass across "junctures" in text marked by punctuation and paragraphing, are more salient than are diffuse patterns of language, such as repeated words or sounds, that create systematic relations among elements of meaning. Cuing (often syntactic), which helps readers manage their cognitive effort by controlling and directing memory, imagination, and attention, is extremely important in creating a sense of flow.

The design of a text—its fully realized and relatively fixed coherence as a meaning object—stabilizes for the reader only in retrospect (and even then is always subject to reinterpretation). The accuracy and detail of this image depend on the reader's pursuing the integrational effort through such means as rereading in a less ordered fashion so as to study the text, perhaps with the aid of note taking or annotation; paying attention to more subtle systems of cues not concentrated at junctures and less consciously inscribed; mapping the text into a visual representation such as an outline; summarizing; and engaging in dialogue with other readers and even the writer. (I am not describing here just the scholarly practice of literary criticism, but methods used throughout a highly literate society—by students learning from texts, by lawyers and judges consulting documents, by intelligence analysts, editors, and many others.)

Design is characteristically timeless, independent both of the virtual time in which the thought process and action of a discourse evolve, and of the real time lived by the reader and writer. Design for the reader is the product of an effort to step back from the immediacy of ongoing integrations to put the textual meaning at a distance and contemplate it. In this moment all the elements of a discourse are simultaneously present and can be interpreted in terms of one another. Thus a word introduced at the beginning of a discourse (like "constructive" or "integrative" here) acquires richness and resonance from its cumulative use in the discourse.

Since, however, human minds cannot maintain all elements and levels of discourse in consciousness with equal attention and emphasis, the appreciation of design as the simultaneous coherence of discourse meanings involves considerable abstraction along with a concentration on selected features. We can see these requirements in the typical topic outline, which drops out microlevels of discourse and reduces propositions to predicates or topics. The more the image encompasses, the more abstract it must become to be grasped all at once, and whole. Through abstraction and condensation aided by iconicity, a reader can contemplate (on the page or in memory) the design of the discourse. In this contemplative state readers are less dependent on the managerial stylistic cuing that helps them to carry out integrations in sequence, and can attend to the less prominent systematic stylistic features throughout the text. The ability to negotiate thought objects of great complexity, depth, and scope in discourse springs from the moment of design, with its possibilities for distanciation, objectification, and contemplation.

The distinction between flow and design as dynamic and static perspectives on coherence suggests a corresponding one between two methods for studying the interaction between textual cues and readers' activities from which integrations emerge. These methods emphasize on the one hand the concentration of diverse stylistic cues at junctures, called "transition," and on the other hand, cuing systems of a single type diffused across the text, called "motif." To explore this last complementary pair, I must present explicitly a distinction running tacitly through this discussion, that between *coherence* and *cohesion*.

The Distinction between Coherence and Cohesion

In the reader's perspective being considered here, the central paradoxes of coherence revolve around the role of a text in stimulating, and to a degree controlling, the reader's experience of discourse as coherent. The text or verbal symbol has been viewed as a system of constraints on readers' integrations of its message as a global structure or situational model. In this section I will consider the nature of texts as such to be a set of directions sytematically related one to another. Just as coherence is the semantic and pragmatic integrity discovered by readers in textual meanings, so cohesion is, broadly, the verbal relatedness of the text as a cuing system. Although there is a sense in which every definable linguistic feature in a text has a cohesive function, we can distinguish roughly between statement and style; I will concentrate on the role of stylistic cues (sometimes expanded to literal statement) that we recognize to be specifically integrative for a given text. The term "cohesion" has this narrower compass here.

After great early confusion between the notions of coherence and cohesion, a distinction between them has firmed up along the lines suggested, although it remains rather vague and inconsistent. A major source of this lingering problem in composition theory is the traditional textbook treatment of coherence as essentially equivalent to the presence in texts of particular kinds of stylistic devices labeled "transitions." The confusion was actually reinforced by the efforts of certain linguists to describe cohesive systems in the grammar, since they were not interested in coherence as an experience and tended to believe that coherence as a property of texts could be formally specified in terms of their verbal relatedness. When confronted with the inadequacies of this account (for example, the fact that coherence in this definition can be faked, or that a nonsensical text can be formally cohesive), they assumed that there must be some formal mechanisms yet undescribed that accounted for the problem.

More recently, however, in composition at least, the term "cohesion" has been reserved for stylistic features of texts (language) in global contrast to their semantic and pragmatic aspects or structures (meaning).[16] My discussion attempts to state this distinction more precisely, as becomes possible with a more fully articulated concept of coherence. Many analyses and some experimental work in composition have focused largely on describing types of cohesive cues in texts, relating these to systems in the grammar, and investigating how writers use them and learn to use them. These are not my concerns in this chapter, and I must leave for some other forum a review of the extensive literature that is just beginning to give clearer theoretical definition and empirical content to many types of stylistic cuing.[17] Here instead are my limited purposes with respect to cohesion: to consolidate the definition just proposed, and to describe two practical methods (adaptable to the classroom) for identifying and studying cohesion in relation to the dynamic and static dimensions of the reader's experience in integrating a text.

Transition and Motif

Consider hypothetically two alternate angles of approach to cohesion in texts that are rooted in the contrasting traditions of linguistic and literary analysis. Composition theorists working in the first tradition (more common in current research) tend to borrow or adapt linguists' taxonomies of cohesive mechanisms or systems in the grammar, and use these to identify instances of cohesion in texts. (For instance, reference, connective words, and topic/comment structure of sentences have all been singled out as resources of the language with specifically cohesive functions.) In this approach an element in a particular text is abstractly defined as cohesive prior to its use there, and the analyst identifies cohesive features in texts on these purely formal grounds. This approach assigns integrative function to a relatively limited number of stylistic features in any given text, distributed there against a neutral background of presumably noncohesive language.

A theorist grounded in literary traditions of analysis comes to a text with very different tacit assumptions and expectations. The language of the text presents itself to this analyst as an intricate pattern of verbal relations whose texture is more or less well knitted out of uncountable, multiple connections at all levels of language systems—sound, lexicon, syntax, visual inscription. These felt linkages are indeterminately various (similarity, association in memory, equivalence, naming of relations, transformation, derivation, etc.) because they rest, like meaning itself, on the relation between abstract structural properties of the language system and the human capacity to make connections. Potentially, any linguistically recognizable feature or system of the grammar can participate in the verbal connectedness of text, but certain features in actual texts will take on stylistic significance for readers as a set of integrative cues. It is the analyst's job to discover the verbal relations most salient for coherence in a given case, by paying attention (through protocols or retrospective studies) to his own or others' experiences in reading, guided by his knowledge about the properties of different aspects of the language system.

It is evident that the claim to study "cohesion" conceals here a fundamental difference between two objects of study. At the most general level, it is the difference between language as system (Saussure's *langue*, Chomsky's "competence") and language as event (*parole*, "performance"). There is cohesion as a systematic resource of the grammar (not limited, I would claim, to any particular systems, although some are used mainly for cohesive purposes), and there is cohesion as a special case of the verbal relatedness of texts—those sets of stylistic features recognized and identified by readers as important to coherence in a particular text.

Composition theorists—who are, paradoxically, theorists of performance—obviously need a functional conception of cohesion to fit the kind of discourse model being developed here. The problem has been in taking systematic, formal statements about the language as functional ones about specific texts. It is a mistake on our part, I think, to translate statements and generalizations too directly from the domain of competence to that of performance, or to adopt the linguist's move from system to text rather than the literary critic's round from reader to text to reader. One can see the problems that develop from such illegitimate transfers through an analogy with the study of word meanings. It is appropriate for linguists or lexicographers to conceive and study words in the dictionary as semiotic entities, that is, as a system of contrastive units associated with finite lists of definitions or "meanings." But it is inadequate to identify these "meanings" of words as defined in the closed sphere of the lexicon with their rich life and indeterminately potential interpretations in the contexts of actual use. Composition theorists need a method of analysis that addresses cohesion functionally, drawing on knowledge of language together with close examination of reading experiences to discover the correlations between cohesion and coherence.

The two practical methods I suggest now for studying cohesion and coherence contextually are a natural extension of the two phases or moments of reading described earlier. Readers pay different kinds of attention, construct meaning differently, and have different experiences of coherence during these two phases of reading. In reading through the text from beginning to end, we saw, the reader performs an anticipatory integration associated with a sense of flow or passage from one point in the text, or in reading time, to another. In retrospective thought or subsequent readings, the reader is able to attend to the structure of meaning as a static design spread out before the mind's eye. This suggests that we can examine cohesive features and their influence on integration in two aspects, correlated with readers' experiences of coherence as flow or design.

In the first method of analysis, we locate ourselves in the ongoing flux of a reading experience and stop the clock. We find ourselves frozen in a moment of transition between two points, looking both forward and backward, trying to integrate some new information into a projected and partially filled-in macrostructure. At this moment, cut out of the flow of reading, cohesive cues appear as a discrete complex of features woven in and around the current sentence from many linguistic systems, performing overlapping and complementary functions. These cues interact to influence at least three aspects of the reading experience. First, they make information in memory salient, for example through a repeated word or pronoun. Second, they focus the current attention of the reader, often through syntactic transformations that move items to the beginning of a sentence or into subject position. Third, they predict structure and content, by introducing new lexical chains, for example. Besides such managerial or "staging" functions, cues at junctures explicitly place current elements into the reader's ongoing representation of the macrostructure through such means as connective phrases and orienting statements.

Transition, then, refers to a perspective on cohesion focusing on the way multiple cues work together at points of juncture in text to create a reader's sense of flow. (This usage corresponds quite well to the traditional notion of transition in composition textbooks.) The question now arises how a reader can identify and isolate significant points of juncture in a particular text.

As textbooks observe, the natural points for transition are defined in texts by sentence and paragraph boundaries, which presumably signal pauses in the stream of processing where readers can gather up new material, internally integrate or project it locally, and assimilate it to an evolving representation of the global structure. Psychological and linguistic studies support this presumption with evidence that reading is a discontinuous process, the reader taking in information from text in short bursts much as the eye sees in a series of fixes or saccades.[18] Readers seem to accumulate bits of information as chunks in working memory up to some limit, then at a point of closure simultaneously integrate downward to put together the chunk of meaning, and upward to grasp it as part of a larger field of meaning. This process takes place at the microlevel roughly in clauselike or sentence chunks, influenced markedly by punctuation.[19]

At a higher level of integration, paragraph indentations and other signals such as titling create junctures or rest stops where readers can integrate larger chunks: abstracting a set of meanings from a stretch of text, dropping out details, consolidating macrostructure, and reorienting themselves to go on. Since indentation probably triggers such integrations, we can expect to find transitional cues concentrated at paragraph junctures, that is, in the sentences that begin new paragraphs and sometimes those that precede indentations. In cases where indentation also marks junctures between stretches of text at even higher levels of structure, the transitional material may expand from one or two sentences to paragraphs or more, and from style to statement. Introductions and conclusions will also have specialized transitional functions, since they mark junctures between text and scène.

Whereas cohesion in its transitional aspect defines points of passage through the text, the study of cohesion as motif focuses on how a single type of stylistic feature affects the reader's experience of coherence as design. This method of analysis pays attention to how such a feature enters into a cohesive system, which through its diffusion across a particular text creates verbal patterns (often subtle) that have a holistic effect. This type of cuing is most fully effective in retrospect, where a cohesive feature has its richest impact because all its instances are in some sense copresent. Any definable verbal feature in a text (for example personal pronouns, or a metaphor and its elaborations, or words in a particular semantic field) can be abstracted from the text and examined as a chain, cluster, or set, most often related by similarity, repetition, or association, establishing a basic continuity or unity within which variation and development of ideas occur. Besides such thematic functions, one may consider how a system of cues contributes to other holistic qualities of coherent structure, such as logical connectivity, periodicity, dialectical tension, or tone.

In both cases, these methods of studying cohesion do not resort to rules or lists of possibilities for cohesive cues, but rely on readers' instincts and experience to pick out points in the text and features that are salient and significant in their ability to integrate coherent meanings. These approaches are, therefore, not foolproof or algorithmic, but depend on educating the sensitivities of readers to their own responses and to the resources of the language as exemplified in actual texts, especially their own. The kind of knowledge these approaches produce is ultimately practical. From a knowledge of the relationships that come into being between real texts and their readers, from observation and discussion of the problems that arise in these encounters, discoursers can learn how to use the systems and conventions of the language in conjunction with context to construct intersubjectively coherent meanings. In this view, discourse analysis is not a science, though it can be rigorous and fruitful: it is the study of performance through participation. As such, discourse analysis itself is a skilled performance (depending on expert reading), and it yields a conscious, but experiential, contextualized knowledge that is of value to the discourser as a writer and reader.

Figure 3 represents schematically the conceptual relations among the family of terms introduced to describe coherence in this chapter.

Figure 3. Coherence on the reader-text axis.

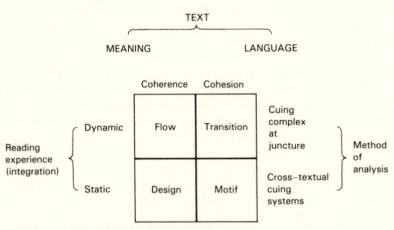

I end this chapter with an acute consciousness of the limitations of my analysis. As a study of coherence, it is merely the first step toward developing an integrative concept, worked out only along the axis of readers and texts, and there just sketchily. Although I have acknowledged the significance of context, I have not done justice to the role of reference in testing coherence, because to say that comprehension is basically contextual is to say that texts make sense of worlds, not just themselves, and that integrations made by readers are not detached from their own beliefs about the world. I must certainly wonder how far a text can stray from a reader's model of the world before it is judged not just fictional or mistaken, but incoherent.

More glaringly, I have completely bracketed (often with great reluctance) the writer's perspective on coherence. I wanted to show that process, or more precisely the intersubjective action of discourse, does not stop when the text is composed, and that texts are themselves dynamic elements in a wonderful, intricate dance of discourse. To rescue texts from their death as "product," I dramatized the role of textual symbols in closely shaping acts of comprehension, whose living texture they thus share, while from the writer they acquire the virtual power to "speak." But to understand this dynamic, we had to set aside another one arising from the fact that texts have a past. To restore the dynamic of texts as historical objects requires that we study them "in process" in a different sense—as they grow during composing. With this shift we encounter a whole new set of interactions and reciprocities focused by the relation between the writer's developing thought and the evolving text. Here arise the intentionality and purposefulness of meanings, essential if a reader is to experience coherence. The relevance of the dialectics worked out here—coherence and cohesion, flow and design, transition and motif—to the writer's perspective remains open to inquiry; surely other concepts will be needed.

Finally, I hope that even an incomplete and inevitably flawed analysis of coherence as an integrative concept will suffice to establish the validity of the goal and the potential of this approach. At the least, it should open a dialogue between two lines of research; at best, it may begin the process of reconciling and integrating them.

Notes

1. The nature of this scholarly consensus is nicely illustrated in Maxine Hairston's article describing an "emerging paradigm" for teaching writing, "The Winds of Change: Thomas Kuhn and the Revolution in the Teaching of Writing," *CCC* 33 (1982), 76-88. Agreement depends on not trying to go beyond a list of features, which conceals profound conflicts and leaves open the question of how these principles might be coherently related.

2. See chapter 6.

3. Work reflecting this trend includes ethnographical research in both classroom and home, attention to the relationships between reading and writing, and advocacy of a more interactive conception of knowledge and inquiry. See my bibliographical essay, "Cross-Sections in an Emerging Psychology of Composition," in *Research in Composition and Rhetoric: A Bibliographical Sourcebook*, ed. Michael G. Moran and Ronald F. Lunsford (Westport, CT: Greenwood Press, 1984), pp. 27-69.

4. I am influenced here by Susanne Langer's recommendation for philosophical thinking in the human sciences, especially psychology, in *Mind: An Essay on Human Feeling* (Baltimore: Johns Hopkins Univ. Press, 1967), vol. 1, xxi-xxiii.

5. Compare expositions of this view from varying disciplinary perspectives: John D. Bransford and Nancy S. McCarrell, "A Sketch of a Cognitive Approach to Comprehension: Some Thoughts about Understanding What It Means to Comprehend," in *Cognition and the Symbolic Processes*, vol. 1, ed. Walter B. Weimer and David S. Palermo (Hillsdale, NJ: Erlbaum, 1974), pp. 189-229; Jesse G. Delia and Barbara J. O'Keefe, "Constructivism: The Development of Communication in Children," in *Children Communicating: Media and Development of Thought, Speech,*

Understanding, ed. Ellen Wartella (Beverly Hills: Sage, 1979), pp. 157-85; Roger Shuy, "A Holistic View of Language," *RTE* 15 (1981), 101-11: Hubert Dreyfus, *What Computers Can't Do: A Critique of Artificial Reason* (New York: Harper, 1972), especially part 3 on the role of the body and the concept of situation; and Paul Rabinow and William M. Sullivan's introduction, "The Interpretive Turn: Emergence of an Approach," in *Interpretive Social Science: A Reader*, ed. Paul Rabinow and William M. Sullivan (Berkeley: Univ. of California Press, 1979), pp. 1-21. The latter is an important collection of primary sources for the interpretive position in the social sciences. Janet Emig takes an interpretive stance for composition in "Inquiry Paradigms and Writing," *CCC* 33 (1982), 64-75.

6. Dreyfus, *What Computers*, p. 173.

7. Bransford and McCarrell, "Sketch," p. 199.

8. This point may seem obvious, but even after cognitive theorists began to consider the role of context in understanding, they tended to postulate rather rigid data structures such as story grammars, with slots to be filled, rather than general, strategic, ad hoc situational models as means to understanding. For developments of a situational model approach, see Bertram C. Bruce, "Plans and Social Actions," in *Theoretical Issues in Reading Comprehension: Perspectives from Cognitive Psychology, Linguistics, Artificial Intelligence, and Education*, ed. Rand J. Spiro, Bertram C. Bruce, and William F. Brewer (Hillsdale, NJ: Erlbaum, 1980), pp. 367-84; and A. J. Sanford and S. C. Garrod, *Understanding Written Language: Explorations of Comprehension beyond the Sentence* (Chichester: Wiley, 1981).

9. Teun A. van Dijk, *Macrostructures: An Interdisciplinary Study of Global Structures in Discourse, Interaction, and Cognition* (Hillsdale, NJ: Erlbaum, 1980), pp. 1-15.

10. See Mary diSibio, "Memory for Connected Discourse: A Constructivist View," *Review of Educational Research* 53 (1982), 163.

11. Heinz Werner, "The Concept of Development from a Comparative and Organismic Point of View," in his *Developmental Processes: Heinz Werner's Selected Writings, General Theory and Perceptual Experience*, vol. 1, ed. Sybil S. Barten and Margery B. Franklin (New York: International Universities Press, 1978), p. 109.

12. Charles Taylor, "Interpretation and the Sciences of Man," in Rabinow and Sullivan, *Interpretive Social Science*, pp. 25-71; and Paul Ricoeur, "Model of the Text: Meaningful Action Considered as a Text," ibid., pp. 73-101.

13. Terry Winograd gives a clear exposition of this view in "A Framework for Understanding Discourse," in *Cognitive Processes in Comprehension*, ed. Marcel Adam Just and Patricia A. Carpenter (Hillsdale, NJ: Erlbaum, 1977), pp. 63-88.

14. Bonnie J. F. Meyer, "What Is Remembered from Prose: A Function of Passage Structure," in *Discourse Production and Comprehension*, vol. 1 of *Discourse Processes: Advances in Research and Theory* (Norwood, NJ: Ablex, 1977), pp. 307-36.

15. The notion of intention is of course highly problematic in literary theory. My position is that ordinary readers take writing to be intended, reflecting their assumption that language is designed to communicate.

16. See Stephen P. Witte and Lester Faigley, "Coherence, Cohesion, and Writing Quality," *CCC* 32 (1981), 189-204, for a recent statement of the distinction, influenced in part by the work of van Dijk.

17. I cannot begin to cite this material even representatively, and there are but few good review articles that sort out concepts, since these are still in a considerable muddle. But see Witte and Faigley's summary of the work of Halliday and Hasan in "Coherence,

Cohesion, and Writing Quality," and William J. Vande Kopple, "Functional Sentence Perspective, Composition and Reading," *CCC* 33 (1982), 50-63, as well as these primary sources: M. A. K. Halliday and Ruqaiya Hasan, *Cohesion in English* (London: Longman, 1976); Joseph Grimes, *The Thread of Discourse* (The Hague: Mouton, 1975), which reviews much important work; and Frantisek Daneš, "Functional Sentence Perspective and the Organization of the Text," in *Papers on Functional Sentence Perspective*, ed. F. Daneš (The Hague: Mouton, 1974), pp. 106-28. Researchers in developmental pragmatics have made significant contributions to pragmatic analysis of child language: see *Developmental Pragmatics*, ed. Elinor Ochs and Bambi Schieffelin (New York: Academic Press, 1979). Robert de Beaugrande attempts a synthesis from a text linguistic perspective in *Text, Discourse, and Process: Toward a Multidisciplinary Science of Texts*, vol. 4 of *Advances in Discourse Processes*, ed. Roy O. Freedle (Norwood, NJ: Ablex), 1980.

18. Wallace L. Chafe, "The Development of Consciousness in the Production of Narrative," in *The Pear Stories: Cognitive, Cultural, and Linguistic Aspects of Narrative Production*, ed. Wallace L. Chafe, vol. 3 of *Advances in Discourse Processes*, ed. Roy O. Freedle (Norwood, NJ: Ablex, 1980), pp. 12-13.

19. J. A. Fodor, T. G. Bever, and M. F. Garrett, *The Psychology of Language: An Introduction to Psycholinguistics and Generative Grammar* (New York: McGraw-Hill, 1974), pp. 271, 342-44.

8

The Third Way: Paul Ricoeur and the Problem of Method

In composition, as in any systematic study, metatheory has a broadly critical function for a set of theories or possible theories. The metatheorist attempts to answer questions like these: what topics and problems should a theory in the field address? What relations hold among theories? What grounds would justify choosing one over another? Corresponding to theories in a field are methods of research and analysis, ways that a given discipline characteristically employs to study its chosen objects and topics. Method is in a sense the dynamic or processual counterpart to theory, so that in linguistics, for example, Chomsky's theory of language introduced a rationalistic method into a discipline dominated to that point by empirical studies. Any comprehensive theory in composition studies implies a corresponding research method that defines a field of knowledge and the terms of a project for deriving knowledge about objects and events in that field. Completing the ratio, then, we would expect a metatheory of composition to have as its dynamic correlate a "metamethod," with the same critical functions regarding methods of inquiry that a metatheory has for discourse theories. In this chapter I want to raise the question of method in composition at this metalevel of analysis, that is, in terms of a possible process for mediating methods.

It might be wondered why such an abstract question is interesting or necessary. The reason for my concern with metamethod is actually a very practical one: the incivility and chaos that attend what might otherwise be thought a productive plurality of methods in composition today. This incessant clash of methodologies poses a seemingly abstract issue with a special urgency and bite. My goal is not to argue for a particular method, but to suggest the possibility of a metamethod— let me call it a philosophic method—as a systematic practice for rigorously characterizing, debating, coordinating, and judging the nature and value of particular working methods for composition studies.

One such practice may be found in the dialectical, mediating habits and commitments of Paul Ricoeur, which I will explore here as they bear on the problem I have defined. The appropriateness and applicability of Ricoeur's attitude to this task of mediation in composition is not coincidental. In fact, the problem of method in composition studies, while highly idiosyncratic and local in certain respects, is exemplary for a fundamental "conflict of interpretations" in modern thought, broadly between positivist or objectivist modes of inquiry and interpretive ones, more relativistic and subjective. It is not surprising to find composition struggling with this problem so intensively, given the history of the modern development of the discipline. Like medicine, engineering, or psychoanalysis, composition grew from a professional practice and seeks knowledge for the sake of action. Originally, this practice was composition teaching in the college classroom, but the limitation was historical and artificial; the logic of inquiry into writing processes has gradually expanded the scope of research and teaching to personal literacy over the lifespan. Even a single instance of writing, reading, or teaching in a classroom demands (if one is to understand it theoretically) knowledge of truly profound and basic aspects of human existence, of language, thought, and social interaction. Initially, at least, and I think characteristically as a mission-oriented field, composition relied heavily on multidisciplinary sources to build up a broad if fragmentary knowledge base about these matters, always scrambling to keep up with its urgent practical needs. In the process it opened the door to the conflict of interpretations. For composition has incorporated from these disciplines not only facts and theories, but also perspectives on human life that are fundamentally different from one another, and in some cases apparently incompatible.

This fact, I think, gives the predicament of composition a more than local interest. The methodological conflicts of the human sciences and natural sciences are internalized by the borrowings of composition, so that it reproduces in miniature, within one field, the problem of method that separates other disciplines. This is not the only respect in which the problem of method in composition has wider implications. In the human sciences generally, as I have implied, method translates into the central contemporary question of how humans constitute knowledge of reality and what that knowledge amounts to. In philosophy, literary theory, psychology, and many other disciplines, this question is currently being posed directly in terms of interpretation, semiotics, rhetoric, and writing. There are therefore important and complex links to be explored between method and discourse, between the practice of inquiry in composition and the more general issue of how language is involved in, or rhetoric governs, the constitution of knowledge in any field. These questions represent a context of opportunity for composition to turn a troubling internal problem into a means of identifying and communicating the relationships between its own concerns and those of related disciplines.

Let me turn, then, more narrowly to what I regard as a fundamental challenge to the constitution of composition as a productive modern discipline: the need to deal in a positive way with the tensions within the field, generated by the eclecticism of its knowledge base and exacerbated by related polarities whose history stretches back to Greek rhetoric. Before I turn to Ricoeur's philosophic method as a possible model of mediation, let me briefly survey the problem itself as it manifests itself in our practices.

The Conflict of Interpretations

The hesitancy in naming our discipline—between composition studies, rhetoric, or some combination—encapsulates certain peculiarities of its modern development. The process that institutionalized the teaching of writing within American college English departments broke, for a time, the continuity of scholarship and praxis within the rhetorical tradition. The freshman English course thus lost its conceptual basis and decayed into a tribal situation of competing methodologies, reflecting the intellectual fads of the day. For this reason the conflict of interpretations appears first in composition as a problem not of inquiry but of teaching.[1]

An apparent babble of arguments for a bewildering range of teaching approaches resolves itself on closer look into something simpler. Over the years of its short history, composition has displayed a set of dichotomies that repeat and continually refigure an underlying fundamental opposition of teaching styles and educational philosophies. Those in the profession react knowingly to the terms of specific disputes as code words for an antinomy so entrenched, irreducible, and wearily familiar in its sterility that we can never debate an issue as a new one, but only recode the antinomy and relocate it in a new context. So we pass from one cycle to another without progress. Yesterday it was the "conjure words" referred to in Richard Beach's report from the 1974 NCTE "unconference" in Kalamazoo: the "behaviorists" versus the "humanists," "structure" versus "openness," and "grammar" or "standard English" versus "the students' right to their own language."[2] Today it is the battle between "back to the basics" and "writing to learn," teaching sentence combining and teaching the composing process, thinking as problem solving and reclaiming the imagination. Granted, in reducing these many different positions, issues, and values to a polarity, I obscure historical change and do an injustice to complex differences and distinctions. Certainly there are many efforts to reconcile the two views or to represent them as compatible, often in the course of arguing that composition is a newly unified and self-coherent discipline.[3] But my point is precisely about the way such problems are perceived, and I think it fair to say that composition has persistently assimilated new debates about teaching methods to an old opposition, whose proponents talk at cross-purposes without, usually, confronting their fundamental disagreements at a philosophical level.

When, in the late 1960s and early 1970s, the profession began to reconceive itself as a discipline in search of its principles and methods, this antinomy manifested itself at a theoretical level, where it became more self-conscious. The underlying theme was recognized (if, perhaps, not extrapolated back to continuing arguments about teaching methods) and identified with broader cultural oppositions such as the Romantic and mechanistic (technologic) sensibilities; innovation and tradition; and most deeply, subjectivist and objectivist perspectives on reality and the problem of human knowledge. In making such conflicts explicit, composition is rising now to a more conscious participation in the dominant Western philosophical tradition flowing from Descartes, which grounded knowledge in the subject/object dichotomy. (Ironically, this occurs at the very moment when modern thought is struggling to surpass that distinction.) In any case, the conflict is not felt primarily as an incompatibility between subjective and objective discourse theories, since there are as yet only fragments, borrowings, and sketches of theories in either mode. In the absence of mature, full, and philosophically founded discourse theories, these themes still clash more directly, and voice their calls more compellingly, in the world of action. And whereas that action was predominantly practical or pedagogical before, now it is increasingly played out in the competition of methods for developing and validating knowledge.

It is here that the problem of interdisciplinary sources arises. In one aspect of this problem, composition must choose which disciplines to draw on for basic knowledge. To rephrase the question, what kind of knowledge do compositionists recognize as akin or foundational to their own? To answer, they must decide what knowledge would be specifically and characteristically theirs, in the sense that knowledge in history is recognizably historical and knowledge in psychology is recognizably psychological. Arriving at such a concept would entail examining more broadly the relation between knowledge and action in a pragmatically motivated discipline.[4]

More saliently, and more centrally for this discussion, the problem poses itself methodologically in this fashion: what fields offer appropriate models for a search for knowledge in composition studies? Here is the cutting edge of the conflict of interpretations. The issue of working research methods arose as soon as composition studies began to cohere around an object of inquiry, initially the writing process. Searching for the one right method that would constitute a research paradigm, composition was seduced by one methodology after another. Educational behaviorism, the linguistic model of appealing to intuitions and constructing generative rules, structuralist analyses, and experimental psychology are major past influences that come to mind, some of them still powerful. Ethnography, text linguistics, literary theory, phenomenology, and cognitive science provide current examples. The mix of influences is curious and revealing—empirical sciences, social sciences, the humanities. Clearly the new discipline remains radically uncertain about what *kind* of field it is, what kind of knowledge is proper to it, and therefore what mode of inquiry is appropriate to its needs.

If we return for a moment to the enduring divisions over teaching methods—free, progressive, child-centered, expressively oriented versus authoritative, traditional or technological, teacher-centered, formally oriented—we can see how they parallel these theoretical positions. Both concern the fundamental philosophical issue of how we know and how we learn what we know. We can view all the different methodologies, pedagogical or scholarly, as playing out different notions of learning and knowing. Both history and contemporary realities play a part in channeling considerably variant conceptions and practices of knowing into inflexible and often fiercely expressed dualities. As I noted, composition internalizes from its contemporary sources the struggle between powerful antagonists, positivist science and interpretive positions in the human sciences. Although positivism is losing ground in this battle (not so much to radically subjective views as to interactional ones that transcend the dualism), and many would argue that philosophically it is discredited, this is not the case in the pragmatic world. Even science itself displays a schizophrenia between the epistemological implications of modern physics, chemistry, and biology on the one hand, and the activity and methodological commitments of routine science on the other. Composition, as Robert Connors points out, remains fascinated by science, being envious of the accomplishments of the classical sciences, desirous of "verifiable knowledge," respectful of quantitative and controlled studies, and regretful at the possibility that it may not fit this mold.[5] At the same time it is not exempt from the tide of change in the intellectual community, so that, as nonpositivist methods show increasing vigor and capacity for innovation, composition theorists are beginning to defend them on broad philosophical grounds.[6]

The second reason that composition suffers such an exaggerated polarization of methodological debates is that the same conflict of world views brought to it by other disciplines finds a responsive echo in its own structure and history. I have suggested (without trying to trace causes and development) that, in its modern phase, composition has seen most ideas about the teaching of writing assimilated to one of two implacably opposed teaching approaches. Historians looking into the origin of these views are now realizing the role of the teaching tradition in maintaining a hidden continuity with classical rhetoric, partly through complex relations among its vestiges and descendants (primarily composition, literary criticism, communication, and speech). They discover, first, the paradoxical oppositions and mutual dependence of a mechanistic and an organic rhetoric, roughly corresponding to the empirical-scientific and humanistic perspectives I have described. Second, they remind us of the antiquity of related distinctions and oppositions in classical rhetoric, which can be traced back to conflicts in Greek thought over the nature of rhetoric and the relations between philosophy and rhetoric. These are battles that modern thought has returned to, and that composition both rediscovers and preserves in its own history.[7]

We find ourselves, then, with a conflict of interpretations, of methodologies, that is rooted in our long history (whereby composition continues the development of rhetoric). It is a conflict reinforced and dogmatized in the modern history of college teaching and textbooks, and exacerbated by our dependence—as an aspiring discipline—on other fields for knowledge and for models of knowledge and inquiry. Between the two poles of method a great chasm has opened up, a chasm that will not be leaped, a wound at the heart of the young discipline that will not heal. Each methodology stakes its claim imperialistically and with a fine contempt for any other way of knowing. Indeed, in the extreme, positivist science does not even grant the status of knowledge to experiential forms of understanding, while literary relativists bring into doubt not only verifiable knowledge but the very possibility of human knowledge, rational inquiry, and communication.

It has been persuasively argued that we are dealing here with two world views that are logically independent and cannot be compromised or merged. This is why proponents literally cannot talk to each other, since they are not operating within the same universe of discourse. Instead they inhabit different worlds governed by a "root metaphor," in Stephen Pepper's phrase.[8] Pepper, who identified four "relatively adequate" root metaphors, argued that each is autonomous and comprehensive, and cannot accommodate or combine with any other. Since, on the other hand, no world hypothesis yet proposed is fully adequate to deal with all aspects of reality as represented in human knowledge, he advocates *"rational clarity in theory and reasonable eclecticism in practice"* (p. 330). In the case of composition, which presents currently the alternative between a dualistic choice or an uncritical eclecticism, the question is how to interpret that advice in practical terms.

Discussing the same polarity in developmental psychologies, Hayne Reese and Willis Overton comment that "the crucial difference is so fundamental and broad in its implications that syncretism is impossible, and the only rapprochement possible is like the parallel play of preschoolers in that the protagonists are separate, but equal and mutually tolerant."[9] But it seems questionable to me that a discipline can successfully constitute itself, much less survive, simply by asserting the goal of mutual tolerance between coexisting and competing spheres of influence whose relation is actually more reminiscent of a cold war. Instead, some mediating principle is called for, one able to bring opposing forces into stable but dynamic relation. I am envisioning a dialectic whereby these forces would play against one another in constantly shifting patterns of enhancement, reciprocity, limitation, catalysis, inhibition, primacy, and emphasis. Such a dialectic is perhaps historically inevitable anyway; but to recognize and practice it systematically might curtail the pendulum swings and permit composition to establish a delicate simultaneous balance of forces as a principle of its nature.

Paul Ricoeur shows that this dilemma reproduces itself at a higher level in the choice that philosophy itself faces in seeking truth.

Don Ihde summarizes: "At one extreme lies the demand of philosophy itself for unity . . . but hidden in this demand is a possible dogmatism, the temptation to a philosophical *hubris.* If one philosophy is 'true,' then all others must be 'false.' On the other extreme lies the alternative of an irreducible plurality of warring philosophies with a temptation to skepticism in which all unity is abandoned or merely imposed by fiat."[10]

Ricoeur rejects this antinomy and offers instead a "third way" based on the infinite postponing of a synthesis, which places philosophy in a "living tension." Ihde continues: "The tension preserves a recognition of limits on one side and a desire, as hope, to probe as fully as possible towards unity on the other. . . . The limit idea of a postponed synthesis becomes a functional rule to protect thought against both hubris and skepticism" (p. 14). It is this notion of mutual limitation that I want to take up as a possible means for bringing into productive relation the two poles of method in composition, acknowledging the impossibility of synthesis but not of complementarity, interplay, and communication. As a method for mediating methods, the third way not only constructs bridges between the opposing extremes, but allows for the development of infinitely varying refigurations along a spectrum of methods, any or all of which can be brought into mutually limiting and revealing relationships.

Ricoeur's understanding of philosophy and the possibility of truth represents the third way at its highest level of abstraction. That vision is expressed more concretely in Ricoeur's specifically dialectical approach to philosophical problems. It is this more concrete sense of the third way (as philosophic method rather than ideal) that corresponds to the metamethod needed to mediate the working methods of research practice in composition. I will next examine Ricoeur's dialectical practice in order to sketch briefly, in the last part, a program for taking the third way in composition. The themes to be discussed are the weighted focus, demythologizing, the diagnostic relation, the wager, and the limit concept.

The Themes of the Third Way

In general, the third way is a strategy for opposing two sides of a polarity in order to discover the limits of each, often through a third term. I will illustrate the themes of this strategy as revealed in Ricoeur's famous encounter with structuralism through a dialectic of structure and event, later repeated in his hermeneutics as a dialectic between explanation and understanding. This encounter and its consequences are at once more accessible and more significant to compositionists than are many ideas in Ricoeur's work, because some of the issues and terms are familiar to them or parallel those in their discipline. Even so, it will be necessary to simplify Ricoeur's richly intricate analysis. The concept of a weighted focus is the starting point of Ricoeur's method.

Broadly, the conflict of methods for Ricoeur, as for composition, represents the opposition of objectivist and subjectivist approaches to the problem of knowledge. In this duel Ricoeur is not neutral: his initial position is phenomenological and, after the "linguistic turn," hermeneutical. In both aspects his starting point is "subjectivist" in the sense that it thematizes the subject and initiates a critique of the object or of naive objectivism (in the form, for instance, of empirical science or structuralist linguistics). Thus, as Ihde has shown and Ricoeur himself has confirmed, his philosophic method consists of taking up a "subjectivist" working method—always some version of phenomenology—as his favored method or weighted focus, and playing against it one or more objectivist countermethods in order to discover how these two mutually diagnose each other's limits.[11]

To call Ricoeur's hermeneutic phenomenology subjectivist, however, is potentially misleading without some clarification of these terms and their relations in his philosophy. It is especially important at least to set some limits on their interpretation, because of the tendency in composition to appropriate glamorous terms such as "phenomenological" without an acute sense of their complexity and conceptual variations in different contexts.[12] In briefly setting forth a notion of what it means to say that Ricoeur practices a hermeneutic phenomenology, I will focus on the opposition of subjective and objective elements in Ricoeur's thought, in order to convey more subtly and accurately his own conception of each stance. Two points will emerge: first, that Ricoeur contrasts his phenomenological attitude with objectivism, especially the empiricist variety, without reducing his own position to a mentalistic subjectivism; and second, that his phenomenological practice anticipates his hermeneutics by incorporating its own distanciating attitude into description of experience.

Ricoeur is said to have "grafted" hermeneutics onto a phenomenological philosophy, radicalizing Husserlian phenomenology by shifting it to a linguistic plane.[13] But another way of looking at the relation is to say that Ricoeur's interpretation of phenomenology prefigured his her-

meneutics in its pattern: always beginning with concrete experience—
objects of mental acts—and, in a reflexive movement, constituting an
indirect, mediated, and finite understanding of the self or subject. In his
hermeneutic phenomenology, language takes the place of the perceptual
world of objects, so that texts become the objects from which human
existence is indirectly understood, or "read." Ricoeur's hermeneutics,
which originally addressed the problem of interpreting mythological and
religious symbols, later developed a notion of text as written language
extending first to cultural artifacts generally and finally to history itself
as an inscription of human existence. Let me expand these points by
examining some of the premises of his phenomenology at the point
where they join hermeneutics.[14]

Ricoeur responds to two injunctions from Husserl: "to return to
things themselves and to abstain from every presupposition" (*PPR*,
p. 70). The first maxim anchors Ricoeur's philosophy in descriptions
of concrete experience. As he explains this starting point, phenomenology attempts to begin with the complex wholes of living experience
and to discover their essential structures. Specifically, phenomenology
aims at expressing the signification or meaning of experience: "Phenomenology makes a wager for the possibility of thinking and of
naming . . . even with regard to the confusion of affective life. Phenomenology wagers that the lived can be understood and said" (*PPR*,
p. 66). Ricoeur points thus to the *logos* in the word "phenomenology"
itself, so that phenomenology is by necessity founded on a hermeneutical or interpretive presupposition (*HHS*, pp. 120–28).

The second premise in which phenomenology and hermeneutics
coincide is the thematic structure of intentionality, which characterizes
every mental act. This structure consists of a correlation between a
directed consciousness and an object of thought, in such modes as
perception, will, memory, and desire. It is closely linked, in Ricoeur's
view, with the phenomenological "epoche," which suspends naive
belief in one's experience in order to signify it and thus to understand
it critically. "Phenomenology begins when, not content to 'live' or
'relive,' we interrupt lived experience in order to signify it" (*HHS*,
p. 116). The epoche amounts to a dispossession from the immediacy of
presence, which applies doubly to the experience of the self. The
subject knows itself only indirectly, through the mediation of an
"object" —the world acting as a mirror or correlate of consciousness.
Hermeneutics repeats this movement with the language of cultural
texts serving as the mediate object by which human beings can understand themselves aesthetically, historically, and morally.

The phenomenological reduction (epoche) incorporates an "objectivist" moment into the pattern of phenomenological understanding itself. Ricoeur's phenomenology is not "subjective" in the sense of privileging consciousness over the world or beginning with a self-founding subject. Just the opposite: he begins with the correlation between world and consciousness and regards the prereflective belonging of humans to the world as a given, prior to all philosophical meditation or science. At the same time, however, he draws a distinction between this kind of object emphasis (which falls on phenomena as experienced and on the way the embodied self participates in and belongs to the world) and the "objectivism" of positivist science. Ricoeur regards the latter as a reduction of the "richness of the real" to a set of observable facts, that is, "objects considered as the correlates of a theoretical consciousness, and . . . reducible to a physico-mathematical model"; whereas "phenomenology giv[es] to lived experience its complete amplitude." The scientific object represents a "second level of elaboration" (physical causality) grounded in the original world of praxis (*PPR*, p. 70).[15]

The development in Ricoeur's work that interests us here, however, is the process by which he projects this attitude of "alienating distanciation" into the human sciences, introducing an objectivist moment into an essentially phenomenological analysis in order to create a dialectic of methods. Before turning to an example, I should make one further point about the meaning of the objective-subjective polarity in Ricoeur's work. Although he does make the contrast in those terms, one might render the relationship more sensitively by translating them into a dialectic of distance and participation. From one perspective his project amounts to theme and variation on the effort to make distanciation productive. Methodologically, this means introducing counter-methods such as structuralism and psychoanalysis as moments of alienation, objectifying analysis, and thus critique, into an act of interpretation. The hope is to recover or reappropriate the sense of participation in the life-world that is primevally given, yet appears lost to humans with the first moment of reflective consciousness. Ricoeur denies that this given is "some sort of ineffable immediacy" along the lines of the metaphysics of presence denounced by Jacques Derrida: "rather [it] is construed as designating the reservoir of meaning, the surplus of sense in living experience, which renders the objectifying and explanatory attitude possible" (*HHS*, p. 119).

Let us turn now to the actual practice of the philosophical method by Ricoeur, which takes the phenomenological working method so far described as a weighted focus and attempts to balance and limit it dialectically through objectivist countermethods. Using a weighted focus rather than pretending neutrality, Ricoeur can both acknowledge his allegiances and undercut them as dogma by deliberately risking them. In a sense, it also represents a commitment of the heart or an expression of faith (depth) that must be balanced by reflection (clarity). In the case of my example, Ricoeur's encounter with structuralism, his weighted focus is a phenomenology of speech symbolized by the notion of discourse as event.[16]

The first step in the play of methods against one another is to take up a critical attitude that is initially directed toward demythologizing structuralism in the sense of limiting its absolutist claim to understand language as the object of a science. But this process brings equally into question the adequacy of a phenomenology of speech to provide a full understanding of human language by grasping it only existentially as a gesture of the body, as the power of expression felt and enacted by the speaking subject.[17] These two enter into an antinomy of structure and event that Ricoeur transforms into a dialectic whereby they mutually limit each other.

The pattern of analysis by which these limits are revealed is called the "diagnostic," the possibility of which arises from the fact that objectivist and subjectivist perspectives constitute two languages for describing the same reality, two universes of discourse. This is why the doctor can use the patient's description of his symptoms to "diagnose" the objective characteristics of a disease. But when we investigate the correspondence of these two languages, we find that it is not total. There are subjective experiences for which there is no objective equivalent, and there are objective phenomena for which there is no subjective awareness. In these instances the language of one universe of discourse "indexes" the other in such a way as to disclose an "obscurity border" between them, which Ricoeur takes as the lower limit placed on the powers of that language to describe, and thus understand, reality. An example of how the diagnostic relation works is the phenomenon of birth, which is objectively known but has no subjective equivalent in the individual's conscious memory. But there is an overlap between the biologist's account and the individual's experience in that, as the individual's memory reaches back into childhood, it fades into an obscurity and silence that suggest a beginning that consciousness cannot reach, the lower limit of the conscious self. Opposed to the lower limit of any language or method is the upper limit of the ideality, that specific power of disclosure toward which it aspires and which it can never reach. In the case of structuralism, that upper limit is the full accounting for language as a system of signs.

To set the dialectic between structure and event in motion, Ricoeur lays out the terms and implications of the opposition as fully as possible. Because his weighted focus is phenomenological, and the event pole of the pair represents a phenomenology of speech, his emphasis falls on structure as the countermethod to be played against his own center. At this point, even as he assumes a critical, demythologizing stance that destroys the first naiveté, whereby one inhabits or "indwells" structuralism as an absolute accounting for language, Ricoeur performs his characteristic reversal into a second naiveté affirming the value of structuralism. This move is the wager, in which Ricoeur gambles that, by practicing a hypothetical (thus critical) but affirmative belief in the countermethod, he will be able to recover its meaning from the shattered antinomy through the discovery of a third term. Beginning an examination of Claude Lévi-Strauss's *The Savage Mind*, he says of this process, "It is in order to give full measure to this method, and especially to allow myself to be instructed by it, that I will seize hold of it in its movement of expansion, starting with an indisputable core" (*CI*, p. 31).

Putting together a composite account of Ricoeur's efforts to "go all the way with the antinomy," we find six contrastive traits of system (language as structure) and discourse (language as event):

1. System is virtual and timeless; discourse is temporal and present.
2. System is semiotic; discourse, semantic. Within the closed system of signs, words have value rather than meaning: they refer only to each other. In use, language is about something: words refer to a world.
3. System is the condition for expression, the codes that make it possible to say something meaningful. Discourse is the act of saying something to someone about something.
   A correlate is that system has no subject, while discourse is self-referential and addressed from one subject to another.
4. System is constraint; discourse, choice.
5. System is by definition static (a state); discourse is creative.

The first phase of the dialectic, then, consists of reinforcing the antinomy of structure and event, the systematic and the historical, opposing, as Ricoeur says, "term for term, the 'event-ual' to the potential, choice to constraint, innovation to institution, reference to closure" (*PPR*, p. 116). He turns now to the task of understanding language as the "incessant conversion" of structure and event into one another in discourse. The mediating third term by which Ricoeur does this is the word, which he discovers by a movement from syntax (the sentence) to semantics (the word).

"Syntax," says Ricoeur, "is on the path of the return of the sign toward reality" (*PPR*, pp. 117–18). Sentences exemplify the interpenetration of the linguistic system, the finite world of signs, with the infinitely creative and new reference of language toward a world. Our ability to generate an infinite number of sentences describing and redescribing reality, through the finite means of the rules drawn from the apparently closed semiotic system, already means that there is an opening and an interchange between structure and event. This interchange is grasped most fully by turning to the semantic order and the problem of the word.

Words and signs are not the same; rather, "words are signs in speech position" (*PPR*, p. 119). It is only in use that the sign has meaning, when it leaves the lexicon and becomes speech event by its insertion in a sentence. But the word is a "trader between the system and the act, between the structure and the event," not only in the sense that it makes the sign actual, but also in the complementary sense of returning the event to the system. For words in natural language, as represented in the dictionary, are polysemous, replete with multiple meanings that do not remain fixed. The polysemy of the lexicon is nothing but a record of the history by which context makes words mean. Here structure and event explicitly limit each other: in speech the word is constantly charged with new use-values, but its possible values at a given moment are constrained (though indefinitely) by the existing values laid down or sedimented in the system, producing a "regulated polysemy." Ricoeur's wager has paid off in this coming to understand the mediation of structure and event by sentence and word, which he later carries to the discourse level in a parallel dialectic for textual interpretation, where structuralism and other distanciating methods provide the critical moment in interpretation to mediate the first naive understanding of a text and the reader's deeper appropriation of its meanings.

Program

In its weaker sense the practice of Paul Ricoeur's philosophic method is the habit of civility and the ability to listen to others' viewpoints with a respectful but critical openness. I believe that many in composition are tired of the imperialism of faddish, absolutist, and often moralistic methodologies characterizing all other approaches as unable to yield knowledge, validate claims, or guide praxis usefully. But in its stronger sense it is something much more specific and rigorous than a vague tolerance. In this last section I would like to speculate on how we might interpret and adapt the third way as a metamethod for composition. It becomes especially important to make this possibility more concrete as the expansion of methodologies in composition continues. In a discipline defined pragmatically rather than logically, there is no principled way to exclude either new information or the perspectives and methods that come with it. Instead we must find a principle for creating a dynamic stability, a constantly postponed synthesis of research methods that incorporates means for critically examining each contribution to the progress of inquiry.

Ricoeur's philosophic method provides general guidelines: the choice of a weighted focus (we must decide whether that is to be a matter for each individual scholar or for the whole discipline); the critical regard for a particular method that demythologizes and simultaneously gives it "full measure"; the wager that, through mutual limitation, two methods played against each other can recover the surplus of meaning that overdetermines all human action and discourse. When I try to think of making this framework concrete, it is the concept of the diagnostic that seems most suggestive and striking. The diagnostic derived originally from Ricoeur's analysis of the relationship between the voluntary and the involuntary in the structure of the human will.[18] My program would build the mediation of methods on a diagnostic that takes intention in written discourse as a special case of human will.

It might be agreed that much composition research is concerned with how intention operates relative to texts, and that intention or purpose has recently come to include both writer and audience as participants in the composing of meaning. In the context of Ricoeur's work, I would ask participants in a discourse event: in what ways do different aspects of written discourse constrain the realization of intention, that is, limit the will of each discourser to mean, to interpret or understand? My concern here is not to answer the question at the level of experience, but to translate it onto the methodological plane. My suggestion, repeating Ricoeur's dialectical figure, is to play methodologies of the subject, concerned with the freedom of the will (intention to mean) against those that impose constraints or represent conditions of possibility for that intention, that is, methods that operate within the realm of objective causality or ideal system. These are, in fact, the two types of alienating distance that Ricoeur identified as possible countermethods to phenomenology—empiricism and structuralism. He came to see the method of language as providing a new model of intelligibility for objectivity or distance, the proper critical instrument for the human sciences, because, unlike the empiricism of the physical sciences, it represented the object world of culture. One might argue that, for the most part, what is experienced as involuntary in human experience is culture rather than a brute physical world.[19]

I would prefer, however, to leave that question open, and consider instead the general problem of a weighted focus for composition, or at least for myself as theorist. It seems inevitable that I choose a subjective method, as did Ricoeur, for the simple reason that discourse is the act of conscious subjects. Such methods, then, as dramatism, phenomenology, contingent practical action (as in contextualized teaching and learning), and case studies or ethnography, which assume the observer's participation, would be favored as the naive starting points of all inquiries into written discourse, since they allow us to focus on the way meaning is personally willed. Each of these methods focuses, in different ways, on motive and on the nature of personal meaning experiences.

Within any such experience, however, Ricoeur's analysis tells us we will experience the resistance of the involuntary. The notion of intention in writing, like free will, is a fundamental possibility, an ideality reaching toward a limit that is never achieved (perfect expression, in which intention fills language, and language expresses all that is willed, and no more). On the other side is an obscurity limit, where intention can neither fathom nor control other forces. These forces include my own body, in particular the brain in its unconscious and tacit operations; language as an institution beyond my control; social and political powers and forces; and the physical technology of writing and reading. Most important of all, perhaps, is the other with whom I enter into the communicative transaction: even when I am my own audience, I internalize a perspective not my own, a fiction with social roots.

I am proposing that it is these involuntary forces and realities that call for objective methods of inquiry, ranging from experimental studies of the brain to the critique of ideology. Such methods are objective both in the sense of analyzing realities causally, perhaps quantitatively, and in taking up a critical distance from the experience of subjects who intend meanings in discourse. By using these methods to counterbalance the intimate and participatory ones of the subject orientation, we may come to terms with the finitude of our own expression and communication, yet understand them in the context of our persistent hope for their success. It is essential, however, that we develop some such characterization (not necessarily this one) of the relationship among methods, and, even more specifically than I have done so far, develop the role, object, and appropriate sphere of different methodologies.

We are on the path of the third way when composition researchers begin to question, not simply systematize and justify, their own practice. In doing so—as we see happening now, for example, with protocol analysis—they acknowledge the transactional nature of knowledge itself. Ironically, at this point we rejoin our own tradition, which has been taken up almost unbeknownst to us by science, philosophy, and the social sciences. For Ricoeur's third way, practiced as philosophic method, is a particularly civilized and perhaps idealized form of a dialogic rhetoric. And if composition has faithfully reflected the conflicts of method within the culture at large, it also can discover in its own past the seeds for a new third way, the dialectical path between intuition and technique, freedom and constraint, generativity and criticism, appropriation and distanciation, Romanticism and formalism, humanism and science.

Notes

1. For early and recent accounts of these conflicts, see Albert R. Kitzhaber, *Themes, Theories, and Therapy: The Teaching of Writing in College* (New York: McGraw-Hill, 1963); Thomas W. Wilcox, *The Anatomy of College English* (San Francisco: Jossey-Bass, 1973); Richard Ohmann, *English in America: A Radical View of the Profession* (New York: Oxford University Press, 1976); and James A. Berlin, *Writing Instruction in Nineteenth-Century American Colleges* (Carbondale, IL: Southern Illinois Univ. Press, 1984).

2. Richard Beach, "Notes from Kalamazoo," *CE* 35 (1974), 838–41.

3. See Maxine Hairston's widely cited article "The Winds of Change: Thomas Kuhn and the Revolution in the Teaching of Writing," *CCC* 33 (1982), 76–88, and a reply by Thomas E. Blom, *CCC* 35 (1984), 489–93. See also Janice Lauer, "Composition Studies: Dappled Discipline," *Rhetoric Review* 3 (1984), 20–29; and Richard L. Graves, "The Way of a Large House: Synthesis in Teaching Composition," *Rhetoric Review* 3 (1984), 4–12.

4. See chapter 9 for an analysis.

5. Robert Connors, "Composition Studies and Science," *CE* 45 (1983), 1–20.

6. For a review of methodology in composition studies, see Christopher C. Burnham, "Research Methods in Composition," in *Research in Composition and Rhetoric:*

A Bibliographic Sourcebook, ed. Michael G. Moran and Ronald F. Lunsford (Westport, CT: Greenwood Press, 1984), pp. 191–210. Janet Emig and W. Ross Winterowd, in the entire body of their work, are perhaps the most eloquent spokespersons for nonpositivist methods: Emig for a "phenomenological gaze," and Winterowd for a dramatistic, transactional perspective influenced by Kenneth Burke.

7. See John C. Briggs, "Philosophy and Rhetoric," in Moran and Lunsford, *Research in Composition and Rhetoric*, pp. 93–124; and *The Present State of Scholarship in Historical and Contemporary Rhetoric*, ed. Winifred Bryan Horner (Columbia: Univ. of Missouri Press, 1983).

8. Stephen C. Pepper, *World Hypotheses: A Study in Evidence* (Berkeley: Univ. of California Press, 1942).

9. Hayne W. Reese and Willis F. Overton, "Models of Development and Theories of Development," in *Life-Span Developmental Psychology: Research and Theory* (New York: Academic Press, 1970), p. 116.

10. Don Ihde, *Hermeneutic Phenomenology: The Philosophy of Paul Ricoeur* (Evanston, IL: Northwestern Univ. Press, 1971), p. 13. This study is an excellent guide to Ricoeur's early work, especially for those more familiar with his studies in language. It follows the development of his thought closely up to the hermeneutical turn, paying careful attention to his dialectical method. See also Paul Ricoeur, "Preface to the First Edition," *History and Truth*, tr. Charles A. Kelbley (Evanston, IL: Northwestern Univ. Press, 1965, pp. 3–14. In this chapter the works of Paul Ricoeur are cited in the text by abbreviated titles, as follows: *CI=The Conflict of Interpretations: Essays in Hermeneutics*, ed. Don Ihde (Evanston, IL: Northwestern Univ. Press, 1974); *HHS=Hermeneutics and the Human Sciences: Essays on Language, Action and Interpretation*, tr. and ed. with an introduction by John B. Thompson (Cambridge: London, 1981); *HT=History and Truth*; *PPR=The Philosophy of Paul Ricoeur*, ed. Charles E. Reagan and David Stewart (Boston: Beacon Press, 1978).

11. Ihde, *Hermeneutic Phenomenology*, pp. 14–20; Paul Ricoeur, "Foreword," ibid., pp. xiii–xvii. See also Ricoeur, "From Existentialism to the Philosophy of Language," chapter 6 in *PPR*, pp. 75–85.

12. See Herbert Spiegelberg, *The Phenomenological Movement: A Historical Introduction*, 3rd ed. (The Hague: Nijhoff, 1982), for a discussion of the phenomenological method and movement, especially in part 5, "The Essentials of the Phenomenological Method." According to Spiegelberg, there is no single concept or value that defines the unity of all phenomenology. Ricoeur's phenomenology is primarily derived from Edmund Husserl and balanced by an existentialist emphasis taken from Gabriel Marcel. His method also owes much to the thought of Kant, Hegel, and Heidegger.

13. Don Ihde, "Editor's Introduction," *CI*, pp. xiv–xvii. See also his introduction to *Hermeneutic Phenomenology*, pp. 3–25.

14. See especially *HHS*, pp. 101–28, and part 2 of *PPR*, pp. 59–93.

15. There is a good discussion of Ricoeur's phenomenology in relation to Husserl and the function of bracketing by Ricoeur's translator Erazim V. Kohak, in "The Philosophy of Paul Ricoeur," his introduction to Ricoeur's *Freedom and Nature: The Voluntary and the Involuntary* (Evanston, IL: Northwestern Univ. Press, 1966), pp. xi–xxix.

16. Among the places that Ricoeur outlines this contrast are *PPR*, pp. 109–19; *CI*, pp. 27–61; and *HHS*, pp. 197–221.

17. See Maurice Merleau-Ponty, *Phenomenology of Perception*, tr. Colin Smith (New York: Humanities Press, 1962), pp. 174–99.

18. The diagnostic is described in *Freedom and Nature*, pp. 2–20 and passim. See chapter 2 in Ihde, *Hermeneutic Phenomenology*, pp. 26–58, for a sense of how this concept developed historically in Ricoeur's work.

19. See Peter L. Berger and Thomas Luckmann, *The Social Construction of Reality: A Treatise in the Sociology of Knowledge* (Garden City, N.Y.: Doubleday, 1969).

Part Three

Application

9

Toward a Human Science
Disciplined by Practical Wisdom

> I cannot really make sense of a *phronēsis* that is supposed
> to be scientifically disciplined, although I can imagine a
> scientific approach that is disciplined by *phronēsis*.
>
> HANS-GEORG GADAMER

The epigraph for this chapter, which inspired its title and theme,
comes from a letter written by Hans-Georg Gadamer to Richard
Bernstein, published as an appendix to Bernstein's book *Beyond Objectivity and Relativism: Science, Hermeneutics, and Praxis.*[1] The term
"phronesis" refers to Aristotle's concept of practical wisdom, or ethical
know-how, as developed in book 6 of the *Nichomachean Ethics.*[2]
Gadamer's work uses phronesis, the case-by-case analysis application
of ethical concepts to concrete practical situations, as a model for
hermeneutical understanding. As I interpret the line quoted (which is
not elaborated in his letter), Gadamer claims that science, in the form
of general laws, cannot tell us precisely how to make practical-moral
decisions in everyday life, while he suggests—somewhat mysteriously—that perhaps the wisdom of experience should "discipline"
science itself. To translate this language into that of composition
debates, Gadamer is saying that theory, at least theory as defined by
the natural sciences, cannot govern daily teaching practices, but that
conceivably it might work the other way around.

In the context of reconstructing composition as a "discipline," a
human science, Gadamer's assertion is profoundly unsettling. That
project rests on the assumed capacity of theoretical knowledge to
direct practical decisions, the very relationship that Gadamer denies
and indeed reverses. Leaders of the reform in composition thought it
self-evident that rigorously developed knowledge—the "theory" pro-

duced by disciplinary inquiry—would provide a better guide to teaching or discourse practices than incoherent, inconsistent, unreflective beliefs and maxims, the content (according to new rhetoricians) of the textbook tradition.[3] That assumption provided the formative impetus for composition to develop and disseminate a new knowledge base for practical-moral action.

The problem is that, even as composition pursues this goal at one level of its discourse, a gap between theory and practice widens at another, like a fault line cracking the foundations of the discipline. Deep in the disciplinary unconscious runs a strong undertow of anti-intellectual feeling that resists the dominance of theory in every institutional context of the field—journals, conferences, writing classrooms, textbooks, teacher education—and even in some forms of theory itself. Despite all the brave talk of a new paradigm, teachers fear and distrust the abstract and they constantly, stubbornly assert the priority of the practical and concrete over "theory." The conflict is perhaps most poignant and fierce when it divides the mind of the theorist-teacher herself, torn between two allegiances.

As a young field determined to establish a scholarly ethos, proud and insecure, composition has been understandably reluctant to admit that these tensions pose a serious threat to its progress. But by repressing and trivializing the resistance to theory, we have only increased its power to distort, even disintegrate the project of reform. In this situation Gadamer's remark administers a therapeutic shock, demanding that we candidly expose and assess the conflictual relation between theory and practice in composition. With the sudden clarity that rouses critical consciousness by denaturalizing a familiar idea or attitude, Gadamer valorizes what we have regarded as the reactionary position—the teachers' stance against theory—and makes it possible to address the previously unthinkable possibility that a discipline might constitute itself without submitting praxis to the domination of theory. His succinct reversal of current values stands for all the efforts of science, philosophy, and rhetoric to reconfigure the traditional oppositions between theoretical and practical wisdom. My concluding chapter undertakes to imagine that possibility for composition, the goal being to construct a new dynamic balance that reflects both theorists' purposes in seeking disciplinarity and teachers' intuitions about the proper role of knowledge in practical-moral activities.

One source of our own particular dilemma is that the two sides have not defined an agenda of arguable issues and hence are talking at cross-purposes. To the practitioner (most acutely, to the new teacher or the teacher new to disciplinary discourse in composition), the point to be argued is whether theory has any relevance to daily practice in the classroom at all. By posing this insistent "practical" question, teachers perform a critical function that is itself theoretical, even though prereflective.[4] Teachers' objections to theory challenge composition scholars to acknowledge and defend (or modify) the assumptions underlying their recommendations to classroom teachers. Among these assumptions are the following: (1) there is inherently a relationship between formal theory and practice; (2) this relationship is well defined and fixed, that is, "good" theory would inform or govern practice in exactly the same (rule-governed) way in any concrete situation; and (3) within such a relationship, theory is automatically the privileged term. One can interpret teachers' resistance as a properly critical demand that these premises be articulated, analyzed, and argued.

But this challenge to theory has not been met or even recognized as such. Instead, in discussions of knowledge about writing, theorists have focused on debating such global issues as whether composition is a science or an art, what type of knowledge is appropriate to composition as a discipline, and what fields should serve as methodological models for writing research. Discussions of application project these questions onto the pedagogical field, where they become conflicts of teaching method. Researchers advocate their own favored forms of theory as the basis for curriculum and teaching method, thus constructing the issue between themselves and teachers as one of salesmanship, rather than serious dialogue over the fundamental relevance of theory and the proper means of application. By failing in this way to confront as arguable the questions teachers raise about relevance, validity, applicability, and the privileging of theory, composition has failed to address one of the constitutive problems of a practical-moral field.

One approach to setting an agenda that overcomes the limitations of both teachers' and scholars' perspectives is to construct a set of questions across a continuum that includes issues and concerns of both sides, but differently framed. Rather than assuming an inherent, single, abstract, fixed relationship between theory and practice, or no relationship at all, let us begin with the hypothesis that this relationship is contextually defined and varies from one situation to another. Each specific case of practice raises anew the question of what theory, if any, is relevant, and how in particular it applies, and with what changes, caveats, and consequences. It is up to the teacher, not the theorist, to make such decisions, although theorists may play a role. We have yet to determine what that role might be, if it is not simply technological and oppressive. The questions generated by this hypothesis will have to do with the grounds and means for seeking out, selecting, evaluating, and adapting knowledge to particular concrete situations. I will try here to reframe the problem of application along such lines. In the process I hope to show how the teacher's own capacity to reflect on experience establishes a dialogic relation between classroom practices and organized inquiry, such that they reciprocally motivate, interpret, and limit each other.

My discussion begins with some definitions and distinctions drawn primarily from the work of John Dewey, Paulo Freire, and Hans-Georg Gadamer (the latter rehabilitating Aristotle's concept of phronesis). These ideas provide a conceptual background for analyzing the concrete problem that theory presents for praxis in teaching composition. From Dewey I will borrow the idea of reflection as a type of deliberate, rigorous thinking, and by extension a critical attitude or relation to phenomena. Reflection at the disciplinary level generates Theory: the process and products of systematic inquiry within a community organized for that purpose. But the formal counterpart or "antistrophe" to Theory is informal reasoning—the reflective processes of hypothesizing, questioning, testing, connecting, and so forth, that characterize everyday life and generate the theories that people live by.[5] Both Dewey and Freire believe that reflective powers are profoundly latent in human experience and can, through deliberate effort and stimulation, be brought out and cultivated. From this possibility Freire develops a conception of praxis as not simply action but thoughtfully articulated activity, a symbiosis of work and word. Gadamer adds phronesis as a model for the situation of context-dependent action that requires reflective judgment.

Conceptual Background

Dewey's Experimental Method

In *Experience & Nature* John Dewey advocates a "denotative [experimental] method" for philosophy analogous to the empiricism of the natural sciences: "the theory of empirical method in philosophy does for experienced subject-matter on a liberal scale what it does for special sciences on a technical scale."⁶ Dewey's advocacy of the experimental method constitutes a critique of any theory that is not rooted in and referred back to firsthand experience (as doing and suffering, praxis and pathos). Dewey indicts philosophy for "intellectualism," the habit of identifying the refined products of reflection (abstractions from experience) with primary reality itself. One of his criticisms is that philosophy, by following a nonexperimental method, denies cognitive content to ordinary experience (and thus fails to recognize the source of its own abstraction). At the same time, nonempirical philosophy does not, as science does, reconnect its formed concepts and theories to nature. Dewey summarizes the results as three "evils": the failure to check abstractions by testing them against raw experience; the inability to enrich the content of experience by placing phenomena and their qualities within a system of objects and meanings; and the consequent irrelevance of philosophical subject matter, which appears arbitrarily abstract.

Dewey does not condemn theory per se. "The charge that is brought against the non-empirical method of philosophizing is not that it depends upon theorizing, but that it fails to use refined, secondary products as a path pointing and leading back to something in primary experience" (*EN*, p. 8). Indeed, he regards reflection as an essential corrective to the tacit prejudices and beliefs picked up by people in normal social intercourse and activity without careful examination and evaluation. Reflection subjects such ideas to critical study and test: "Thoughtful persons . . . weigh, ponder, deliberate—terms that imply a careful comparing and balancing of evidence and suggestions, a process of evaluating what occurs to them in order to decide upon its force and weight for their problem."⁷ They seek to understand phenomena not merely relationally, but in terms of exact relationships that can be exhibited in ordered chains of reasoning. In Dewey's view, the cultivation of reflection as a skilled, disciplined form of thought is a primary goal of education: "*upon its intellectual side education consists in the formation of wide-awake, careful, thorough habits of thinking*" (*HWT*, p. 78).

Dewey wants to restore to philosophic method the full richness of reflection when it maintains a link to common experience. In natural science experience itself is highly formalized by procedures of observation and experimentation that constrain the answers nature may give to human questions. But Dewey's experimental method takes everyday experience itself for the laboratory in which philosophical concepts are tested. The justification for subjecting philosophy to praxis in this fashion is that experience is itself prereflectively intelligent and capable of creating values. Experience is specifically experimental in its very form, a process of hypothesizing and checking, responding to challenge and change, transforming self and environment.

> Experience is not a rigid and closed thing; it is vital, and hence growing. When dominated by the past, by custom and routine, it is often opposed to the reasonable, the thoughtful. But experience also includes the reflection that sets us free from the limiting influence of sense, appetite, and tradition. Experience may welcome and assimilate all that the most exact and penetrating thought discovers. Indeed, the business of education might be defined as an emancipation and enlargement of experience. . . . Abstract thought is imagination seeing familiar objects in a new light and thus opening new vistas of experience. Experiment follows the road thus open and tests its permanent value. (*HWT*, p. 202)

In short, Dewey's experimental method reintegrates reflection and experience so that they complement and incorporate each other. Experience is the source for the refined methods and products of philosophy (for which we may read Theory in composition). At the same time it is the testing ground (praxis) where reflective concepts can be experimentally verified. The process of verification involves taking theoretical concepts as designating abstract meanings that can be tested for their power to illuminate and enlarge primary experience when they are reinserted into personally experienced contexts.

Dewey does maintain a distinction between the reflection of participants embedded in experience, which through education can become deepened, more rigorous and critical, and the explicit, precise, elaborated products of specialist inquiries (whether in science or philosophy). Thus, translating into our own framework, his philosophy of experience suggests how we may relate teachers' praxis as writers, readers, and instructors in composition classrooms to the knowledge products presented to them as Theory. The teacher's own capacity to reflect—to weigh, compare, experiment, judge—is the crucial mediating element. Teachers test concepts drawn from Theory against their own theories developed from and within the matrix of practical experience. Simultaneously, they test their own concepts against those of systematic inquiry, to see in what degree the meanings of each check, constrain, and enrich the other.

Let us try rewriting Dewey's premises into a preliminary characterization of theory-praxis relations in composition:

Composition Theory has its origin in primary experiences of discourse (by people in the roles of teachers, learners, writers, readers, speakers, listeners) that set problems to be solved and circumstances to be explained. (This statement does not apply necessarily to Theory developed in other disciplines that is appropriated for composition.)

Theory must be (re)tested in daily personal experience regardless of how it has been previously validated in its disciplinary context.

Teaching praxis itself is an arena for reflection and theorizing, including experimentation to test reflective concepts developed directly in and from primary experience. In this sense the teacher is a lay scientist or philosopher.

One function of Theory, and of teacher education, can be to articulate and deepen teachers' reflective powers within praxis, making these more systematic and sustained. In this sense, Theory serves to activate experience as a searching, inquiring, critical praxis.

By virtue of these relationships, as in Dewey's philosophic method, teachers' personal and collective experience logically has priority over the products of systematic inquiry, since such experience is both source and ultimate testing ground for theoretical conceptions.

Freire's Redefinition of Praxis

So far I have not attempted to deal with the complexities introduced into these relationships by the fact that students are themselves human subjects in the composition classroom, and the further complication that they are themselves *learning to reflect* via written language. For this purpose I turn to Paulo Freire's *Pedagogy of the Oppressed.* Just as Dewey redefines experience as inherently cognitive, Freire redefines true praxis as an inseparable relation between reflection and action. For each man it is education (in essence, exposure to Theory) that brings about the integration and thus liberates the human imagination and reason for critical and creative activity. Freire describes praxis without reflection as activism, tending toward oppression, whereas reflection without action is mere verbalism. He sketches these symmetries:

$$\left.\begin{array}{l} \text{Action} \\ \text{Reflection} \end{array}\right\} \quad \text{word} = \text{work} = \text{praxis}$$

Sacrifice of action = verbalism
Sacrifice of reflection = activism.[8]

What Freire adds to the framework developed so far is the element of *dialogue* whereby teachers' praxis interacts with those capacities for reflection and action that are simultaneously developing within their students. Dialogue is the means by which reflection creates, re-creates, and transforms the knowledge that each side brings to the dialogic situation. Freire explains this notion through a negative example, the "banking concept" of education in which knowledge is deposited by teachers into students' minds. He sums up banking education in this list of its attitudes and practices:

(a) the teacher teaches and the students are taught;

(b) the teacher knows everything and the students know nothing;

(c) the teacher thinks and the students are thought about;

(d) the teacher talks and the students listen—meekly;

(e) the teacher disciplines and the students are disciplined;

(f) the teacher chooses and enforces his choice, and the students comply;

(g) the teacher acts and the students have the illusion of acting through the action of the teacher;

(h) the teacher chooses the program content, and the students (who were not consulted) adapt to it;

(i) the teacher confuses the authority of knowledge with his own professional authority, which he sets in opposition to the freedom of the students;

(j) the teacher is the Subject of the learning process, while the pupils are mere objects (p. 59).

Against this oppressive model of education Freire counterposes his own concept of "problem-posing education" based on communication. Problem-posing education treats both teachers and students as Subjects. Both are incomplete beings in the process of becoming, their knowledge in the process of making and remaking, as are their worlds. In this relation the object of study is the middle term that relates the reflection of both actors (teachers and students). The classroom is the site for the creation of new knowledge, which arises collaboratively. "Through dialogue, the teacher-of-the-students and the students-of-the-teacher cease to exist and a new term emerges: teacher-student with students-teachers" (p. 67). The teacher

does not regard cognizable objects as his private property, but as the object of reflection by himself and the students. In this way, the problem-posing educator constantly re-forms his reflections in the reflection of the students. The students—no longer docile listeners—are now critical co-investigators in dialogue with the teacher. The teacher presents the material to the students for their consideration, and re-considers his earlier considerations as the students express their own. (p. 68)

Dialogue in this sense is a practice of freedom expressed in the respect that dialoguers have for one another's capacity to speak, to name the world. Freire characterizes dialogue as both critical and creative. It promotes critical as distinct from naive thinking: "thinking which perceives reality as process, as transformation, rather than as a static entity—thinking which does not separate itself from action, but constantly immerses itself in temporality without fear of the risks involved" (p. 81). Because this critical spirit implies, and is founded in, humility, faith, the hope of transforming reality, and the courage to love life and humanity, it is inherently generative.

Freire's concept of dialogue enriches the view already developed from Dewey's analysis that makes the teacher's own praxis reflective and experimental, by extending those qualities into an intersubjective situation. From another angle, one may regard the teacher's position relative to Theory as analogous to the student's position relative to the teacher's knowledge:

$$\frac{student}{teacher} = \frac{teacher}{Theory}$$

That is to say, between the teacher and Theory exist the same possibilities for oppression or freedom that Freire discovers in the teacher-student relation.

Freire's characterization of banking education translates with uncomfortable precision into a description of what is all too often the relationship that teachers form with Theory:

(a) Theory instructs and the teacher is taught;
(b) Theory knows everything and the teacher knows nothing;
(c) Theory thinks and the teacher [practice] is thought about;
(d) Theory talks and the teacher listens

and so forth. To use another of Freire's metaphors, theorists often disseminate Theory to teachers on the model of agricultural extension by which peasants are taught new technologies without regard to the environment in which they farm, their intimate knowledge of needs and problems in that setting, and their prior invention and adaptation of methods and means for their own purposes. Theorists' purposes impose themselves on teachers in the guise of new methods and means to the same ends; actually, though, in this technological application Theory becomes an end in itself, supplanting teachers' own highly local knowledge of constantly varying ends and appropriate means.

But the alternate possibility equally exists. Theory is not inherently oppressive; it becomes so only when it is transmitted to the teacher's mind—and received—as a solid, invariant chunk of meaning closed to interpretation, so that she can only reproduce it or fill in the slots of a rigid schema. The other way is for teachers and theorists to treat Theory as plastic, not an indigestible lump but a heterogeneous, multiplistic text or open system of meanings capable of entering into a communicative relation with other knowledge systems. One can think of the ensuing dialogue either individually or communally, depending on whether the focus is on the individual's knowledge base or on the collective understanding of an interpretive community. The teacher has her personal model of the events and acts to which Theory applies, representing the goals, methods, actors, responsibilities, ideals, and other dimensions of practical situations and decisions. But this personal model is embedded in a teaching community where it participates in subtle interchanges, affinities, and oppositions with other models of discourse and teaching. The whole may be thought of as a set of interlocking texts, narratives, and their interpretations that are constantly modifying one another. These models in turn interact with those being formed and tested by students in the classroom.

In the dialogic ideal, teachers and students participate in an unrestricted exchange (though in different roles) whereby they coconstruct interpretations of Theory and apply these to their own personally experienced models and contexts of discourse. The teacher in this instance is not the object of Theory, but a Subject who mediates between the systematic knowledge-creation of disciplinary communities and the reflection of learners who are developing critical consciousness through the praxis of written communication. He is thus the key player in a complex nested set of dialogues: between Theory and teacher, student and teacher, thus student and Theory, where in each case abstract products of reflection are not reified but re-created in the form of new meanings, new hypotheses and plans for action to be tested in experience.

This complex ratio reveals a moral dimension to teaching praxis for which we need the concept of phronesis. It is not possible, given the framework suggested by Dewey and Freire, to regard teaching as a Method that applies knowledge in the strictly technological sense. Instead it is a situation in which ends (what is to be taught or learned, its effects on the student) are not predetermined but are constantly shaped by means and context, so that no prescriptions are possible. Such a circumstance calls for practical wisdom in applying knowledge to particular context-bound cases. For a better understanding of that task, I turn to Gadamer's reading of Aristotle on ethical know-how.

Gadamer's Treatment of Phronesis

In *Truth and Method* and elsewhere, Gadamer sought to characterize "understanding" as a mode of knowledge appropriate to the human sciences (also called the moral, cultural, or historical disciplines), for which text interpretation is paradigmatic.[9] By modeling understanding on Aritstotle's concept of phronesis, Gadamer effectively fuses hermeneutics and praxis. His analysis identifies hermeneutics with phronesis because in each case it is impossible to separate knowledge from application. Bernstein explains: "*Phronēsis* is a form of reasoning and knowledge that involves a distinctive mediation between the universal and the particular. This mediation is not accomplished by any appeal to technical rules or Method (in the Cartesian sense) or by the subsumption of a pregiven determinate universal to a particular case. The 'intellectual virtue' of *phronēsis* is a form of reasoning, yielding a type of ethical know-how in which what is universal and what is particular are codetermined" (*Beyond Objectivism*, p. 146).

Aristotle's analysis of practical wisdom in the *Nichomachean Ethics* makes a distinction among forms of knowledge, contrasting *episteme* (knowledge for its own sake) with two kinds of know-how, *phronēsis* (knowledge directed toward right conduct) and *techne* (knowledge directed toward the production or making of objects). All know-hows share the characteristic of being learned at least partly in experience, while as knowledge they are developed for and oriented toward experience. Their goal is application of the universal or general to the specific case, as means to end.

To this point I have conflated the notions of "form of knowledge" and "form of reasoning," since Aristotle's discussion itself attempts to distinguish types of knowledge. Gadamer's effort to characterize understanding, insofar as it focuses on specific qualities of the historical or hermeneutical sciences, seems to do the same. But Gadamer's discussion modulates from *type of knowledge as determined by object* (phronesis as knowledge about ethical action) to *form of reasoning as determined by the situation of application*, where phronesis becomes, as practical reason, the prototype for a certain relation between knowledge and action, general and particular. In the broader interpretation, the difference between application on the model of techne and application on the model of phronesis becomes crucial. Gadamer's analysis of phronesis becomes a characterization and defense of practical reasoning against what Gadamer regards as the inappropriately technical application of scientific knowledge to praxis. In such cases what should be personal decisions are turned over to experts, allowing (in our terms) theory to discipline praxis by subjecting it to rule.

In Gadamer's interpretation, phronesis comes to stand for all situational use of knowledge, where knowledge is bound to context and changed by it, in contrast to the situation of (technological) application wherein a particular is subsumed under a general law by virtue of its regularity (predictability) according to that law. In practical reasoning, neither the means nor the ends nor their relation is fixed. In a discussion of one of Gadamer's favorite examples of application, the case of interpreting the law, Joel Weinsheimer explains:

> Application is reciprocal. The judge applies his understanding to the law—that is, tries to understand the law according to his best lights with reference to the case at hand; but he also applies the law to his understanding, for he wants to understand the case at hand with reference to the law and not to his own understanding alone. . . . This reference to the case at hand implies that there is always a tension between the sense of the legal or biblical text as it is written and the sense arrived at by its application to the particular situation, the particular case. The situation of application is continually varied and continually new. (*Gadamer's Hermeneutics*, p. 186)

Thus Gadamer argues that application is a constitutive moment in hermeneutics as well as in ethics, "not a calibration of some generality given in advance" ("Problem," p. 145).

The problem of application identifies in praxis itself a reflective moment, since practical reasoning involves judgment. Weinsheimer defines judgment as "the skill (for which there is no rule) to apply rules. Judgment is needed because there is always a tension between the general rule and the particular instance. . . . Such judgment is not impulsive but deliberate. It cannot merely subsume the particular under the general, and thus it requires a weighing of both. It requires reflecting and deliberating with oneself. This is phronesis, the virtue of reflective deliberation that determines right application" (p. 191). Gadamer speaks of knowledge applied on the phronetic model as simply a sketch or schema that guides the reflection of the *phronimos*, the wise person (*TM*, p. 286).

There is a sense in which we might quite justly describe Theory as a text, that which is written and must be interpreted or applied. Indeed, for most teachers Theory presents itself literally in the form of text (journal articles, books, speeches, courses of instruction) to be interpreted and applied. In Gadamer's terms the teacher is in a hermeneutical situation that ideally produces self-understanding and self-transformation. But "self" here does not refer in psychological terms to the teacher as person. Rather, Theory reads different aspects and elements of the whole classroom situation (the situation of teacher-in-relation-to-learners) and is read in turn by the teacher-student dialogue. Insofar as it is hermeneutical, the relation between classroom praxis and Theory is *like* phronesis with respect to the uniqueness of the individual case, the indeterminate relation of ends and means, the need for critical judgment, and so on. However, the limit to this comparison is that teaching involves activity with practical-moral consequences for others, so that it is not only formed on the model of phronesis (in being hermeneutical), but actually *is* phronesis in the original sense of conduct subject to regulative ideas of right and good. The teacher brings Theory into the classroom responsibly as phronimos, thus forming and reforming herself as a "good" teacher.

Earlier I redefined phronesis in the paradigmatic sense as a form of reasoning triggered by situation rather than pertaining only to particular kinds of knowledge (ethical, historical, etc.). This conception allows us to account for the radical eclecticism of composition in drawing on and making use of all kinds of knowledge. Gadamer hints at this possibility: "The problem of the application of science already presupposes that science as such possesses its self-certain and autonomous existence prior to all application and free from all reference to possible application; but thanks to just this freedom from purpose, its knowledge is available for any application whatsoever, precisely because science has no competence to preside over its application."[10] What I am suggesting is that *any* kind of knowledge, including the epistemic knowledge of science, becomes phronetic by its incorporation into human situations where it is tested in personal experience. For example, epistemic knowledge about the physics of bicycles or bobsleds and the physiology of humans that ride them is subjected to practical reasoning when it is brought to bear strategically in racing. Techne itself need not be technologically applied (in Gadamer's sense, as rule to instance), but can be subsumed to ethical ends, as in various conceptions of rhetoric (Platonic, Ciceronian, Augustinian) that place a technology of persuasion in the service of values—truth, the social good, God. It is clear that in the activities with which composition is concerned—writing, reading, educational interactions—we cannot neatly separate out ethical acts that depend on ethical knowledge, artistic decisions that depend on techne, textual interpretations that represent hermeneutical knowledge, and so on. Instead, there is a whole situation in which phronesis is the form of reasoning by which teachers constantly adapt for new circumstances knowledge that is itself mixed and subject to change.

The problem of Theory is a question, then, of what H. S. Broudy calls "knowing with," in that it involves appropriating conceptual knowledge within praxis and making it effective.[11] Experience in "knowing with" produces "know-how," which is not really a kind of knowledge but a habit and potential for bringing tacit knowledge to bear productively in new situations. In the next section I will practice phronesis myself, interpreting Gadamer's abstract framework in the light of my own teaching experience so as to venture a speculative analysis of application in composition. To simplify matters, I will restrict myself to the teacher's choices as teacher. (I am bracketing, for example, the teacher's experience as discourser, or the student's contribution to choices regarding Theory.) My goal is to bring out the underlying structure of application as a concrete activity of mediation between Theory and teaching practice.

Application as Dialogic Engagement: A Speculative Outline

Analyzing the process by which teachers apply Theory to praxis presents all the classic problems of describing any process, which compositionists discovered when they began to study composing. In isolating any elements in the process and presenting them discursively, one implies—and in a naive analysis professes—a simplistic stage theory in which discrete parts succeed one another in lineal sequence. Making these stages recursive does not help very much, because the description is still obdurately digital (i.e., it treats components as independent, however one shuffles the sequence or multiplies the links). Applying contextualist principles, I propose to discriminate *strands* from a *texture*; in a time frame, I will also use the phenomenological term "moment," which implies no sequence or no fixed sequence.[12] Texture characterizes the complex wholeness of an experience, object, or event. Here, that whole is the activity of applying theory to everyday teaching practice. As observers, of necessity participant-observers, we can differentiate strands interwoven in that experience in order to understand the texture of the whole (its multiplicity, internal difference, conflict, harmonies, progressions, and so on), and in so doing we may capture truths about the process, even though the strands we identify represent only one way of sorting out these complex relationships. It is understood that strands are not discrete except by our convention, although, if we define them wisely, they do embody possibilities of difference or opposition or change in the texture of the process.

In this way of thinking about processes, then, when I discriminate strands and present them, necessarily in some sequence, I do not imply a determinate order in which they are experienced. Instead, I assume that these strands relate to one another in many shifting patterns, both simultaneous and sequential. Descriptions select one or more configurations for such patterns within an experiential time frame. In this case, the strands represent mind-sets toward Theory that one falls into at particular moments, attitudes that might characterize any period of time from a momentary flicker of attention to a sustained global activity incorporating other orientations within it. However, once a teacher takes action in terms of one of these attitudes (for example, chooses to treat a particular concept or claim analytically), certain constraints begin to operate on what can happen next and in what terms, over a range of still indeterminate and uncountable possibilities. In other words, history determines options in a given instance that cannot be foreseen in general.

I intend to describe three strands in the texture of application, each being an orientation toward Theory characterized by typical activities, operations, and responses on the part of teachers:

1. Preselective attention, a state of relaxed attunement.
2. Critical examination, a more selective critical attention involving analytical work.
3. Experimentation in practice.

However, first I want to sharpen the characterization given so far to the texture of application.

Earlier I showed that composition had polarized choices so that there seemed to be only two relations to Theory: teachers could naively accept it (along the lines of the banking model of education), or they could reject it as impractical, overly abstract, and irrelevant. To escape this dilemma I proposed a context-sensitive form of application in which teachers could reflectively consider Theory and apply it in a form of phronesis, making case-by-case judgment of which principles and strategies are appropriate, and adapting such general truths or insights to fit the particular situation at hand. Following Freire, I called this relationship "dialogue," which in his terms places the teacher in a "critical relation" to Theory. Freire's use of "critical" is too inclusive for my purposes, since I want to distinguish between critical and affirmative aspects of the teacher's relation to Theory. A better term to characterize the complex attitudinal texture of application might be "dialogic engagement." By this phrase I mean to capture a tension between two complementary stances that a teacher might adopt toward Theory, one critical (distancing, objectifying, analytical, skeptical) and the other affirmative or creative. If one thinks of rejection and naive assimilation of Theory as the polar extremes, forming the dichotomy we have been working to reconstruct, dialogic engagement rearticulates the two categories as a dialectic pair:

Attitudes Toward Theory

1. current: [rejection]   vs.   [naive assimilation]

2. proposed: (critical judgment $<>$ constructive appropriation)

Within the dynamic structure of application, teachers engage themselves dialogically with Theory through an internal dialectic between critical and appropriative attitudes, one that can take many forms and paths. The three moments of this structure described below are not simplistically differentiated as either critical or appropriative; rather, these impulses are balanced differently in each mode.

Attunement

Preselective attention to Theory means being attuned to it in an ongoing state or mode of selective alertness to theoretical ideas encountered or sought out in one's intellectual environment. Of course I am referring specifically to ideas understood as relevant to understanding discourse and teaching composition (in its broadest definition), but there is no reason why such ideas have to be formulated in or for that framework. It is the receptive practitioner who decides that abstractions are relevant to his own future activity and that of his students in the classroom. The question is, then, given such an indeterminately broad and ill-defined field of potential sources, how does the teacher know what Theory to apply? How does he search for relevant Theory or come upon it, and how does he know it is or might be applicable?

The concept of attunement comes from ecological psychology, where it was proposed as an alternative to theories of memory as search through storage.[13] Bransford and his colleagues trace it to J. J. Gibson's theory of perception, which posits that "learning involves the attunement of the system to invariant information."[14] Past experience (that is, learning) "sets the stage" for the organism to grasp not only the sameness of information, but its novelty. This process is one of differentiating the new from the invariant information, rather than of matching a template—memory traces or schemas—to new input. The ecological psychologists extend the notion of attunement to other cognitive processes, including memory and language comprehension, where the interpreter's knowledge of word meanings and syntactic structures sets the stage for the construction of new meanings that are not simply the sum of discrete components.

In the case of composition pedagogy, attunement is a readiness on the part of teachers to perceive a theoretical idea as relevant and productive, not merely to existing problems but to unknown situations yet to be encountered. It involves at least two judgments, both tending to be vague and anticipatory in nature. First, the teacher senses a "match" between theory and experience—not a simple truth correspondence, but relations such as similarity, analogy, precise articulation of what intuition suggests, and harmony with a perspective or framework. The second judgment teachers make is that the idea in question intimates something unknown but desired: an enlarged or corrected insight, capable of generating new hypotheses, goals, or plans of action.

If this description sounds familiar, it is because it follows closely the account that scientists and artists have given of problem solving and creativity, specifically the moments of search and insight. In fact, we will see strikingly throughout my analysis of application that the teacher seems to parallel and replay the processes of inquiry that produced Theory in the first place. Michael Polanyi's discussion most vividly evokes the "heuristic passion" with which the scientist (and by extension here, the teacher) anticipates finding what is sought.[15] As he points out, prior to any rules or laws or methods of science comes the scientist's personal gamble that a particular problem is interesting (i.e., that it promises contact with a fundamental reality), and his affirmation of a "heuristic intimation" pointing to the directions of possible solution. Says Polanyi, "even though we have never met the solution, we have a conception of it in the same sense as we have a conception of a forgotten name. . . . The admonition to look at the unknown really means that we should *look at the known data, but not in themselves, rather as clues to the unknown; as pointers to it and parts of it"* (pp. 127–28). Polanyi emphasizes the conviction of rightness and truth that motivates intellectual search; similarly, the choice to select and enact Theory rests on personal confidence, a sense of rightness and fitness, the gamble that one's tentative commitment will be confirmed by experience.

Attunement is in the most general mode a kind of background state of attention by which one continually sifts information and ideas for what might be useful in some context that is not presently focal. Already the tuning filter is both creative and critical in operation: judgment excludes as irrelevant or uninteresting most of what one is exposed to, while the creative or assimilative impulse occasionally "notices" something and begins to make connections, cross-checks and references, projections, and intertextual linkages. A good bit of this may happen without conscious awareness as we read or engage in conversation. Furthermore, one tunes not only to what is current input but also to what is in memory, so that applicable Theory may rise to the surface of attention long after the initial exposure. (In the meantime, unless swallowed whole in an undigested lump, it will have undergone a sea change, having been inserted into multiple networks of meaning in the constant, dynamic reconstruction of experience.)

It should be clear that this process of sieving does not net only fully developed, comprehensive, well-articulated theories: Theory constitutes a great deal more. It is a bank of concepts, images, frames, bits of language, traces of thought—anything in the explicitly intellectualized background of cultural ideas to which the attuned mind responds. Since theory clusters themselves, however well formed, are subject to dissolution into and reconstitution of their parts, application, if not oppressive or fanatical, is always a process of intertextualization and recontextualization of ideas rather than of placing events under a rule that explains, predicts, or prescribes action.

At times one focuses the tuning process deliberately, in at least two ways: a tight-beamed search for the abstract tools one needs to solve a practical problem; or the systematic study of ongoing changes in a discipline, which provides a fuller and constantly updated source of general understandings for application. Since not every teacher can engage in such continual surveying of the field, some of this sifting and synthesis is done by what I call "translators," compositionists who carry out for practitioners the preselective work that identifies and gives teachers access to ideas in and out of composition that the translators find promising for application. (At best, they do so in a critical spirit that accomplishes some of the testing necessary in the next phase.) However, one of the functions Theory can have for teachers is to attune them to be their own scanners across a wider base of knowledge or acquaintance with ongoing developments in the discipline.

Critical Examination

I have remarked on the similarity between the structure of application and the structure of creative problem solving. According to Gadamer, text interpretation is also an analogue. Paul Ricoeur has described textual interpretation in terms of three phases: (1) initial understanding (a guess or intuition); (2) explanation; and (3) comprehension or appropriation.[16] My strand of critical examination is, like his "explanation," the sustained work of analysis (structural description, comparison, imaginative variation, thought experiments) necessary to evaluate Theory at an intellectual level, in contrast to the third orientation (experimentation), where it is evaluated at the level of action. The work of critical examination supports two types of screening or checking: first, a process of validating Theory within its original disciplinary context; second, one of judging and verifying its fitness for the specific situation(s) at hand. The first type of screening is difficult for teachers to do in every case with great rigor, so we must consider how they can rely on the larger community to help. The second type, however, requires case-by-case judgment that, although it can be guided by general observations and the experience of others, must be made again and again by individual teachers for new situations. In this respect they are like doctors who, while they rely on research to provide them with general principles of health and pathology as well as descriptions of typical medical events, must wisely invoke their own experience and judgment to calibrate diagnosis and treatment for individual patients. Furthermore, these judgments are not solely medical but incorporate other factors—technological, economic, ethical.

Assume for the moment that in principle any kind of knowledge might be relevant to composition practice. There are many systems of categorizing and subcategorizing knowledge and processes of inquiry. Figure 4 shows one such scheme, arraying types of knowledge roughly on a continuum from practical-moral know-how to philosophy and critique.[17] Examples in some of these categories for composition include, under empirical-analytic, studies of brain processes and structures; under structural-critical, analyses of language as system or of schooling as an institution; under techne, codification of stylistic options and their effects; under dramatistic-hermeneutical, concepts of ethos and audience.

The point here is not to argue distinctions and values we might attribute to different types of knowledge, but to suggest that for each well-recognized type there are self-defined, institutionalized standards of validity. Behind these standards, which are open and well argued, although frequently controversial both within and between fields, lie less fully explicit forms of discourse. These forms of discourse demarcate discourse communities within which certain conventions of language and argumentation operate, determining what counts as topic, as evidence, as legitimate argumentation, as method, as theory. These differences present a number of problems for compositionists, who must translate ideas from one to another of these discourses and into the theoretical and pragmatic languages of composition. Hybrid research presents special difficulties, since it is not clear what criteria of validation apply.

In order to screen Theory for application, teachers or their surrogates (translators) must indwell a particular research context that establishes the terms of validation for its own theoretical constructs. This is the case whether one is borrowing ideas from other fields or applying composition theory itself, which internalizes the research languages of various fields. The principle is not to select Theory *because* it is valid in its own terms, but *in view of* those terms and the claims they support, so that application is critical rather than naive. The horizon for pragmatic decisions includes not simply method in the original field, but the placement of Theory in the full context of disciplinary issues, arguments, and beliefs as they play out within a sociohistorical frame. Judgments must also take account of other evaluations and applications; some seminal ideas whose validity is contested or disallowed within their home discipline gain it through recontextualization, as in the case of Freudian psychoanalysis.

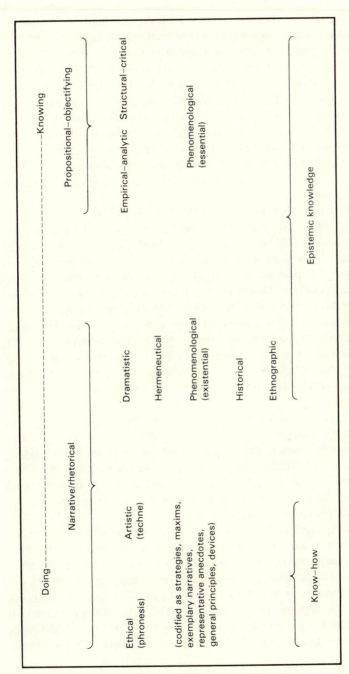

Figure 4. Schema for types of knowledge applied in composition.

One value, however, in checking validity of Theory first within its original context is to avoid inappropriately applying normative standards from one field or method to the product of another, failing to recognize or respect the kind of claim being made. In particular, natural science cannot set the standards for "knowledge" in all branches of study, for example in aesthetics, ethics, or theology. I have made the point that knowledge brought to bear in composition practice may not even be Theory in the strict sense of epistemic knowledge; teachers may draw on any source of insight including various nonverbal arts and skills. (Indeed, performances and teaching styles in such fields as music, acting, and sports are a fertile source of ideas for teaching practice.)

Obviously no practitioner, indeed no individual, is in a position to check personally the evidence and context of argumentation for most Theory that he encounters. Normally it is the person who "notices" Theory as relevant for practice who first examines its validity in the primary context and presents the broader case for its use in composition. Unfortunately, this is not a task that can be done once and for all. Attitudes toward Theory and evaluation in the original and extended contexts change constantly as Theory is interpreted, reinterpreted, appropriated, criticized, modified, rediscovered, and resituated. For these reasons, compositionists must not only check initially, but continue to refer to and make salient the changing contexts of Theory that they have borrowed or wish to apply to practice.

Composition has often failed to do this checking adequately in its enthusiastic and eclectic borrowing of Theory from other fields, and practitioners sometimes pick up composition theory itself in a faddish, uncritical way. While urging remedies for this problem, one must also acknowledge and accept the degree to which we are dependent on authority for guaranteeing the validation of Theory according to appropriate disciplinary standards.

Polanyi, in his description of the "conviviality" of science, demonstrates how much science depends on a consensus that jointly authorizes its achievements. His account suggests a model for practitioners to act as a community in analogous ways to support the activities of the three modes of application. According to Polanyi, the consensus of scientific opinion "is a joint appraisal of an intellectual domain, of which each consenting participant can properly understand and judge only a very small fraction." He explains how it works: "Each scientist watches over an area comprising his own field and some adjoining strips of territory, over which neighboring specialists can also form reliable first-hand judgments." There is a constant adjusting of standards across the network thus created, "and the system is amply supplemented also by somewhat less certain judgments made by scientists directly on professionally more distant achievements of exceptional merit. Yet its operation continues to be based essentially on the 'transitiveness' of neighboring appraisals—much as a marching column is kept in step by each man's keeping in step with those next to him" (*Personal Knowledge*, p. 217).

We are, as a community of practitioners, dependent on this community of science that Polanyi describes, and our dependence amounts to a personal commitment of confidence in that social system. At the same time, Polanyi points out, "[e]very acceptance of authority is qualified by some measure of reaction to it or even against it" (p. 208). We accept, but critically; we check, if not personally, as a community. In selecting or evaluating knowledge for possible application, we rely not only on the consensus of science (including our own composition theorists), but on the careful watchkeeping of translators and other practitioners to alert us to its type, methodological standards, and status within a disciplinary context as well as its role in applications other than our own. A good example of both our dependence and the increasing critical consciousness of the composition community is the application of the work of Thomas Kuhn to understanding the evolution of composition theory and teaching. Originally, these discussions were innocent of the context for his work within the philosophy of science and its reception and application in a wider community. Now our own applications are becoming more informed; one lesson is that there is normally a time lag between noticing Theory (and beginning to use it) and the work of analysis and judgment that supports richer appropriation.

There is a second type of screening that must in large part be repeated by every individual for every case, because it is the core of phronesis. This is the crucial testing of applicability to the case at hand. While I am separating for purposes of discussion the selective from the experimental phase, in practice the two merge because one first anticipates (in thought experiments and hunches) the applicability of Theory and then tests or verifies that guess experientially. However, testing here is not simply trying out, using Theory as rule, formula, predictor, or prescription. Experiment is itself not only judgmental but also inventive. In the process of phronetic testing, teachers in a sense *make* Theory appropriate, rather than simply finding it so.

Focusing then on the selective phase, let us consider some criteria for phronetic screening. Three principles that come to mind are *relevance, truth,* and *fitness.*

Clearly, we make a judgment that a particular concept or conceptual set is relevant to the case at hand. (I speak as if the case at hand were concrete; however, in the screening phase it is often an amalgam of cases remembered or anticipated, cases from which the teacher has abstracted a prototypical situation or problem.) It is hard to explain relevance; it is really an undefined primitive. To see Theory as relevant to a situation is essentially to make intuitive connections among phenomena and ideas. Such connections are potentially infinite in a contextualist universe, but not all are equally available, already foregrounded and made explicit within an intellectual or practical context. In this sense relevance is not intrinsic to the situation or relation (at least not usefully), but is created by the interpreter for current purposes. Hence application is not restricted to Theory developed *for* particular purposes (i.e., to explain this particular situation), since the teacher can apply ideas from any context that she has found or made relevant.

It is considered bold these days to propose truth as a criterion for anything, including application. Yet I believe that teachers look to Theory for truth, if we understand the meaning of truth as the power to give insight into phenomena. Without getting into philosophical complexities about truth, let us recognize a distinction (argued by Ricoeur in relation to religious language) between truth as *adequation* and truth as *manifestation.*[18] Adequation provides a negative criterion for phronesis, in the sense that a teacher might reject Theory because it did not correspond to her own experience or her understanding of that experience. Teachers must ultimately be free to make such a judgment. However, the concept of truth as manifestation suggests that their judgments will be too limited if they conceive of Theory as describing (or predicting) only what they have already experienced. As Ricoeur explains it, to judge by the criterion of manifested truth is to ask what possible ways of understanding, acting, or being are opened up by a text (here, by Theory taken as text). This criterion is similar to that which we might apply in attributing "truth" to a work of art.

Following the logician Gottlob Frege's distinction between sense and reference, Ricoeur defines truth as reference to a world: "The reference is the truth value of the proposition, its claim to reach reality" ("Philosophy," p. 78). Truth in this sense is opposed to difference, which determines the value of words in a semiotic system taken independent of world. For religious language, as for literary texts, Ricoeur describes a second-order reference, which does not refer directly to a real world but discloses new ways of being in possible worlds. "The moment of understanding responds dialectically to being in a situation, as the projection of our ownmost possibilities in those situations where we find ourselves. . . . [W]hat is to be interpreted in a text is a proposed world, a world that I might inhabit and wherein I might project my ownmost possibilities" (p. 80).

What I am suggesting, then, is that teachers judge the truth of Theory with regard to cases at hand not merely in terms of adequation to past experience, but in terms of its capacity to redescribe that experience and point to new ways of being and doing. Theory taken this way embodies the "reality of the possible." It is neither an adequate description of what has passed nor a prediction of what will happen, but a manifestation of what might happen if . . .

To argue that manifestation is one criterion of truth is not to exclude the criterion of adequation, the ability of Theory to explain and account for experience comprehensively and satisfyingly. Teachers properly test the adequacy of Theory to account for their own experiences and those of other practitioners. The mode of informal reasoning they use is a logic of good reasons or common sense for which Walter Fisher has proposed the term "narrative paradigm."[19] Fisher argues persuasively for narration as a general theory of symbolic action, intended to account for and reconcile two traditional strands in the history of rhetoric: the argumentative, persuasive theme and the literary, aesthetic theme" ("Narration," p. 2). Here I am using his notion merely to point to a type of reflection whereby teachers engage Theory. Regardless of the general status of the narrative paradigm, it is an appropriate mode of evaluation for teachers to use because, from the practical perspective, Theory makes a claim about reality *as humanly experienced.* (It is this fact that gives priority within composition praxis to dramatistic and hermeneutical knowledge.)

Here is Fisher's characterization of the narrative paradigm in terms of a set of premises:

(1) humans are essentially storytellers;
(2) the paradigmatic mode of human decision-making and communi-
     cation is "good reasons" which vary in form among communica-
     tions situations, genres, and media;
(3) the production and practice of good reasons is ruled by matters of
     history, biography, culture, and character. . . .
(4) rationality is determined by the nature of persons as narrative
     beings—their inherent awareness of *narrative probability*, what
     constitutes a coherent story, and their constant habit of testing
     narrative fidelity, whether the stories they experience ring true
     with the stories they know to be true in their lives. . . .
(5) the world is a set of stories which must be chosen among to live
     the good life in a process of continual recreation. ("Narration,"
     pp. 7–8)

From this perspective we might say that teachers test the stories
provided by Theory against their own stories, guided by a sense of
narrative probability and fidelity, so as to judge the adequacy of
Theory to describe and explain experience. However, narrative judgments themselves are more complex than simple decisions about adequation. In the first place, they are two-way: they permit teachers to
judge not only Theory but their own hypotheses on the same grounds.
Second, narratives invoke practical-moral criteria regarding good or
right stories and what might or should come true in practical worlds;
they are not restricted to historical fact. Thus Fisher would claim that
the narrative paradigm has bearing not only on the truths of adequation but those of manifestation.

The last criterion I propose for phronetic screening is contextual appropriateness or situational fit. I will discuss this criterion
under the heading of *kairos*, a principle of Greek rhetoric reappro-
priated for composition by James Kinneavy, who traces it to Gorgias
and Plato.[20]

In Greek thought time had two aspects, *chronos* and *kairos*, but
chronos has dominated the Western tradition to the neglect of its
complement. According to John E. Smith, chronos refers to "the
uniform time of the cosmic system . . . time as measure, the *quantity*
of duration, the length of periodicity, the age of an object or artifact
and the rate of acceleration of bodies whether on the surface of the
earth or in the firmament beyond." Kairos points to *qualitative* rather
than quantitative time: "to the special position an event or action
occupies in a series, to a season when something appropriately

happens that cannot happen just at 'any time,' but only at *that* time, to a time that marks an opportunity which may not recur."[21]

In addition to "right time," a meaning that makes kairos a historical and situational concept, kairos also means "right measure" or proportion. In this dual sense of situational fitness kairos was applied in Greek rhetoric to human action, but Smith points out that kairos has an ontological dimension as well. He argues against attributing kairos to human affairs and chronos to the cosmos: instead, "both aspects of time are ingredient in the nature of things and both have practical import" (p. 5). Human choices reflect human purposes and understandings responsive to the relationship of chronos and kairos in the structure of "the order of happening," a structure of nature and culture that presents situational opportunities for right action.

The idea of kairos as explicated by Smith and Kinneavy resembles the notion of bifurcation points put forth by Ilya Prigogine, who takes a similar view of time.[22] Prigogine locates the possibility of qualitative novelty and thus human freedom and history in the bifurcation points characteristic of open systems. From our perspective, application is kairotic in two senses: situations arise that call for human choice (right time); and teachers acting in response to this situation use kairos as a criterion of choice. Kinneavy draws on Paul Tillich's analysis of kairos as distinct from *logos* in a way that brings out the relevance of kairos to application.[23] According to Kinneavy, Tillich sees logos thinking as "characterized by an emphasis on timelessness, on form, on law, on stasis, on method"; while he stresses kairos because "it brings theory into practice, it asserts the continuing necessity of free decision, it insists on the value and norm aspects of ideas, it champions a vital and concerned interest in knowledge because knowledge always is relevant to the situational context" ("*Kairos*," p. 90). Smith further points out that kairos implies problem solving in response to particular situations of conflict and tension.

Judging the fitness of Theory to organize thinking or action in practical cases divides conveniently into three questions: (1) the fitness of method (and thus conclusions) of inquiry to the object studied; (2) the fitness of concepts or abstractions to the situation (time, place, purpose, etc.); and (3) the fitness of knowledge to the nature and state of the individual who will use it.

Fitness of method to the object studied is a crucial issue for teachers, even though the choice of method is actually a problem within Theory itself, as a practice of inquiry. There are very complex problems involved, first, in theorists' making conceptual judgments regarding the nature of the object studied and the relation of method to that object; and second, in teachers' making practical choices in light of a full understanding of the former decision. Teachers are prejudiced toward understanding human beings as Subjects or signs, since they are concerned with human action and discourse, and deal with concrete individuals who understand and present themselves as Subjects. Does this mean that teachers should reject a method of inquiry that treats teachers as objects either by not letting them speak (meaningfully, within the inquiry itself); or by treating their discourse as something other than discourse, as unself-conscious revelation (e.g., as clue to cognitive processes); or by quantifying them?

The answer to this question cannot be simple—for example, that we need to reject for composition praxis all inquiry based on non-dramatistic or nonhermeneutical methods. Instead, it seems that we must first make as precise and explicit as possible the assumptions of a particular inquiry regarding its object of study, that is, the mode in which the inquirer conceives the object, or perhaps the aspect of the object being studied (i.e., hormones rather than moods). That has not been done, and many arguments in composition—for example, debates about protocol methods—rest on misconceptions of particular research on this score. Second, the teacher must make a principled decision regarding the use of Theory that depends on a clear understanding of the relation between the way Theory treats an object of study, the claim Theory makes in these terms, and the way a practitioner or discourser conceives the same "object."

The bias of the teacher is always toward understanding and/or controlling or shaping life *as* experience. However, objectifying methods can be enormously useful to teachers in providing concepts that are not based directly on personal experience to deal with objective realities that are either not psychologically real, not consciously available, or not under the control and scope of the individual's will. (By "objective" realities I mean that they are understood by a distanced and discursive, critical consciousness; that they are intersubjectively confirmed; and/or that they represent the situatedness by which an individual is subject to the facticity of a world.) For example, discrepancies between what I believe about my composing or teaching acts and what an observer reports of them may be highly valuable to me in comprehending my experience and deciding on future action. For this reason teachers must judge case by case the ways whereby methods in composition representing countermethods to their dramatistic bias can be useful to them in practical decisions and actions.

Just as teachers cannot judge Theory simplistically with respect to method, they cannot judge Theory as appropriate to context solely on the basis of what they already know about prior or current situations and purposes, because of the potential power of Theory to manifest novel and unanticipated meanings within future situations. That is why we will say that praxis disciplines but cannot dominate Theory. Theory has its own purposes and situations; indeed, it is a practice in its own right.

However, this is not to deny that Theory often responds, and should respond, to practical needs. One way that studying Theory might help teachers is to enable them to define more clearly to theorists what needs to be conceptualized, and in what ways appropriate to practice. For example, teachers might have said to theorists much earlier that they needed a conception of reading and interpretation appropriate to the activity of reading student texts, drafts in process, as distinct from theories of literary criticism (which takes a different object and, currently, omits writers from the transaction) and cognitive processing (which has focused largely on sentences and treated reading as information processing rather than as experience or purposeful action).

Similarly, teachers might now ask for an "ecological grammar" appropriate for consciously thinking and talking about writers' linguistic and stylistic choices. This idea is modeled on the development of an "ecological physics" by psychologists whose aim is to describe the environment as biologically significant, with objects or events defined in terms of the value or meaning they have for an animal or species. Different aspects of the environment (space, surfaces and layout, detached objects, other people) "afford" for particular animals such possibilities as burning, eating, swimming, carrying, or conversing. "Affordances constitute a partitioning of an environment with an organism in mind instead of, say, the more neutral partitioning of the environment of energy flux into observer-independent properties by classical physics."[24]

We may think of long-term knowledge as an internal environment that affords cognition. In the case of composing, people draw on metalinguistic and metacognitive knowledge to afford choices of many kinds including syntactic ones. At least part of this knowledge is consciously available in the sense that people can articulate it retrospectively or simultaneously with choice, as in protocols. Thus we might ask theorists to formulate grammatical descriptions as a meta-language designed to meet the needs of composers as they make stylistic choices at the point of utterance and in editing; or to facilitate discussion and commentary on surface features of text between writers and readers, teachers and learners. Such descriptions would supplement rather than replace descriptions of language competence like that of Chomsky which are not designed to account for how people think and talk *about* language.

Finally, teachers must judge whether Theory suits the person who will use it. This decision is tricky because it involves the double hermeneutic—the fact that students are not merely the objects of Theory (through the teachers' praxis) but the Subjects to whom Theory may be offered. On the one hand, Theory may sometimes be the silent force hidden from students that guides a teacher's own behavior—making assignments, responding to a text, choosing what to say and not say. But teachers do not simply enact Theory, they also offer it to students directly as text, comment, or tool, so that students may appropriate it to organize their discourse practices and learning processes. When teachers thus focalize what is tacit in discourse and enter into discussions of it in the metalanguage of Theory, they are making a judgment for and on behalf of another Subject. They are deciding what that person should know and when. The decision has a developmental context, because the issue is not only whether particular knowledge is appropriate to a discourse situation or process (for example, selecting the right moment in composing to offer information about genre constraints or state a punctuation convention), but whether it fits the developmental state of the learner.

It seems to me inevitable that a teacher should introduce Theory, in the sense of formal, focalized knowledge about discourse, to students; there is no way to avoid it other than utter silence. The problem we need to debate is not whether to do so, but how to do so according to the principles of kairos: specifically, what knowledge is appropriate at given moments of development and process; how to introduce it most productively; how to engage students in a dialogue about it rather than impose it as rule; how, once knowledge becomes formal and focal, it can become tacit in use again.

Experimentation

Experimentation refers to teachers' praxis in its aspect as a process of validating, or revalidating, Theory. All that has just been said regarding the selective phases holds for experimentation, since the choices made on the level of thought experiment and anticipation in these phases are carried out or made again during concrete activity and experience in the classroom. Like the other phases, experimentation is simultaneously and alternately creative and critical, appropriation and judgment. Teachers do not simply choose a method of teaching based on a theory and then carry it out mechanically; they design approaches and improvise within them, in the process constantly reformulating as well as evaluating Theory (and their own theories—their own stories making sense of what happens) in terms of their new experiences. The whole process is, in the ideal, collaborative and dialogic both within the classroom and through participation in the community of practitioners.

One way of conceiving the process of experimentation is as reading researchers in education (influenced by literary theory) have recently begun talking about text comprehension—in terms of intertextuality.[25] In this view Theory is in a given case not a cognitive schema to be instantiated, but a text to be mapped onto experience. Such mapping is inherently intertextual, in two senses. In the first place, the theory that we are calling a text is heterogeneous and multiplistic even within itself, its parts communicating intertextually with one another in partially conflictual and dialectical ways. It cannot be reduced to a single, total structure or interpretation. In the second place, the text of Theory is open and contingent; both comprehension and application of it depend on cross-referencing and constructing new links between it and other texts within situations, a process of creating a new "code" or hypothesis specific to a particular context. Rand Spiro, from whom this account is drawn, speaks of intertextuality as a general phenomenon of content area comprehension in "ill-structured domains" such as medical cases, literary works, and historical events. The classroom is such an ill-structured domain, and the comprehension of Theory as text in this domain is inseparable (as Gadamer has told us) from the moment of application, or phronesis.

Phronesis has a habitual aspect, in that for Aristotle phronesis was an intellectual virtue formed as a habit of wisdom acquired through experience. To be a phronimos is to be able to make wise decisions incorporating both general principles and strategies for adapting them to situations. The process of experimentation that builds such wisdom is repetitive and social, so that teachers do not carry out single confirming or disconfirming experiments isolated from one another or from other classrooms. Rather they engage

Theory dialectically in company with other teachers and with students. In this process of dialectic engagement teachers imagine, try out, observe, adapt and refine, test and retest ideas, not only as individuals but as members of different communities that share practical purposes and conversations about them. There is no reason to believe that what has worked once in one situation will work in the same way, or at all, in the next. Experimentation has a historical rather than a determinate function in preparing the way for making decisions in new circumstances.

Similarly, Kenneth Gergen has pointed out that research in psychology does not establish reliable relationships between environmental factors and human responses such that it would be possible to predict individual development.[26] He describes the confluence of factors affecting development as a "cross-time emergent" dependent on specific sociohistorical conditions. For example, psychologists have shown that age cohorts are so different that generalizations made from study of one generation do not hold for the next. He therefore argues for an "aleatory change template" to understand developmental sequences. Theory in an aleatory science offers historically sensitive explanations of the past that permit only limited predictions of human behavior (something like weather forecasting), limited both in accuracy and in scope of application. It provides not prescriptions for practice but a framework for thinking about it, in terms of meaning, values, and a multidimensional, stochastic (probabilistic) causality.

Striking a New Balance

In chapter 2 I proposed an abstract conception of the activities of composition as a dialectic between reflection and experience occurring within and across three regions of responsibility: (1) organized inquiry (Theory), (2) teaching, and (3) personal literacy. (See Figure 1, p. 73.) My discussion of dialogic engagement in the previous section attempted to make the relation between organized inquiry and teaching more concrete, bracketing for the moment the perspective of the student (and the teacher as developing and practicing personal literacy). Although I will continue this bracketing, we can pause to imagine the full dialectic as a grid specifying the possibilities of dialogic engagement for all three regions of responsibility:

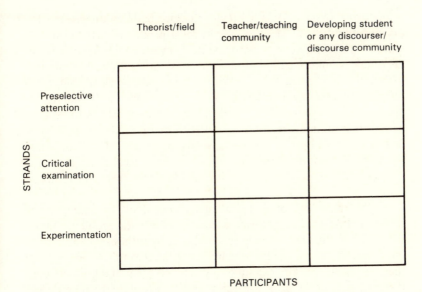

Figure 5. Theory-praxis grid: dialogic engagement across the regions of responsibility.

Like the original figure, this grid attempts to represent composition as a field organized by the special character of the theory-praxis relation. Phronesis together with the universality of reflection as a human potential creates for composition a structure that is not primarily hierarchical, but parallel and interactive. In each region, theory constructs in different ways the relationships between reflection and experience, the individual and the community; these regions are multiply linked and interdependent by virtue of their relations of dialectic and dialogue.

For some disciplines such as mathematics, praxis is not part of their self-understanding *as* disciplines. This is not the case for composition, whose distinctiveness lies in the experimental relationship it establishes between the general principles of inquiry posited and systematically pursued in science and philosophy, and the normative practice of these principles in ordinary discourse and everyday life. The role of Theory and personal theory in a teacher's life is therefore a crucial question for composition's very definition as a discipline.

The immediate purpose of setting forth a new hypothesis about the relationship between theory and praxis was to generate a new set of questions that, unlike the previous choice between oppressive theory and unreflective practice, would set a productive agenda for research. The framework constructed here, in which application is understood as contextually variable, purposeful, and free but situated within dialogue, poses this general challenge: to empirically and theoretically characterize application as a process. We have come to see application as a process in the same profound sense that composing is, or that textual interpretation is, and with many similar or analogous features. As such, it is worthy of study by means of the tools and methods already developed for these other processes, as part of a project to develop a theory of praxis within a metatheory of composition.

The framework of dialogic engagement does, by changing the terms of the question, generate a new set of specific problems, about which my outline here merely speculates or hypothesizes. These ideas are useless if not pursued in research projects that follow out and test their implications. For example, my scheme for judging fitness calls for us to redescribe prior research in order to explain the relationship it inscribes between method and object, and to evaluate the appropriateness of that relationship for the goals of the research and for varying circumstances of practice. Such redescriptions would give us a better theoretical basis for arguing certain issues such as the status of the subject in empirical studies of composing or teaching. Besides study, this framework, if accepted, would demand a reorganization of teacher education from the current alternatives (a banking style or an atheoretical approach) to problem-posing pedagogy. Also, it suggests the need to refine our emerging conception of teacher research to account more concretely for the role of formal Theory in shaping teachers' own reflections and experiments. These are only a few examples of the consequences for research and praxis of adopting the framework of dialogic engagement.

The broader goal of this analysis was to strike a new balance between theory and praxis, acknowledging the purposes and values of both theorists constructing a discipline and teachers enacting a practice. The beginning of an answer lies in rethinking what we mean by "discipline" as a verb. In light of the unforeseen journey taken in this chapter, which began long ago as an attempt to justify Theory to practitioners, I would now argue that Theory and praxis mutually discipline each other and that each has its own sphere of action not to be dominated by the other.

I have tried to demonstrate how praxis disciplines Theory, because for a theorist that is a less obvious truth, and because I came to see that it was necessary to attack the naive logocentrism that gave Theory hegemony over praxis. Praxis disciplines Theory by demonstrating its limits, destroying its absolutist pretensions to be the sole foundation and ultimate reality on which practice depends. While the truths of Theory do surpass the known, actual, historical, and transitory in the situations that composition embraces, the meanings of Theory (like those of the language system) are only virtual. To have force in a world, they must realize themselves in event, depending on the interpretation and subject to the authority of teachers and other players in those events. In turn, just as word use changes the semiotic system, practical experimentation does not simply revalidate Theory but critiques and changes it.

We must not forget that Theory itself is a praxis. As such it has intrinsic goals, purposes, developmental principles, scope, and so forth, that praxis cannot dictate. As in the relationship between science and technology, Theory in composition cannot be restricted to what (teaching) praxis already knows it wants, although it may respond to those needs, because it has an intrinsic function to develop new meanings according to criteria of manifest truth as well as adequation. On the other hand, praxis has a right to ask of Theory Dewey's question, which forms a "first-rate test of any philosophy which is offered us: Does it end in conclusions which, when they are referred back to ordinary life-experiences and their predicaments, render them more significant, more luminous to us, and make our dealings with them more fruitful? Or does it terminate in rendering the things of ordinary experience more opaque than they were before, and in depriving them of having in 'reality' even the significance they had previously seemed to have?" (*EN*, pp. 9–10).

If Theory cannot tell teachers what to do, what good is it to them? Why is not the teacher's own reflection sufficient, especially when placed within a collaborative context, a community in which observations and ideas are shared and tested against one another? (This is the well-meaning but ultimately anti-intellectual philosophy that governs too many of our best efforts to educate and develop the reflective powers of classroom teachers.)

In general, the answer is the same reason why human culture needs science, philosophy, art, and other systems for extending the resources of individuals and communities. Each of us is finite, and so are our local communities, the knowledge of those people with whom we have direct dialogic contact. Cultural systems of knowledge, being written and systematic, cumulative (though not static), and rigorous, represent the continual potential for infusing new energy into local and individual knowledge bases. Restricted to a small group of inter-acting partners in dialogues, we would effectively be closed systems, ultimately degenerating to gossip. In contact with the intellectual context, we become open systems with greater resources to enhance our capacity for novelty, invention, interconnection.

Kenneth Gergen, a social psychologist, gives some more specific answers in developing a view of Theory for the social sciences that is peculiarly appropriate for composition as praxis ("Stability," pp. 135–40). He cuts the connection that is normally made between two criteria for a good theory: comprehensive understanding (the degree to which it fully and satisfyingly explains phenomena) and prediction (its ability to make predictions of new phenomena based on the theoretical superstructure). Gergen lists four values of Theory understood as providing comprehensive understanding independent of its predictive validity. First, theoretical understanding allows us to *organize experience* in terms of categories and patterns that guide response. Second, it provides a *sense of coherence* by embedding events or objects within analytic frameworks, which Gergen sees as giving a sense of control over phenomena and reducing their possible danger. Third, Theory has a *sensitizing role*. "Although it [social theory] may seldom serve as a base for precise prediction, theory may provide an indication of what is possible in social life, what has occurred in the past, and possible reasons for its occurrence" (p. 137). Finally, Theory unsettles and *decomposes common understandings*. By constantly challenging per-sonal and social knowledge systems, theories make us aware of the relativity and finitude of concepts. In this sense they serve, as I sug-gested earlier, as critical moments both for other theories and for our own reflective understanding or unreflective acceptance of conceptual frameworks.

For Theory to function in all these ways within the praxis of composition teachers, those teachers must respect the possibility that Theory can get at truth, despite the finitude and historical situatedness of science itself. To Polanyi science (Theory) represents the "objective" and its call upon ourselves, in these senses: "(*a*) A theory is something other than myself. . . . (*b*) A theory, moreover, cannot be led astray by my personal illusions. . . . (*c*) Since the formal affirmations of a the-ory are unaffected by the state of the person accepting it, theories may be constructed without regard to one's normal approach to experience" (*Personal Knowledge*, p. 4). We accept a theory, Polanyi says, "in the hope of making contact with reality; so that, being really true, our theory may yet show forth its truth through future centuries in ways undreamed of by its authors" (p. 5). In this sense, Theory, disciplined by our own freedom to reflect and to experience, is for composition praxis an enabling fiction, and science and art are not, after all, so far apart.

Notes

1. Hans-Georg Gadamer, letter of June 1, 1982, in Richard J. Bernstein, *Beyond Objectivism and Relativism: Science, Hermeneutics, and Praxis* (Philadelphia: Univ. of Pennsylvania Press, 1983), pp. 261–65.

2. Aristotle, book 6, *Nichomachean Ethics*, in *Introduction to Aristotle*, ed. Richard McKeon (New York: Random House, 1947).

3. See for example Richard E. Young, "Paradigms and Problems: Needed Research in Rhetorical Invention," in *Research on Composing: Points of Departure*, ed. Charles R. Cooper and Lee Odell (Urbana, IL: NCTE, 1978), pp. 29–47; and calls for theory by John Warnock, "Who's Afraid of Theory?" *CCC* 27 (1976), 16–20, and Nancy I. Sommers, "The Need for Theory in Composition Research," *CCC* 30 (1979), 46–49.

4. Cf. the antitheory debate in literary studies, *Against Theory: Literary Studies and the New Pragmatism*, ed. W. J. T. Mitchell (Chicago: Univ. of Chicago Press, 1985).

5. See Robert Price, "Some Antistrophes to the Rhetoric," *Philosophy and Rhetoric* 1 (1968), 145–64, for an explanation of the antistrophic arts, including rhetoric.

6. John Dewey, *Experience & Nature*, 2nd ed. (1929: rpt. La Salle, IL: Open Court, 1971), p. 5. Cited hereafter as *EN*.

7. John Dewey, *How We Think: A Restatement of the Relation of Reflective Thinking to the Educative Process* (1933; rpt. Chicago: Regnery, 1971), p. 76. Cited hereafter as *HWT*.

8. Paulo Freire, *Pedagogy of the Oppressed*, tr. Myra Bergman Ramos (New York: Continuum, 1982), p. 75, n. 2.

9. Hans-George Gadamer, *Truth and Method* (New York: Seabury, 1975), pp. 274–305 (cited hereafter as *TM*); "The Problem of Historical Consciousness," in *Interpretive Social Science: A Reader*, ed. Paul Rabinow and William M. Sullivan (Berkeley: Univ. of California Press, 1979), pp. 103–60. For discussions, see Bernstein, *Beyond Objectivism*, part 3, "From Hermeneutics to Praxis"; David Couzens Hoy, *The Critical Circle: Literature and History in Contemporary Hermeneutics* (Berkeley: Univ. of California Press, 1978), pp. 41–72 and passim; and Joel C. Weinsheimer, *Gadamer's Hermeneutics: A Reading of Truth and Method* (New Haven: Yale Univ. Press, 1985), pp. 184–99.

10. Hans-Georg Gadamer, "Welt ohne Geschichte," in *Truth and Historicity*, ed. Hans-Georg Gadamer (The Hague: Nijhoff, 1972), p. 8, quoted in Weinsheimer, pp. 188–89, n. 52.

11. H. S. Broudy, "Types of Knowledge and Purposes of Education," in *Schooling and the Acquisition of Knowledge*, ed. Richard C. Anderson, Rand J. Spiro, and William E. Montague (Hillsdale, NJ: Erlbaum, 1977), pp. 12–15.

12. Stephen C. Pepper, *World Hypotheses: A Study in Evidence* (Berkeley: Univ. of California Press, 1942), pp. 232–79. For an example of a textural analysis see James J. Jenkins, "Remember That Old Theory of Memory? Well, Forget It!" in *Perceiving, Acting, and Knowing: Toward an Ecological Psychology*, ed. Robert Shaw and John Bransford (Hillsdale, NJ: Erlbaum, 1977), pp. 413–29.

13. Jenkins, "Remember"; John D. Bransford et al., "Toward Unexplaining Memory," in Shaw and Bransford, *Perceiving, Acting, and Knowing*, pp. 431–66. See also James A. Anderson, "Neural Models with Implications," in *Basic Processes in Reading: Perception and Comprehension*, ed. David Laberge and S. Jay Samuels (Hillsdale, NJ: Erlbaum, 1977), pp. 27–90, on the brain as a radio.

14. Bransford et al., "Toward," p. 433. See J. J. Gibson, *The Senses Considered as Perceptual Systems* (Boston: Houghton-Mifflin, 1966).

15. Michael Polanyi, *Personal Knowledge: Towards a Post-Critical Philosophy* (Chicago: Univ. of Chicago Press, 1962), pp. 142–45, 395–96, and passim.

16. Paul Ricoeur, *Interpretation Theory: Discourse and the Surplus of Meaning* (Fort Worth, TX: Texas Christian Univ. Press, 1976), pp. 71–88.

17. Among the sources that influenced this schematic are Gerald Radnitzky, *Continental Schools of Metascience*, vol. 2 of *Contemporary Schools of Metascience* (Göteborg, Sweden: Akademiförlaget, 1968); and the works of Aristotle, Kenneth Burke, and Paul Ricoeur.

18. Paul Ricoeur, "Philosophy and Religious Language," *Journal of Religion* 54 (1974), 72.

19. Walter R. Fisher, "Narration as a Human Communication Paradigm: The Case of Public Moral Argument," *Communication Monographs* 51 (1984), 1–22. See also *Human Communication as Narration: Toward a Philosophy of Reason, Value, and Action* (Columbia: Univ. of South Carolina Press, 1987).

20. James L. Kinneavy, "*Kairos*: A Neglected Concept in Classical Rhetoric," in *Rhetoric and Praxis: The Contribution of Classical Rhetoric to Practical Reasoning*, ed. Jean Dietz Moss (Washington, D.C.: Catholic Univ. of America Press, 1986), pp. 79–105.

21. John E. Smith, "Time and Qualitative Time," *Review of Metaphysics* 40 (1986), 4.

22. Ilya Prigogine and Isabelle Stengers, *Order Out of Chaos: Man's New Dialogue with Nature* (Boulder: Shambhala, 1984).

23. Paul Tillich, "Kairos and Logos," in *The Interpretation of History*, tr. N. A. Rasetzki and Elsa Talmey (New York: Scribner's, 1936), cited in Kinneavy, pp. 89–90.

24. William M. Mace, "James J. Gibson's Strategy for Perceiving: Ask Not What's Inside Your Head, but What Your Head's Inside of," in Shaw and Bransford, *Perceiving, Acting, and Knowing*, p. 59. See also James J. Gibson, "The Theory of Affordances," ibid., pp. 67–82.

25. "Expanding Our Notions of Discourse Processing: Intertextuality as a Search for Multiple Connections," Symposium at the National Reading Conference, Austin, Texas, December 1986. The session was chaired by Robert J. Tierney, with Rand J. Spiro presenting a synthesis and commentary on the papers presented.

26. Kenneth J. Gergen, "Stability, Change, and Chance in Understanding Human Development," in *Life-Span Developmental Psychology: Dialectical Perspectives on Experimental Research*, ed. Nancy Datan and Hayne W. Reese (New York: Academic Press, 1977), pp. 135–58.

Works Cited

Adler, Mortimer, and Charles Van Doren. *How to Read a Book*. Rev. ed. New York: Simon and Schuster, 1972.

Anderson, James A. "Neural Models with Cognitive Implications." In *Basic Processes in Reading: Perception and Comprehension*, ed. David Laberge and S. Jay Samuels. Hillsdale, NJ: Erlbaum, 1977, pp. 27–90.

Anderson, Myrdene. "Synthetic Potential within, beyond, and through Semiotics." In *Semiotics*, ed. John Deeley. Lanham, NY: University Press of America, 1985, pp. 363–72.

Anderson, Myrdene, et al. "A Semiotic Perspective on the Sciences: Steps toward a New Paradigm." *Semiotics* 52 (1984), 7–47.

Aristotle. *Nichomachean Ethics*. In *Introduction to Aristotle*, ed. Richard McKeon. New York: Random House, 1947.

Arnold, N. Scott. "Research Methods and the Evaluation of Hypotheses: A Reply to Kinney." *Rhetoric Society Quarterly* 10 (1980), 149–55.

Augustine, Dorothy, and W. Ross Winterowd. "Intention and Response: Speech Acts and the Sources of Composition." In *Convergences: Transactions in Reading and Writing*, ed. Bruce T. Petersen. Urbana, IL: NCTE, 1986, pp. 127–48.

Austin, J. L. *How to Do Things with Words*. Cambridge, MA: Harvard Univ. Press, 1962.

Bakhtin, M. M. *The Dialogic Imagination: Four Essays*. Tr. Caryl Emerson and Michael Holquist. Ed. Michael Holquist. Austin: Univ. of Texas Press, 1981.

Bateson, Gregory. *Steps toward an Ecology of Mind*. New York: Ballantine, 1972.

Beach, Richard. "Notes from Kalamazoo." *CE* 35 (1974), 838–41.

Beaugrande, Robert de. *Text, Discourse, and Process: Toward a Multidisciplinary Science of Texts*. Vol. 4 of *Advances in Discourse Processes*, ed. Roy D. Freedle. Norwood, NJ: Ablex, 1980.

Berger, Peter L., and Thomas Luckmann. *The Social Construction of Reality: A Treatise in the Sociology of Knowledge*. Garden City, NY: Doubleday, 1969.

Berlin, James. *Writing Instruction on Nineteenth-Century American Colleges*. Carbondale, IL: Southern Illinois Univ. Press, 1984.

Bernstein, Richard J. *Beyond Objectivism and Relativism: Science, Hermeneutics, and Praxis.* Philadelphia: Univ. of Pennsylvania Press, 1983.

Bissex, Glenda L. "The Child as Teacher." In *Awakening to Literacy: The University of Victoria Symposium on Children's Response to a Literate Environment: Literacy before Schooling,* ed. Hillel Goelman, Antoinette A. Oberg, and Frank Smith. Exeter, NH: Heinemann, 1984, pp. 87–101.

———. *GYNS at WRK: A Child Learns to Write and Read.* Cambridge, MA: Harvard Univ. Press, 1980.

Bizzell, Patricia. "On the Possibility of a Unified Theory of Composition and Literature." *Rhetoric Review* 4 (1986), 174–80.

Bleich, David. *Subjective Criticism.* Baltimore: Johns Hopkins Univ. Press, 1978.

Bleicher, Josef. *Contemporary Hermeneutics: Hermeneutics as Method, Philosophy and Critique.* London: Routledge, 1980.

———. *The Hermeneutic Imagination: Outline of a Positive Critique of Scientism and Sociology.* London: Routledge, 1982.

Blom, Thomas E. Reply to Maxine Hairston, *CCC* 35 (1984), 489–93.

Bohm, David. "Science as Perception-Communication." In *The Structure of Scientific Theories,* ed. F. Suppe. Urbana, IL: Univ. of Illinois Press, 1974.

———. *Wholeness and the Implicate Order.* London: Routledge, 1980.

Booth, Wayne. *Modern Dogma and the Rhetoric of Assent.* Chicago: Univ. of Chicago Press, 1974.

Boulding, Kenneth. *The Image.* 1956; rpt. Ann Arbor: Univ. of Michigan Press, 1961.

Bransford, John D., et al. "Toward Unexplaining Memory." In *Perceiving, Acting, and Knowing: Toward an Ecological Psychology,* ed. Robert Shaw and John Bransford. Hillsdale, NJ: Erlbaum, 1977, pp. 431–66.

Bransford, John D., and Nancy S. McCarrell. "A Sketch of a Cognitive Approach to Comprehension: Some Thoughts about Understanding What It Means to Comprehend." In *Cognition and the Symbolic Processes,* vol. 1, ed. Walter B. Weimer and David S. Palermo. Hillsdale, NJ: Erlbaum, 1974, pp. 189–229.

Briggs, John C. "Philosophy and Rhetoric." In *Research in Composition and Rhetoric: A Bibliographic Sourcebook,* ed. Michael G. Moran and Ronald F. Lunsford. Westport, CT: Greenwood Press, 1984, pp. 93–124.

Britton, James, et al. *The Development of Writing Abilities: 11–18.* London: MacMillan, 1975.

Bronfenbrenner, Urie. *The Ecology of Human Development: Experiments by Nature and Design.* Cambridge, MA: Harvard Univ. Press, 1979.

Bronowski, J. *Science and Human Values.* Rev. ed. New York: Harper, 1965.

Broudy, H. S. "Types of Knowledge and Purposes of Education." In *Schooling and the Acquisition of Knowledge*, ed. Richard C. Anderson, Rand J. Spiro, and William E. Montague. Hillsdale, NJ: Erlbaum, 1977, pp. 12–15.

Brown, Harold I. *Perception, Theory, and Commitment: The New Philosophy of Science*. Chicago: Univ. of Chicago Press, 1977.

Bruce, Bertram C. "Plans and Social Actions." In *Theoretical Issues in Reading Comprehension: Perspectives from Cognitive Psychology, Linguistics, Artificial Intelligence, and Education*, ed. Rand J. Spiro, Bertram C. Bruce, and William F. Brewer. Hillsdale, NJ: Erlbaum, pp. 367–84.

Bruner, Jerome S. *Beyond the Information Given: Studies in the Psychology of Knowing*, ed. Jeremy M. Anglin. New York: Norton, 1973.

———. "Language, Mind, and Reading." In *Awakening to Literacy: The University of Victoria Symposium on Children's Response to a Literate Environment: Literacy before Schooling*, ed. Hillel Goelman, Antoinette A. Oberg, and Frank Smith. Exeter, NH: Heinemann, 1984, pp. 193–200.

Burke, Kenneth. *Language as Symbolic Action: Essays on Life, Literature, and Method*. Berkeley: Univ. of California Press, 1968.

———. *The Philosophy of Literary Form: Studies in Symbolic Action*. 3rd ed. Berkeley: Univ. of California Press, 1973.

———. *A Rhetoric of Motives*. 1950; rpt. Berkeley: Univ. of California Press, 1969.

Burnham, Christopher C. "Research Methods in Composition." In *Research in Composition and Rhetoric: A Bibliographic Sourcebook*, ed. Michael G. Moran and Ronald L. Lunsford. Westport, CT: Greenwood Press, 1984, pp. 191–210.

Cairns, Robert B. *Social Development: The Origins and Plasticity of Exchanges*. San Francisco: Freeman, 1979.

Calkins, Lucy McCormick. *Lessons from a Child: On the Teaching and Learning of Writing*. Exeter, NH: Heinemann, 1983.

Capra, Fritjof. *The Tao of Physics: An Exploration of the Parallels between Modern Physics and Eastern Mysticism*. Boulder: Shambhala, 1975.

———. *The Turning Point: Science, Society and the Rising Culture*. New York: Simon and Schuster, 1982.

Carr, David. "Husserl's Problematic Concept of the Life-World." In *Husserl: Expositions and Appraisals*, ed. Frederick Elliston and Peter McCormick. Notre Dame, IN: Univ. of Notre Dame Press, 1977, pp. 202–12.

Chafe, Wallace L. "The Deployment of Consciousness in the Production of a Narrative." In *The Pear Stories: Cognitive, Cultural, and Linguistic Aspects of Narrative Production*, ed. Wallace L. Chafe, Vol. 3 of *Advances in Discourse Processes*, ed. Roy O. Freedle. Norwood, NJ: Ablex, 1980, pp. 9–50.

Charmé, Stuart L. "Paul Ricoeur as Teacher: A Reminiscence." *Pre/Text* 4 (1983), 289–94.

Clark, Katerina, and Michael Holquist. *Mikhail Bakhtin.* Cambridge, MA: Harvard Univ. Press, 1984.

Connors, Robert J. "Composition Studies and Science." *CE* 45 (1983), 1–20.

Csikszentmihalyi, Mihaly, and Olga V. Beattie. "Life Themes: A Theoretical and Empirical Exploration of Their Origins and Effects." *Journal of Humanistic Psychology* 19 (1979), 47–48.

Culler, Jonathan. *On Deconstruction: Theory and Criticism after Structuralism.* Ithaca: Cornell Univ. Press, 1982.

Daneš, Frantisek. "Functional Sentence Perspective and the Organization of the Text." In *Papers on Functional Sentence Perspective,* ed. Frantisek Daneš. The Hague: Mouton, 1974, pp. 106–28.

Delia, Jesse G., and Barbara O'Keefe. "Constructivism: The Development of Communication in Children." In *Children Communicating: Media and Development of Thought, Speech, Understanding,* ed. Ellen Wartella. Beverly Hills: Sage, 1979, pp. 157–85.

DeLoach, Bill. "On First Looking into Ricoeur's *Interpretation Theory*: A Beginner's Guide." *Pre/Text* 4 (1983), 225–36.

Derrida, Jacques. *Of Grammatology.* Tr. Gayatri Chakravorty Spivak. Baltimore: Johns Hopkins Univ. Press, 1976.

———. *Speech and Phenomena and Other Essays on Husserl's Theory of Signs.* Tr. David B. Allison. Evanston, IL: Northwestern Univ. Press, 1973.

Dewey, John. *Experience and Nature.* 2nd ed. 1929; rpt. La Salle, IL: Open Court, 1971.

———. *How We Think: A Restatement of the Relation of Reflective Thinking to the Educative Process.* 1933; rpt. Chicago: Regnery, 1971.

diSibio, Mary. "Memory for Connected Discourse: A Constructivist View." *Review of Educational Research* 52 (1982), 149–74.

Dixon, Roger A., and John R. Nesselroade. "Pluralism and Correlational Analysis in Developmental Psychology: Historical and Philosophical Perspectives." In *Developmental Psychology: Historical and Philosophical Perspectives,* ed. Richard M. Lerner. Hillsdale, NJ: Erlbaum, 1983, pp. 113–45.

Donaldson, Margaret. *Children's Minds.* New York: Norton, 1978.

Dowst, Kenneth. "The Epistemic Approach: Writing, Knowing, and Learning." In *Eight Approaches to Teaching Composition,* ed. Timothy R. Donovan and Ben W. McClelland. Urbana, IL: NCTE, 1980, pp. 65–85.

Dreyfus, Hubert. *What Computers Can't Do: A Critique of Artificial Reason.* New York: Harper, 1972.

Dyson, Anne Haas. "Emerging Alphabetic Literacy in School Contexts: Toward Defining the Gap between School Curriculum and Child Mind." *Written Communication* 1 (1984), 3–55.

Eagleton, Terry. *Literary Theory: An Introduction.* Minneapolis: Univ. of Minneapolis Press, 1983.

Eco, Umberto. *A Theory of Semiotics.* Bloomington: Indiana Univ. Press, 1976.

Ede, Lisa, and Andrea Lunsford. "Audience Addressed/Audience Invoked: The Role of Audience in Composition Theory and Pedagogy." *CCC* 35 (1984), 155-71.

Elbow, Peter. "Preface 4: The Doubting Game and the Believing Game." *Pre/Text* 3 (1982), 339-51.

Emig, Janet. "Inquiry Paradigms and Writing." *CCC* 33 (1982), 64-75.

———. "The Tacit Tradition: The Inevitability of a Multi-Disciplinary Approach to Writing Research." In *Reinventing the Rhetorical Tradition*, ed. Aviva Freedman and Ian Pringle. Conway, AK: L & S Books, 1980, pp. 9-17.

———. *The Web of Meaning: Essays on Writing, Teaching, Learning, and Thinking.* Ed. Dixie Goswami and Maureen Butler. Upper Montclair, NJ: Boynton/Cook, 1983.

"Expanding Our Notions of Discourse Processing: Intertextuality as a Source for Multiple Connections." Symposium at the National Reading Conference. Austin, TX, December 1986.

Faigley, Lester. "Competing Theories of Process: A Critique and a Proposal." *CE* 48 (1986), 527-42.

Feldman, David Henry. *Beyond Universals in Cognitive Development.* Norwood, NJ: Ablex, 1980.

Ferreiro, Emilia, and Ana Teberosky. *Literacy before Schooling.* Tr. Karen Goodman Castro. Exeter, NH: Heinemann, 1982.

Feyerabend, Paul. *Against Method: Outline of an Anarchistic Theory of Knowledge.* London: Berso, 1975.

Fischer, Michael. *Does Deconstruction Make Any Difference?: Post-Structuralism and the Defense of Poetry in Modern Criticism.* Bloomington: Indiana Univ. Press, 1985.

Fisher, Walter R. *Human Communication as Narration: Toward a Philosophy of Reason, Value, and Action.* Columbia: Univ. of South Carolina Press, 1987.

———. "Narration as a Human Communication Paradigm: The Case of Public Moral Argument." *Communication Monographs* 51 (1984), 1-22.

Flavell, John H. "Metacognition and Cognitive Monitoring: A New Area of Cognitive-Developmental Inquiry." *American Psychologist* 34 (1979), 906-11.

Fodor, J. A., T. G. Bever, and M. F. Garrett. *The Psychology of Language: An Introduction to Psycholinguistics and Generative Grammar.* New York: McGraw-Hill, 1974.

Foucault, Michel. "What Is an Author?" In *Textual Strategies: Perspectives in Post-Structuralist Criticism*, ed. Josué V. Harari. Ithaca: Cornell Univ. Press, 1979, pp. 141-60.

Freedle, Roy O., ed. *New Directions in Discourse Processing.* Vol. 2 of *Advances in Discourse Processes.* Norwood, NJ: Ablex, 1979.

Freedman, Aviva, and Ian Pringle, eds. *Reinventing the Rhetorical Tradition.* Conway, AK: L & S Books, 1980.

Freire, Paulo. *Education for Critical Consciousness.* New York: Continuum, 1981.

———. *Pedagogy of the Oppressed.* Tr. Myra Bergman Ramos. New York: Continuum, 1982.

Gadamer, Hans-Georg. "The Problem of Historical Consciousness." In *Interpretive Social Science: A Reader,* ed. Paul Rabinow and William M. Sullivan. Berkeley: Univ. of California Press, 1979, pp. 103–60.

———. *Truth and Method.* New York: Seabury, 1975.

Gardner, Howard. *Art, Mind, and Brain: A Cognitive Approach to Creativity.* New York: Basic Books, 1982.

Gergen, Kenneth J. "Stability, Change, and Chance in Understanding Human Development." In *Life-Span Developmental Psychology: Dialectical Perspectives on Experimental Research,* ed. Nancy Datan and Hayne W. Reese. New York: Academic Press, 1977, pp. 135–58.

Gerhart, Mary. "Genre as Praxis: An Inquiry." *Pre/Text* 4 (1983), 273–88.

Gibson, James J. *The Senses Considered as Perceptual Systems.* Boston: Houghton-Mifflin, 1966.

———. "The Theory of Affordances." In *Perceiving, Acting, and Knowing,* ed. Robert Shaw and John Bransford. Hillsdale, NJ: Erlbaum, 1977, pp. 67–82.

Giddens, Anthony. *Profiles and Critiques in Social Theory.* Berkeley: Univ. of California Press, 1982.

Giroux, Henry A. "The Politics of Educational Theory." *Social Text* 5 (1982), 86–107.

Goelman, Hillel, Antoinette A. Oberg, and Frank Smith, eds. *Awakening to Literacy: The University of Victoria Symposium on Children's Response to a Literate Environment: Literacy before Schooling.* Exeter, NH: Heinemann, 1984.

Goodman, Yetta. "The Development of Initial Literacy." In *Awakening to Literacy: The University of Victoria Symposium on Children's Response to a Literate Environment: Literacy before Schooling,* ed. Hillel Goelman, Antoinette A. Oberg, and Frank Smith. Exeter, NH: Heinemann, 1984, pp. 102–9.

Goody, Jack. *The Domestication of the Savage Mind.* Cambridge: Cambridge Univ. Press, 1977.

Graves, Donald H. *Writing: Teachers and Children at Work.* Exeter, NH: Heinemann, 1983.

Graves, Richard L. "The Way of a Large House: Synthesis in Teaching Composition." *Rhetoric Review* 3 (1984), 4–12.

Grimes, Joseph. *The Thread of Discourse.* The Hague: Mouton, 1975.

Habermas, Jurgen. *Knowledge and Human Interests.* Tr. Jeremy L. Shapiro. Boston: Beacon Press, 1971.

Hairston, Maxine. "Breaking Our Bonds and Reaffirming Our Connections." *CCC* 36 (1985), 272–82.

———. "The Winds of Change: Thomas Kuhn and the Revolution in the Teaching of Writing." *CCC* 33 (1982), 76–88.

Halliday, M. A. K., and Ruqaiya Hasan. *Cohesion in English.* London: Longman, 1976.

Harari, Josué V. "Critical Factions/Critical Fictions." Introduction to *Textual Strategies: Perspectives in Post-Structuralist Criticism.* Ithaca: Cornell Univ. Press, 1979, pp. 17–72.

———, ed. *Textual Strategies: Perspectives in Post-Structuralist Criticism.* Ithaca: Cornell Univ. Press, 1979.

Harris, Wendell V. "Toward an Ecological Criticism: Contextual versus Unconditioned Literary Discourse." *CE* 48 (1986), 116–31.

Harste, Jerome C., Virginia A. Woodward, and Carolyn L. Burke. "Examining Our Assumptions: A Transactional View of Literacy and Learning." *RTE* 18 (1984), 84–108.

———. *Language Stories and Literacy Lessons.* Portsmouth, NH: Heinemann, 1984.

Havelock, Eric A. *Preface to Plato.* Cambridge, MA: Harvard Univ. Press, 1963.

Hayward, Jeremy W. *Perceiving Ordinary Magic: Science and Intuitive Wisdom.* Boulder: Shambhala, 1984.

Heath, Shirley Brice. "Being Literate in America: A Sociohistorical Perspective." In *Issues in Literacy: A Research Perspective,* 34th yearbook of the National Reading Conference, ed. Jerome A. Niles and Rosary V. Lali. Rochester, NY: NRC, 1985, pp. 1–18.

———. *Ways with Words: Language, Life and Work in Communities and Classrooms.* Cambridge: Cambridge Univ. Press, 1983.

Hirsch, E. D., Jr. *The Philosophy of Composition.* Chicago: Univ. of Chicago Press, 1977.

———. *Validity in Interpretation.* New Haven: Yale Univ. Press, 1967.

Hoffman, Robert R. "Context and Contextualism in the Psychology of Learning." *Cahiers de psychologie cognitive* 6 (1986), 215–32.

Hoffman, Robert R., and James M. Nead. "General Contextualism, Ecological Science and Cognitive Research." *Journal of Mind and Behavior* 4 (1983), 507–60.

Hollander, Lorin. "Child's Play: Prodigies and Possibilities." *Nova,* PBS, March 16, 1985.

Horner, Winifred Bryan, ed. *Composition and Literature: Bridging the Gap.* Chicago: Univ. of Chicago Press, 1983.

———, ed. *The Present State of Scholarship in Historical and Contemporary Rhetoric.* Columbia: Univ. of Missouri Press, 1983.

Howard, Roy J. *Three Faces of Hermeneutics: An Introduction to Current Theories of Understanding.* Berkeley: Univ. of California Press, 1982.

Hoy, David Couzens. *The Critical Circle: Literature and History in Contemporary Hermeneutics.* Berkeley: Univ. of California Press, 1978.

Husserl, Edmund. *The Crisis of European Sciences and Transcendental Phenomenology: An Introduction to Phenomenological Philosophy.* Tr. David Carr. Evanston, IL: Northwestern Univ. Press, 1970.

———. *Ideas Pertaining to a Pure Phenomenology and to a Phenomenological Philosophy. First Book: General Introduction to a Pure Phenomenology.* Tr. F. Kersten. The Hague: Nijhoff, 1983.

Ihde, Don. *Existential Technics.* Albany: State Univ. of New York Press, 1983.

———. *Experimental Phenomenology: An Introduction.* New York: Putnam, Capricorn Books, 1977.

———. *Hermeneutic Phenomenology: The Philosophy of Paul Ricoeur.* Evanston, IL: Northwestern Univ. Press, 1971.

Jaggar, Angela, and M. Trika Smith-Burke, eds. *Observing the Language Learner.* Newark, DE: International Reading Association and NCTE, 1985.

Jakobson, Roman. "Closing Statement: Linguistics and Poetics." In *Style in Language,* ed. Thomas A. Sebeok. Cambridge, MA: MIT Press, 1960.

Jantsch, Erich. *The Self-Organizing Universe: Scientific and Human Implications of the Emerging Paradigm of Evolution.* Oxford: Pergamon, 1980.

Jenkins, James J. "Remember That Old Theory of Memory? Well, Forget It!" In *Perceiving, Acting, and Knowing: Toward an Ecological Psychology,* ed. Robert Shaw and John Bransford. Hillsdale, NJ: Erlbaum, 1977, pp. 413–29.

Just, Marcel Adam, and Patricia A. Carpenter, eds. *Cognitive Processes in Comprehension.* Hillsdale, NJ: Erlbaum, 1977.

Keller, Evelyn Fox. *A Feeling for the Organism: The Life and Work of Barbara McClintock.* New York: Freeman, 1983.

Kinneavy, James L. "*Kairos:* A Neglected Concept in Classical Rhetoric." In *Rhetoric and Praxis: The Contribution of Classical Rhetoric to Practical Reasoning,* ed. Jean Dietz Moss. Washington, DC: Catholic Univ. of America Press, 1986, pp. 79–105.

———. "A Pluralistic Synthesis of Four Contemporary Models for Teaching Composition." In *Reinventing the Rhetorical Tradition,* ed. Aviva Freedman and Ian Pringle. Conway, AK: L & S Books, 1980, pp. 37–52.

———. "Restoring the Humanities: The Return of Rhetoric from Exile." In *The Rhetorical Tradition and Modern Writing,* ed. James J. Murphy. New York: MLA, 1982, pp. 19–28.

_____ . *A Theory of Discourse*. Englewood Cliffs, NJ: Prentice-Hall, 1971.

Kinney, James. "Composition Research and the Rhetorical Tradition." *Rhetoric Society Quarterly* 10 (1980), 143-48.

_____ . "A Rhetoric of Dismissing Differences: A Reply to Arnold." *Rhetoric Society Quarterly* 10 (1980), 156-59.

Kitzhaber, Albert R. *Themes, Theories, and Therapies: The Teaching of Writing in College*. New York: McGraw-Hill, 1963.

Kneupper, Charles W. "Revising the Tagmemic Heuristic: Theoretical and Pedagogical Considerations." *CCC* 31 (1980), 160-68.

Kohak, Erazim V. "The Philosophy of Paul Ricoeur." Introduction to *Freedom and Nature: The Voluntary and the Involuntary*. Evanston, IL: Northwestern Univ. Press, 1966, pp. xi-xxix.

Krashen, Stephen. *Writing: Research, Theory, and Application*. New York: Pergamon, 1984.

Kroll, Barry M. "Writing for Readers: Three Perspectives on Audience." *CCC* 35 (1984), 172-85.

Kuhn, Thomas S. *The Essential Tension: Selected Studies in Scientific Tradition and Change*. Chicago: Univ. of Chicago Press, 1977.

_____ . "Reflections on My Critics." In *Criticism and the Growth of Knowledge*, ed. Imre Lakatos and Alan Musgrave. Cambridge: Cambridge Univ. Press, 1970, pp. 231-78.

_____ . *The Structure of Scientific Revolutions*. 2nd ed. Chicago: Univ. of Chicago Press, 1970.

Lakatos, Imre. "Falsification and the Methodology of Scientific Research Programmes." In *Criticism and the Growth of Knowledge*, ed. Imre Lakatos and Alan Musgrave. Cambridge: Cambridge Univ. Press, 1970, pp. 91-196.

Lakatos, Imre, and Alan Musgrave, eds. *Criticism and the Growth of Knowledge*. Cambridge: Cambridge Univ. Press, 1970.

Lakoff, George. "Linguistic Gestalts." *Papers from the 13th Regional Meeting, Chicago Linguistic Society*, 1977. Pp. 236-87.

Langer, Susanne K. *Mind: An Essay on Human Feeling*. Vols. 1-3. Baltimore: Johns Hopkins Univ. Press, 1967, 1972, 1982.

_____ . *Philosophical Sketches*. Baltimore: Johns Hopkins Press, 1962.

_____ . *Philosophy in a New Key: A Study in the Symbolism of Reason, Rite, and Art*. 3rd ed. Cambridge, MA: Harvard Univ. Press, 1963.

Larson, Richard. "Structure and Form in Non-Fiction Prose." In *Teaching Composition: Ten Bibliographical Essays*, ed. Gary Tate. Fort Worth, TX: Texas Christian Univ. Press, 1976, pp. 45-71.

Lauer, Janice M. "Composition Studies: Dappled Discipline." *Rhetoric Review* 3 (1984), 20-29.

Lawlor, Leonard. "Event and Repeatability: Ricoeur and Derrida in Debate." *Pre/Text* 4 (1983), 317-34. Special issue on *Ricoeur and Rhetoric*, ed. Louise Wetherbee Phelps.

Leichter, Hope Jensen. "Families as Environments for Literacy." In *Awakening to Literacy: The University of Victoria Symposium on Children's Response to a Literate Environment: Literacy before Schooling*, ed. Hillel Goelman, Antoinette A. Oberg, and Frank Smith. Exeter, NH: Heinemann, 1984, pp. 38–50.

Lentricchia, Frank. *After the New Criticism*. Chicago: Univ. of Chicago Press, 1980.

Lerner, Richard M. "The History of Philosophy and the Philosophy of History in Developmental Psychology: A View of the Issues." In *Developmental Psychology: Historical and Philosophical Perspectives*, ed. Richard M. Lerner. Hillsdale, NJ: Erlbaum, 1983.

————, ed. *Developmental Psychology: Historical and Philosophical Perspectives*. Hillsdale, NJ: Erlbaum, 1983.

Lerner, Richard M., and Nancy A. Busch-Rossnagel. "Individuals as Producers of Their Development: Conceptual and Empirical Bases." In *Individuals as Producers of Their Development: A Life-Span Perspective*, ed. Richard M. Lerner and Nancy A. Busch-Rossnagel. New York: Academic Press, 1981, pp. 1–36.

————, eds. *Individuals as Producers of Their Development: A Life-Span Perspective*. New York: Academic Press, 1981.

Lewis, Philip. "The Post-Structuralist Condition." *Dialectics* 12 (1982), 2–24.

Lock, Andrew. *The Guided Reinvention of Language*. New York: Academic Press, 1980.

Luetkemeyer, Jean, Caroline Van Antwerp, and Gloria Kindell. "Bibliography of Spoken and Written Language." In *Coherence in Spoken and Written Discourse*, ed. Deborah Tannen. Vol. 12 of *Advances in Discourse Processes*, ed. Roy O. Freedle. Norwood, NJ: Ablex, 1984, pp. 265–81.

McDermott, John J. *The Culture of Experience: Philosophical Essays in the American Grain*. New York: New York Univ. Press, 1976.

Mace, William M. "Ecologically Stimulating Cognitive Psychology: Gibsonian Perspectives." In *Cognition and the Symbolic Processes*, ed. Walter B. Weimer and David S. Palermo. Hillsdale, NJ: Erlbaum, 1974, pp. 137–64.

————. "James J. Gibson's Strategy for Perceiving: Ask Not What's Inside Your Head, but What Your Head's Inside Of." In *Perceiving, Acting, and Knowing*, ed. Robert Shaw and John Bransford. Hillsdale, NJ: Erlbaum, 1977, pp. 43–65.

Magnusson, David, and Vernon L. Allen, eds. *Human Development: An Interactional Perspective*. New York: Academic Press, 1983.

Matsuhashi, Ann. "Explorations in the Real-Time Production of Written Discourse." In *What Writers Know: The Language, Process, and Structure of Written Discourse*, ed. Martin Nystrand. New York: Academic Press, 1982, pp. 269–90.

Meacham, John A. "Political Values, Conceptual Models, and Research." In *Individuals as Producers of Their Development: A Life-Span Perspective*, ed. Richard M. Lerner and Nancy A. Busch-Rossnagel. New York: Academic Press, 1981, pp. 447–74.

Merleau-Ponty, Maurice. *Phenomenology of Perception*. Tr. Colin Smith. New York: Humanities Press, 1962.

Meyer, Bonnie, J. F. "What Is Remembered from Prose: A Function of Passage Structure." In *Discourse Production and Comprehension*. Vol. 1 of *Discourse Processes: Advances in Research and Theory*. Norwood, NJ: Ablex, 1977, pp. 307–36.

Michaels, Walter Benn. "The Interpreter's Self: Peirce on the Cartesian 'Subject.'" In *Reader-Response Criticism: From Formalism to Post-Structuralism*, ed. Jane P. Tompkins. Baltimore: Johns Hopkins Univ. Press, 1980, pp. 185–200.

Mitchell, W. J. T., ed. *Against Theory: Literary Studies and the New Pragmatism*. Chicago: Univ. of Chicago Press, 1985.

Moran, Michael G., and Ronald F. Lunsford, eds. *Research in Composition and Rhetoric: A Bibliographic Sourcebook*. Westport, CT: Greenwood Press, 1984.

Mudge, Lewis S. "Paul Ricoeur on Biblical Interpretation." In Paul Ricoeur, *Essays on Biblical Interpretation*. Philadelphia: Fortress Press, 1980.

Nilsson, Lars-Göran, ed. *Perspectives on Memory Research: Essays in Honor of Uppsala University's 500th Anniversary*. Hillsdale, NJ: Erlbaum, 1979.

Nold, Ellen W., and Brent E. Davis. "The Discourse Matrix." *CCC* 31 (1980), 141–52.

Norman, Donald A. "Twelve Issues for Cognitive Science." In *Perspectives on Cognitive Science*, ed. Donald A. Norman. Norwood, NJ: Ablex, 1981, pp. 265–95.

Ochs, Elinor. "Planned and Unplanned Discourse." In *Syntax and Semantics*, ed. T. Givon. Vol. 12 of *Discourse and Syntax*. New York: Academic Press, 1979, pp. 51–80.

——— . "Social Foundations of Language." In *New Directions in Discourse Processing*. Vol. 2 of *Advances in Discourse Processes*, ed. Roy O. Freedle. Norwood, NJ: Ablex, 1979, pp. 207–21.

Ochs, Elinor, and Bambi B. Schieffelin, eds. *Developmental Pragmatics*. New York: Academic Press, 1979.

Ohmann, Richard. *English in America: A Radical View of the Profession*. New York: Oxford Univ. Press, 1976.

Olson, David R. "See! Jumping! Some Oral Language Antecedents of Literacy." In *Awakening to Literacy: The University of Victoria Symposium on Children's Response to a Literate Environment: Literacy before Schooling*, ed. Hillel Goelman, Antoinette A. Oberg, and Frank Smith. Exeter, NH: Heinemann, 1984, pp. 185–92.

Ong, Walter. *Orality and Literacy: The Technologizing of the Word.* London: Methuen, 1982.

————— . "Reading, Technology, and Human Consciousness." In *Literacy as a Human Problem*, ed. James C. Raymond. University, AL: Univ. of Alabama Press, 1982, pp. 179–84.

Palmer, Richard E. *Hermeneutics.* Evanston, IL: Northwestern Univ. Press, 1969.

Peirce, Charles S. *Philosophical Writings of Peirce.* Ed. Justus Buchler. New York: Dover Publications, 1955.

————— . *Selected Writings.* Ed. Philip P. Wiener. New York: Dover Publications, 1958.

Pepper, Stephen C. *World Hypotheses: A Study in Evidence.* Berkeley: Univ. of California Press, 1942.

Perelman, Chaim, and L. Olbrechts-Tyteca. *The New Rhetoric: A Treatise on Argumentation.* Tr. John Wilkinson and Purcell Weaver. Notre Dame, IN: Univ. of Notre Dame Press, 1969.

Perry, William G., Jr. *Forms of Intellectual and Ethical Development in the College Years: A Scheme.* New York: Holt, 1968.

Petrosky, Anthony. "From Story to Essay: Reading and Writing." *CCC* 33 (1982), 19–36.

Phelps, Louise Wetherbee. "Acts, Texts, and the Teaching Context: Their Relations within a Dramatistic Philosophy of Composition," retitled "Composition in a New Key." Diss., Case Western Reserve Univ., 1980.

————— . "Cross-Sections in an Emerging Psychology of Composition." In *Research in Composition and Rhetoric: A Bibliographical Sourcebook*, ed. Michael G. Moran and Ronald F. Lunsford. Westport, CT: Greenwood Press, 1984, pp. 27–69.

————— . "The Domain of Composition." *Rhetoric Review* 4 (1986), 182–95.

————— , ed. *Ricoeur and Rhetoric.* Special issue, *Pre/Text* 4 (1983).

Philibert, Michel. "The Philosophic Method of Paul Ricoeur." In *Studies in the Philosophy of Paul Ricoeur*, ed. Charles E. Reagan. Athens, OH: Ohio Univ. Press, 1979, pp. 133–39.

Polanyi, Michael. *Personal Knowledge: Towards a Post-Critical Philosophy.* Chicago: Univ. of Chicago Press, 1962.

————— . *The Tacit Dimension.* 1966; rpt. Garden City, NY: Doubleday, 1967.

Pratt, Mary Louise. *Toward a Speech Act Theory of Literary Discourse.* Bloomington: Indiana Univ. Press, 1977.

Price, Robert. "Some Antistrophes to the Rhetoric." *Philosophy and Rhetoric* 1 (1968), 145–64.

Prigogine, Ilya, and Isabelle Stengers. *Order Out of Chaos: Man's New Dialogue with Nature.* Boulder: Shambhala, 1984.

Progoff, Ira. "The Humanic Arts: Proposal for a New Degree in the Experiential Study of Man." *Forum for Correspondence and Contact* 1 (1968), 36–43.

Rabinow, Paul, and William M. Sullivan, eds. *Interpretive Social Science: A Reader.* Berkeley: Univ. of California Press, 1979.

———. "The Interpretive Turn: Emergence of an Approach." Introduction to *Interpretive Social Science: A Reader,* ed. Paul Rabinow and William M. Sullivan. Berkeley: Univ. of California Press, 1979, pp. 1–21.

Radnitzky, Gerard. *Continental Schools of Metascience.* Vol. 2 of *Contemporary Schools of Metascience.* Göteborg, Sweden: Akademiförlaget, 1968.

Reagan, Charles. "Hermeneutics and the Semantics of Action." *Pre/Text* 4 (1983), 239–55.

Reese, Hayne W., and Willis F. Overton. "Models of Development and Theories of Development." In *Life-Span Developmental Psychology: Research and Theory.* New York: Academic Press, 1970, pp. 115–45.

Rico, Gabrielle. *Writing the Natural Way: Using Right-Brain Techniques to Release Your Expressive Powers.* Los Angeles: Tarcher, 1983.

Ricoeur, Paul. *The Conflict of Interpretations: Essays in Hermeneutics.* Ed. Don Ihde. Evanston, IL: Northwestern Univ. Press, 1974.

———. "Creativity in Language." Tr. David Pellauer. *Philosophy Today* 17 (1973), 129–41.

———. *Freedom and Nature: The Voluntary and the Involuntary.* Tr. Erazim V. Kohak. Evanston, IL: Northwestern Univ. Press, 1966.

———. *Freud and Philosophy: An Essay on Interpretation.* Tr. Denis Savage. New Haven: Yale Univ. Press, 1970.

———. *Hermeneutics and the Human Sciences: Essays on Language, Action, and Interpretation.* Ed. and tr. John B. Thompson. Cambridge: Cambridge Univ. Press, 1981.

———. *History and Truth.* Tr. Charles A. Kelbley. Evanston: Northwestern Univ. Press, 1965.

———. *Husserl: An Analysis of His Phenomenology.* Tr. E. G. Ballard and L. E. Embree. Evanston, IL: Northwestern Univ. Press, 1967.

———. "Ideology and Utopia as Cultural Imagination." *Philosophic Exchange* 2 (1976), 16–28.

———. *Interpretation Theory: Discourse and the Surplus of Meaning.* Fort Worth, TX: Texas Christian Univ. Press, 1976.

———. "Model of the Text: Meaningful Action Considered as a Text." In *Interpretive Social Science: A Reader.* Ed. Paul Rabinow and William M. Sullivan. Berkeley: Univ. of California Press, 1977, pp. 73–101.

———. *Paul Ricoeur: An Anthology of His Work.* Ed. Charles E. Reagan and David Stewart. Boston: Beacon Press, 1978.

———. "Philosophy and Religious Language." *Journal of Religion* 54 (1974), 71–85.

———. Preface to 1st ed. In *History and Truth*. Tr. Charles A. Kelbley. Evanston, IL: Northwestern Univ. Press, 1965, pp. 3–14.

———. Ricoeur issue, *Philosophy Today* 17, Summer 1973.

———. *The Symbolism of Evil*. Tr. Emerson Buchanan. New York: Harper, 1967.

———. "Toward a 'Post-Critical Rhetoric'? A Reply." *Pre/Text* 5 (1984), 9–16.

Riegel, Klaus F., and John A. Meacham. "Dialectics, Transaction, and Piaget's Theory." In *Perspectives in Interactional Psychology*, ed. Lawrence A. Pervin and Michael Lewis. New York: Plenum, 1978, pp. 23–47.

Rorty, Richard. *Philosophy and the Mirror of Nature*. Princeton: Princeton Univ. Press, 1979.

Rosenblatt, Louise M. "Viewpoints: Transaction versus Interaction—a Terminological Rescue Operation." *RTE* 19 (1985), 96–107.

Sanford, A. J., and S. C. Garrod. *Understanding Written Language: Explorations of Comprehension beyond the Sentence*. Chichester: Wiley, 1981.

Sarbin, Theodore R. "Contextualism: A World View for Modern Psychology." In *Nebraska Symposium on Motivation, 1976*, ed. Alvin W. Landfield. Lincoln, NB: Univ. of Nebraska Press, 1977, pp. 1–41.

Saussure, Ferdinand de. *Course in General Linguistics*. Tr. Wade Baskin. Ed. Charles Bally and Albert Secheyaye in collaboration with Albert Riedlinger. New York: McGraw-Hill, 1959.

Scholes, Robert. *Textual Power*. New Haven: Yale Univ. Press, 1985.

Schrag, Calvin O. *Radical Reflection and the Origin of the Human Sciences*. West Lafayette, IN: Purdue Univ. Press, 1980.

Scribner, Sylvia, and Michael Cole. *The Psychology of Literacy*. Cambridge, MA: Harvard Univ. Press, 1981.

Searle, John R. *Speech Acts: An Essay in the Philosophy of Language*. Cambridge: Cambridge Univ. Press, 1969.

Shaw, Robert, and John Bransford. "Introduction: Psychological Approaches to the Problem of Knowledge." *Perceiving, Acting, and Knowing: Toward an Ecological Psychology*. Ed. Robert Shaw and John Bransford. Hillsdale, NJ: Erlbaum, 1977, pp. 1–39.

———, eds. *Perceiving, Acting, and Knowing: Toward an Ecological Psychology*. Hillsdale, NJ: Erlbaum, 1977.

Shuy, Roger W. "A Holistic View of Language." *RTE* 15 (1981), 101–11.

Smith, David H. "Communication Research and the Idea of Process." *Speech Monographs* 39 (1972), 174–82.

Smith, John E. "Time and Qualitative Time." *Review of Metaphysics* 40 (1986), 3–16.

Sommers, Nancy I. "The Need for Theory in Composition Research." *CCC* 30 (1979), 46–49.

Spiegelberg, Herbert. *The Phenomenological Movement: A Historical Introduction*. 3rd ed. The Hague: Nijhoff, 1982.

Spiro, Rand J. "Constructive Processes in Prose Comprehension and Recall." In *Theoretical Issues in Reading Comprehension: Perspectives from Cognitive Psychology, Linguistics, Artificial Intelligence, and Education*, ed. Rand J. Spiro, Bertram C. Bruce, and William F. Brewer. Hillsdale, NJ: Erlbaum, 1980, pp. 245–78.

Spiro, Rand J., Bertram C. Bruce, and William F. Brewer, eds. *Theoretical Issues in Reading Comprehension: Perspectives from Cognitive Psychology, Linguistics, Artificial Intelligence, and Education*. Hillsdale, NJ: Erlbaum, 1980.

Sticht, Thomas G. "Comprehending Reading at Work." In *Cognitive Processes in Composition*, ed. Marcel Adam Just and Patricia A. Carpenter. Hillsdale, NJ: Erlbaum, 1977, pp. 221–46.

Swearingen, C. Jan. "Between Intention and Inscription: Toward a Dialogical Rhetoric." *Pre/Text* 4 (1983), 257–71.

———. "The Rhetor as Eiron: Plato's Defense of Dialogue." *Pre/Text* 3 (1982), 289–336.

Tannen, Deborah. "Oral and Literate Strategies in Spoken and Written Narratives." *Language* 58 (1982), 1–21.

———. "What's in a Frame? Surface Evidence for Underlying Expectations." In *New Directions in Discourse Processing*. Vol. 2 of *Advances in Discourse Processes*, ed. Roy O. Freedle. Norwood, NJ: Ablex, 1979, pp. 137–81.

Tate, Gary, ed. *Teaching Composition: Ten Bibliographical Essays*. Fort Worth, TX: Texas Christian Univ. Press, 1976.

Taylor, Charles. "Interpretation and the Sciences of Man." In *Interpretive Social Science: A Reader*, ed. Paul Rabinow and William M. Sullivan. Berkeley: Univ. of California Press, 1979, pp. 25–71.

Taylor, Denny. *Family Literacy: Young Children Learning to Read and Write*. Exeter, NH: Heinemann, 1983.

Taylor, Insup, and M. Martin Taylor. *The Psychology of Reading*. New York: Academic Press, 1983.

Teale, William H. "Toward a Theory of How Children Learn to Read and Write 'Naturally': An Update." In *Changing Perspectives on Research in Reading/Language Processing and Instruction*, 33rd yearbook of the National Reading Conference, ed. Jerome A. Niles and Larry A. Harris. Rochester, NY: NRC, 1984, pp. 317–22.

Thompson, John B. *Critical Hermeneutics: A Study in the Thought of Paul Ricoeur and Jurgen Habermas*. Cambridge: Cambridge Univ. Press, 1981.

Tillich, Paul. "Kairos and Logos." In *The Interpretation of History*, tr. N. A. Rasetzki and Elsa Talmey. New York: Scribner's, 1936.

Toulmin, Stephen. "The Construal of Reality: Criticism in Modern and Postmodern Science." In *The Politics of Interpretation*, ed. W. J. T. Mitchell. Chicago: Univ. of Chicago Press, 1983, pp. 99–117.

Trungpa, Chögyam. *Cutting through Spiritual Materialism.* Ed. John Baker and Marvin Casper. Boulder: Shambhala, 1973.

——— . *Meditation in Action.* Boulder: Shambhala, 1969.

van Dijk, Teun A. *Macrostructures: An Interdisciplinary Study of Global Structures in Discourse, Interaction, and Cognition.* Hillsdale, NJ: Erlbaum, 1980.

van Dijk, Teun A., and Janos S. Patöfi. Editorial introduction. *Text* 1 (1981), 1–3.

Van Peursen, Cornelius. "The Horizon." In *Husserl: Expositions and Appraisals,* ed. Frederick Elliston and Peter McCormick. Notre Dame, IN: Univ. of Notre Dame Press, 1977, pp. 182–201.

Vande Kopple, William J. "Functional Sentence Perspective, Composition, and Reading." *CCC* 33 (1982), 50–63.

Vygotsky, L. S. *Thought and Language.* Tr. and ed. Eugenia Hanfmann and Gertrude Vakar. Cambridge, MA: MIT Press, 1962.

Warnock, John. "Who's Afraid of Theory?" *CCC* 27 (1976), 16–20.

——— . "The Writing Process." In *Research in Composition and Rhetoric: A Bibliographic Sourcebook,* ed. Michael G. Moran and Ronald F. Lunsford. Westport, CT: Greenwood Press, 1984, pp. 3–26.

Weaver, Constance. "Parallels between New Paradigms in Science and in Reading and Literary Theories: An Essay Review." *RTE* 19 (1985), 298–316.

Weimer, Walter B. "A Conceptual Framework for Cognitive Psychology: Motor Theories of the Mind." In *Perceiving, Acting, and Knowing: Toward an Ecological Psychology.* Hillsdale, NJ: Erlbaum, 1977, pp. 267–311.

——— . *Notes on the Methodology of Scientific Research.* Hillsdale, NJ: Erlbaum, 1979.

Weimer, Walter B., and David S. Palermo, eds. *Cognition and the Symbolic Processes.* 2 vols. Hillsdale, NJ: Erlbaum, 1974, 1982.

Weinsheimer, Joel C. *Gadamer's Hermeneutics: A Reading of Truth and Method.* New Haven: Yale Univ. Press, 1985.

Werner, Heinz. "The Concept of Development from a Comparative and Organismic Point of View." *Developmental Processes: Heinz Werner's Selected Writings,* vol. 1, *General Theory and Perceptual Experience.* Ed. Sybil S. Barten and Margery B. Franklin. New York: International Univ. Press, 1978, pp. 107–29.

White, Hayden. *Tropics of Discourse: Essays in Cultural Criticism.* Baltimore: Johns Hopkins Univ. Press, 1978.

Wilcox, Thomas W. *The Anatomy of College English.* San Francisco: Jossey-Bass, 1973.

Winograd, Terry. "A Framework for Understanding Discourse." In *Cognitive Processes in Comprehension,* ed. Marcel Adam Just and Patricia A. Carpenter. Hillsdale, NJ: Erlbaum, 1977, pp. 63–88.

Winterowd, W. Ross. *Composition/Rhetoric: A Synthesis*. Carbondale, IL: Southern Illinois Univ. Press, 1986.

———. *Contemporary Rhetoric: A Conceptual Background with Readings*. New York: Harcourt, 1975.

———. "The Purification of Literature and Rhetoric." *CE* 49 (1987), 257–73.

Witte, Stephen P., and Lester Faigley. "Coherence, Cohesion, and Writing Quality." *CCC* 32 (1981), 189–204.

Young, Richard E. "Arts, Crafts, Gifts and Knacks: Some Disharmonies in the New Rhetoric." In *Reinventing the Rhetorical Tradition*, ed. Aviva Freedman and Ian Pringle. Conway, AK: L & S Books, 1980, pp. 53–60.

———. "Paradigms and Problems: Needed Research in Rhetorical Invention." In *Research on Composing: Points of Departure*, ed. Charles R. Cooper and Lee Odell. Urbana, IL: NCTE, 1978, pp. 29–47.

Young, Richard E., Alton Becker, and Kenneth L. Pike. *Rhetoric: Discovery and Change*. New York: Harcourt, 1970.

Yussen, Steven R., Samuel R. Mathews II, and Elfrieda Hiebert. "Metacognitive Aspects of Reading." In *Reading Expository Material*. Ed. Wayne Otto and Sandra White. New York: Academic Press, 1982, pp. 189–218.

Zukav, Gary. *The Dancing Wu Li Masters: An Overview of the New Physics*. New York: William Morrow, 1979.

Name Index

Subject Index

Addressivity, 56, 69
Alterity, 53, 56–57
Amplifier, cultural, 123
Anthropology, philosophical, 30, 77
Application, 24, 207–8, 216–41
  attunement in, 220–23
  critical examination in, 223–34
  and dialogic engagement, 219–38
  experimentation in, 227–28, 234–38
Axis of simultaneities vs. axis of
  successions, 133

Beginner's mind, 126
Believing game, 92
Bidirectionality, 34

Cartesian anxiety, 21–22
Cartesian-Newtonian worldview, 5, 31,
  40, 136, 142–43
Chronos, 230–31
Clarity vs. depth, 26, 90, 111, 124, 126, 196
Coherence, 160–82
  cohesion, 173–80
  cuing, stylistic, 166–67, 172–78
  definition of, 170–71
  design, 171–73, 176–79
  flow, 171–73, 176–9
  motif, 173, 178–79
  transition, 173, 177–79
Cohesion. See Coherence, cohesion
Composition, discipline of. See also
  Literacy; Process; Rhetoric;
  Writing
  "composing" as a concept, 65–67

conceptual framework for studying,
  viii–xi, 41–42, 52–57, 160–63
cultural ground for, 4–7, 34–35, 41
developmental orientation of, 42, 65,
  70–72, 75–76
ecology of, 3–4, 41, 45, 49, 77–79
experience as principle of, 42, 65,
  71–77
as humanic art, 76
as human science, 76–77, 205
levels of responsibility in, 42, 65,
  70–72
metatheory of, ix–xi, 99, 183, 238
organizing principles of, 42, 64–67,
  73, 76–77, 236–37
as praxis, xi, 42, 55–56, 70–77, 126,
  184, 205–42
psychology of, 99–102
reflection as principle of, 42, 64–80,
  208, 211–14, 236–37, 241
regions of responsibility in, 72–73,
  77, 236–37
in relation to other disciplines, 45,
  76–80, 99–102, 106, 184–88
self-understanding, project of, ix–xi,
  3–4, 109
structure of, 41–42, 61–80, 132
subject matter of, 42, 53, 65, 70–76
values of, 52–57, 74–80, 132
Conflict of interpretations, 184–90
Conscientização, 88–89
Consciousness, critical. See Literacy
Constructivism, 15, 103, 113, 164–66
Contextualism. See also Process
  and contextualist form of analysis,
  58, 60–61, 105, 162–63, 219